Confessions of a Rabbi

Other books by Jonathan Romain

Signs and Wonders (Beginners' Hebrew)

The Jews of England

Faith and Practice (A Guide to Reform Judaism Today)

Tradition and Change (with Anne Kershen)

Till Faith Us Do Part (Couples who Fall in Love across the Religious Divide)

Renewing the Vision (Rabbis Speak Out on Modern Jewish Issues)

Your God Shall Be My God (Religious Conversion in Britain)

Reform Judaism and Modernity (A Reader of Reform Theology)

God, Doubt and Dawkins (ed.)

Really Useful Prayers (ed.)

Great Reform Lives (ed.)

A Passion for Judaism (ed.)

Royal Jews (A Thousand Years of Jewish Life in Berkshire)

Assisted Dying (ed.)

Terror, Trauma and Tragedy (ed. with David Mitchell)

CONFESSIONS OF A RABBI

Jonathan Romain

\Bb\

Biteback Publishing

First published in Great Britain in 2017 by
Biteback Publishing Ltd
Westminster Tower
3 Albert Embankment
London SE1 7SP
Copyright © Jonathan Romain 2017

ISBN 978-1-78590-189-8

10 9 8 7 6 5 4 3 2 1

A CIP catalogue record for this book is available from the British Library.

Set in Minion

Printed and bound in Great Britain by
CPI Group (UK) Ltd, Croydon CR0 4YY

This book is dedicated to the memory of Hugo Gryn
– my teacher and mentor

Contents

Foreword
by Samira Ahmed

I have a confession of my own to make: Rabbi Jonathan Romain is my favourite rabbi. Over the years I've had the pleasure of interviewing him on various religion and ethics programmes, about everything from the desperately serious to the trivial. And when I've been writing about difficult issues, he's the first person I think to call for a point of view and insight.

We've discussed whether you actually have to believe in God to be Jewish; the afterlife; the story of King Saul and the Witch of Endor; and I've had the honour of being a guest at Maidenhead Synagogue's Passover dinner and experiencing the warm regard in which he is held by his congregation.

What stands out about Rabbi Romain has been his combination of experience and open-mindedness. Also, the fact that he has had the courage to change his point of view to acknowledge the complexity of difficult ethical dilemmas, such as the so-called right to die (he is now in favour).

Perhaps that is the benefit of being a good listener. Someone who can offer comfort, support and advice, not necessarily judgement. And perhaps in these stories shared there is a kind of release and, if nothing else, a kind of admiration for what the human heart can and does endure.

A personal note

Should the secrets of the confessional stay secret? As it happens, the confession box is a Catholic institution and we do not have it in Judaism. Still, I have protected individuals by changing their names where appropriate, but the episodes themselves are all true. The real revelation is not the identity of those written about, but whether we recognise aspects of ourselves in the incidents, be it with a wry smile or sense of alarm.

Some of the stories relate to my community at Maidenhead, but most are from people I have met elsewhere through other involvements, whether as police chaplain, prison chaplain, working nationally with mixed-faith couples or the countless individuals throughout the country who write to me about their situation following broadcasts on the BBC they have seen or heard.

The well-used phrase 'you couldn't make it up if you tried' applies to many of the cases, whether they be the examples of appalling recklessness or instances of magnificent endeavour. As the Yiddish saying goes, 'life is with the people', and there is no greater source of richness than the astonishing escapades that people get up to.

As for my own community, I can attest that although members of Maidenhead have their share of personal problems, the community itself lacks any serious offenders or major fault-lines. Comprising over 800 households, it may not be an oasis of perfection, but it is certainly a joy to be part of.

Jonathan Romain

Note on the text
Jewish terms in italics can be found in the Glossary at the end of the book.

1

Sexual misdemeanours

The temptress

I had known Deirdre for some years. Her husband, Patrick, was an Irish Catholic, but totally lapsed and never went to church. In fact, he knew me better than the local priest and was often at the synagogue on a Sunday morning when he brought their two daughters to the Religion School. It was a good marriage and they seemed a typical happy family. The story then began to take on a tragic element that came out of the blue for them, but which will be horribly familiar to many others who have experienced something similar. He began to feel unwell, enduring constant headaches; the doctors suggested various remedies, all of which failed. Eventually it was decided to investigate worst-case explanations, and, sadly, a brain tumour was discovered: inoperable. He was kept as comfortable as possible through medication and, with the help of Macmillan nurses, his wife ensured that he was looked after at home, never spent a night away from her, and he died in his own bed a few months later.

Throughout this period, she had been fighting on all fronts
– supporting him, his parents, their two girls, nursing him,
keeping home life going as normally as possible for the sake
of the children, and dealing with her own grief at the impending loss, not to mention the financial implications she
was facing. I rang her the week after the funeral, then again
a month after that. On both occasions she said that life was
tough, and that, after giving such intense care – physically
and emotionally – she was drained, but she was function-
ing and knew she would be OK. I told her to get in touch if
ever she wanted to chat about matters or if she hit a really
difficult period.

A few months later, Deirdre rang. Could we meet? We
fixed a time and she came round to the synagogue office. She
had always been an attractive woman, and although she had
neglected her personal appearance when her husband had
begun to decline, she was back to her old self: smartly dressed
and expertly made up. It was a small office, with space just
for a desk and some old bookcases, not the larger room I
have now, which has a 'chatting area' with some comfortable
chairs opposite each other that create a more suitable atmosphere for personal conversations. With hindsight, I was very
grateful for just having that impedimentary desk at the time.
I sat one side of it and she the other. We chatted generalities
for a while, me asking about her work and how the girls were
adjusting, and then she suddenly interrupted the flow and
said: 'I want to talk about me.' That was what I was expecting,
so no surprise there, but I did notice that she said it in a very
unusual way and was looking at me very intensely. 'It's hard
being a widow,' she continued. I nodded sympathetically,

assuming she meant being alone or being the only adult bringing up the children. 'It's not so much being alone or being the only adult bringing up the children,' she said, as if reading my thoughts, although she was saying the words in a semi-breathless way, very slowly and pointedly. 'No, the problem is being a woman alone' – the breathlessness turned into heavy breathing – 'a woman who needs a man.'

I began to sense that this conversation was going into a direction I might find difficult. This was confirmed when, without taking her gaze off me, she undid the top button of her blouse. I made some incoherent remark about how much must have changed in her life. She leant back in the chair and opened her legs as wide as the skirt would allow. Yes, this was definitely heading in the wrong direction. But, at the same time, there was no denying that she was attractive. When I was a teenager, I read an article that claimed that whenever a man saw a woman, part of his brain always wondered what she would be like in bed. I remember being indignant at the time, thinking how crude and sexist this was, and totally alien to my teenage idealism and my belief in the purity of true love. Maybe the article had a point, however, and we blokes are genetically disposed to judge women in that way. Of course, what counts is what we do about it, and hopefully the more evolved, less Neanderthal part of our brain stops us from clunking women over the head with a club and dragging them by the hair into our cave. Instead, we value a person for their character, respect their individuality and judge them according to whatever talents they have. Meanwhile, Deirdre had undone another button and her breasts were heaving.

The one thing I knew I was not going to do was what she clearly wanted – for me to leap over the desk and take her in my arms. But what to do instead? Tell her I was appalled and disgusted (albeit mildly flattered) and send her packing? But that would not help her self-respect at a time when she was in emotional free-fall, while it would also mean she was unlikely to ever come back and so would lose the support that came from being part of the community.

I decided it was better to play the dullard who was oblivious to her desires and undeserving of her charms. 'Yes,' I said with idiotic firmness, 'having a man around the place is so important.' I stood up and continued: 'I know just the person, a member of the community who has learning difficulties but is great at DIY and can do any jobs around the house you need. Leaking taps, broken shelves. He's great. What's more, he is much cheaper than most professionals and just as good.' Opening the door for her and indicating that she was better off outside than inside – a sentiment which she was fast beginning to realise herself – I added chirpily: 'I don't have his phone number on me now, but I'll post it to you in the next few days, so that you've always got it if something breaks and needs fixing.' By now she had buttoned up, having come to the rapid conclusion that such an oafish rabbi was of no use to her and she was wasting her time in his office. She stayed a member, I contacted her periodically and everything was conducted as if it had been a normal bereavement counselling session. She kept her pride and I kept my virtue. But each of us could so easily have lost both.

Did he die with a smile on his face?

Priscilla was born in India, as her grandfather had been a civil servant there and her parents had often gone there for long stays. She was schooled and brought up in England, but always loved the lure of travelling, and spent her early twenties abroad, where she met her Muslim husband. They returned to England and settled down. It turned out she was infertile, a regret she never openly expressed but sometimes hinted at. Still, at least it was a blissfully happy marriage. It sort of ended that way too. They were making love and he had a massive heart attack, dying immediately. He was a large man, and her superb cooking had meant he also carried a fair weight. She, by contrast, was very slender. Her horror at the turn of events was compounded by the fact that she could not move. His dead body was pinning her to the bed. She started pummelling the man she adored. She still could not shift him off her. Not only was she finding it hard to breathe, but a sense of rising panic made her feel she might either be crushed to death or suffer a heart attack of her own.

Moreover, the one person she would normally summon to help her if any problem arose was not only dead but the cause of her distress. She stopped trying to throw him off and instead adopted a slower and more measured way of inching out of his grasp. Eventually she engineered herself free. She lay still for a while, exhausted physically and distraught emotionally. Her thoughts leapt about wildly. What was she going to tell her friends – the full story or an edited version? Should she even tell the police, whom she knew she must soon call? If she had been able to summon help immediately, might he still be alive? She did tell her rabbi, which is why I know the story, but not the imam who actually carried out the funeral. She was informed by the coroner, who thought it might help her to know, that sex did not necessarily cause the heart attack and the timing was purely coincidental.

From a technical point of view, sex is akin to climbing two flights of stairs or taking a brisk walk, and so does not increase the risk of cardiovascular problems. This is not the first time such a death has occurred, nor will it be the last. It lends itself to gratuitous remarks about 'how to die happy!' – it is virtually impossible not to think that, even if one refrains from actually saying it – but, for the Priscillas of this world, it turned what might have been the comforting memory of their last moment of intimacy together into a nightmare that has haunted her ever since.

I was familiar with a variant case of the above, the non-Jewish partner of a member of the community, where the husband concerned also died while having sex, but this time with someone who was not his wife. His wife was informed of the exact circumstances, though not the vicar who took the service. It meant that the funeral was particularly difficult for her, leaving her seething rather than grieving, and cursing him rather than mourning for him. I reckon I had the easier case with which to deal.

Au pairs should be seen but not bedded

There was no question that the wife needed an au pair to help her. Caroline had been involved in a bicycle accident that left her with a broken leg and fractured hip. It meant she was able to do very little other than sit and recuperate, initially at hospital and then back home. Meanwhile, her three teenage sons needed feeding and ferrying, and the horse needed mucking out. Her husband had taken two weeks off work after the accident, but he had now gone back to work. The au pair seemed decent enough, but as the weeks went by her attitude changed markedly. At first, she had been helpful and solicitous; but she gradually became more and more haughty. It was as if, Caroline felt, she owned the house and was deigning to let Caroline live there. What was even more worrying was that the three boys also seemed to be different. The phrase she used was 'more cocky'. At first, she put it down to the fact that she was injured and, therefore, in their eyes perhaps, useless and deserving less respect. It would be nice to think that they would still treat her the same as when she was rushing around doing things for them, but, OK, teenagers can be very self-centred. It was only when her husband started acting strangely – as if embarrassed to talk to her – that she decided that either she was going insane or that something was happening that she needed to investigate.

By now, she had begun to hobble around the house and she noticed that the au pair – who had gone out on some errand – had left her handbag balanced perilously on the edge of a chair. As she moved it, a packet of Durex contraceptives fell out, half-empty. She had never enquired what the au pair did on her days off, when she tended to go to the local pub, so the discovery did not particularly shock her, and she put them back. It was ten minutes later, though, when she froze, transfixed by the thought that maybe they had been for use inside the house rather than outside it. It then occurred to Caroline that the au pair occasionally said about an event or conversation, 'Oh, I must put that in my diary.' Might the diary reveal more? Caroline limped upstairs and went into the au pair's bedroom. Careful to keep an ear open for her return, Caroline looked around. It only took a few moments to find the diary in one of the drawers. As she read through the entries for recent weeks, she grew increasingly agitated. Her worst suspicion was totally unwarranted, for the situation was considerably blacker than that. Not only had the au pair had sex with her husband, she had also slept with all three of her sons. Whether they each knew they were part of her serial seduction of the male members of the family was not clear, but Caroline knew and was appalled. She chose to ignore the door opening and kept reading until the au pair came upstairs. Caroline held up the diary, uttered a stream of abuse that she had no idea she was capable of giving, and told her she was dismissed. The au pair replied with equal vehemence, only pausing to point out that she had been doing everyone a favour. She was also kind enough to inform Caroline how much they had enjoyed it. Caroline went downstairs and left her to pack. It did occur to Caroline that as one of the boys was under-age – fifteen – she could instigate criminal proceedings, but she had no wish to drag the family through the courts and felt that expelling her would be victory enough. She never told the boys she knew, although she did inform her husband about her knowledge of his infidelity. Even so, she did not let on that he had been sharing the same person as all of his sons. She wanted him to be on best behaviour for the rest of the marriage, but not ruin his relationship with them. It was the first serious hiccup in the marriage and Caroline was strong enough to let it pass. As it turned out, she made the right decision and it lasted successfully until her death eighteen years later from cancer. Personally, I am just grateful that the au pair did use contraceptives, as sorting out a paternity suit could have proved highly traumatic should she have fallen pregnant.

The home help who was definitely not helpful

When Ronald decided to get a home help, his older brother Charles was greatly relieved. Ronald was seventy-nine, reasonably fit but not as healthy as he once was, and after four years of being a widower, he needed some help around the house. His only daughter had died several years earlier in a boating accident. She had never married, leaving Charles his closest living relative and feeling responsible for him. What Charles and his own family had not expected was that the home help spent the first ten minutes looking round the house and then went to bed with Ronald. It was not that Charles was prudish, but he was worried about her intentions. It would be one thing to slide between the sheets if a relationship developed after she had got to know him well, but after ten minutes? That seemed more like a plan of action. Yes, she did do some cleaning and cooked for him, but did she really care about him or did she see him as a meal ticket? The massive age gap also fuelled suspicions. A 79-year-old might find a 34-year-old attractive – but the other way round? Worst of all was the fact that she had the habit of disappearing for three or four days at a time. It was not so much that it disrupted his routine, but that it raised questions about what she was doing. Was she bedding another septuagenarian and sprinkling his life with fantasies about the future too?

The family might be able to reconcile themselves to a gold-digger who at least made Ronald happy in his final years, but not to one who cheated on him and treated him uncaringly. There was also the matter of inheritance. As a childless widower, much of his estate would pass to Charles's children and grandchildren; but if the home help persuaded Ronald to propose to her and ended up as his wife, the situation would be very different. They were good people and did try not to let that influence their thinking, but that conflict of interest further added to their angst. There was also the worry that, once married, she might be much less helpful and more demanding. And would her periods of absenteeism continue? Charles did try to raise the issue with Ronald, but to no avail, as he dismissed any such discussion with the words: 'You're over-reacting. We are very fond of each other and I'm surprised you can't see that.' As the weeks passed, Ronald's growing attachment to her made them increasingly anxious about her true nature. When Ronald announced they were going on a two-week cruise together and might have 'plans' thereafter, Charles's daughter suggested hiring a private detective to investigate her background. It was a wise move. It turned out that five years earlier she had married someone in his eighties who now had Alzheimer's and was living in a care home. But the person she went off to see was never her aged husband, rather the man who had been her partner for more than a decade and by whom she had a child. Charles was doubly distressed. It was not pleasant for him to have to tell his brother he was the victim of an emotional scam. What was even worse was having to destroy the happy glow Ronald had acquired. It would have evaporated at some point in the future, but it had transformed his life so far, however deceptively. Going back to being a lonely widower would not be easy. Charles decided to at least let him enjoy the cruise before breaking the news to him.

The love child

Shirley and Craig had both grown up in Glasgow, but only met in their thirties when working in London. After a few months' courtship, they had married and later moved to Leeds. Two sons followed, and although home life had its usual ups and downs, all four would describe themselves as part of a close and loving family. That perception came under great strain when Shirley answered the phone one day and a voice said: 'Hello, this is your daughter Emilie.' Fortunately, Craig had taken the two boys to a violent gangster movie at the local cinema that Shirley had no desire to see, so she had a bit of time alone to adjust to the call and its implications. Emilie was the daughter she had conceived when living together with her first long-term partner, Neil, on a commune and completely cut off from her own family. The relationship ended when Emilie was only four months old. For a range of financial and career reasons, it seemed best that Emilie remain with Neil, while it was mutually agreed that it would be best for Emilie's emotional development if she bonded with Neil's new partner and sever ties completely with Shirley. The problem was that, as her way of coping with the sense of loss, and perhaps also of failure, Shirley had completely blocked out all memory of Emilie and had never told anyone about her. Nobody knew at all. Now, aged twenty-eight, Emilie had located her mother and wanted to meet. Could she come to visit that weekend? Shirley realised that even if she dissuaded her from coming then, Emilie would make contact again and she had to tell Craig and the boys before they found out through some other source. It was a difficult series of conversations.

After the boys had gone to bed, she told Craig. She had expected him to understand and put it down to the indiscretions of youth. Instead, he looked at her incredulously, tried to splutter a response but found he was unable to keep his voice level, and so got up to leave the house, saying: 'I'll be back in a while. Wait for me.' As he explained on his return, what shocked him was not the existence of the girl, but that Shirley had never told him. 'It wouldn't have made any difference to our relationship,' he said, 'but I can't understand why you held back on such a major part of your life and which happened only a few years before we met.' The following morning, they jointly told the boys, who reacted very differently from each other. The elder felt highly slighted that he had suddenly lost his status as the firstborn. The younger was more intrigued to know if they looked like each other. Having adjusted to the new reality, Craig had a series of practical concerns: if Emilie wanted to visit more frequently, would that cause friction by distracting Shirley's attention from him and the boys? Depending on what sort of person she was, might she be a bad influence on the boys at a time when they were very impressionable? And might she be looking for financial support from Shirley that would put strain on the family resources?

It was with some nervousness, therefore, that the family awaited Emilie's arrival that weekend. It turned out that she had decided to contact Shirley after watching episodes of the BBC programme exploring family history, *Who Do You Think You Are?*, and wanted to discover her own roots. To everyone's relief, she appeared to be neither a gold-digger nor a malign cuckoo, very keen not to alter her own way of life, but wanting to feel the potential warmth of an extended family. When she was about to go and asked if she could keep in touch, Shirley looked towards Craig who nodded affirmatively. Afterwards, he chided Shirley again for keeping her secret. Although the meeting had gone well, it was clear that, in his mind, there had been a breach of trust that would not heal for some time. He also felt that the family structure had changed: from being part of a totally inter-dependent foursome, he was now married to someone who had three children, only two of whom were his. It made him feel a disconnection with his wife that was a totally new experience and very unsettling. Emilie's phone call had helped answer her own personal needs, but had caused contentious ripples across previously placid family waters.

Sadly, she had to seduce him

Patricia was attractive and outgoing, so she was never short of boyfriends. Shortly after meeting Will, she realised that this was the man she wanted to marry. He felt the same way about her and the wedding duly took place. Immediately after the reception, they went to Heathrow and headed off for their honeymoon. As they got into bed, he said: 'It's been a wonderful day but I'm exhausted,' turned over and went to sleep. The same thing happened the rest of the week, and then once they were back home. After a while, he did not even say anything but just kissed her goodnight. Patricia was hurt and confused. Her problem in the past had been stopping boyfriends having sex on their first date and making them wait until she was ready for it. Will had made it clear early on that he did not believe in sex before marriage and, although slightly bemused, it had added to her respect for him. Now it seemed that he did not believe in sex *after* marriage either. Or maybe it was her fault? Maybe she was not as attractive physically as she'd thought? Having been used to postponing other people's sexual desires, she was the one being denied. The strange thing was, the rest of the time, everything was fine between them. The sparkle that existed between them when they were dating continued unabated. She did try to raise the issue with him, but every time, he batted it away. She also tried taking the lead once in bed, trying to stimulate him, but he had firmly resisted and said that 'now's not the time'. She was becoming increasingly desperate and wondered whether non-consummation was grounds for divorce. She knew she should talk to family or friends, but felt it was both too intimate and too ridiculous to admit. She had mentally prepared for several possible issues they might face – over money or certain friends – but marital celibacy had never occurred to her.

On their first anniversary, Will took her to a restaurant she had once mentioned she would love to go to. It was great of him to remember and they had a truly lovely evening, but she could not enjoy it properly knowing that, although that night might be a suitable time for him to start their sexual relationship, she was sure it would not happen. She was right. It triggered her to seek professional help. She brushed away the suggestion that his reticence was a sign of a malaise in the relationship, which was otherwise very good. She also gave short shrift to the idea that Will was gay. The two of them concluded it was clearly an emotional or psychological blockage, perhaps relating to his childhood or a traumatic experience of some kind later on. The best solution was for Will himself to stop avoiding the issue and seek professional help. When Patricia put the idea to him, he was too furious that she had mentioned it to someone else to even consider what had been said. Patricia did start to think more seriously about divorce, but decided to hold back for two reasons. First, she had made a commitment that she had not undertaken lightly and felt duty-bound to honour as much as possible. Second, she and Will did get on very well; it was only night time that was the problem.

The solution came by accident. Another couple – old friends of his from university days that she had got to know and come to like immensely – were due to come for dinner one Saturday evening. She went to a lot of trouble to arrange a fine meal and deck the table out. An hour before they were due to come, they phoned very apologetically to say they could not make it as one of their children had taken ill and they did not want to leave him with a babysitter. 'Oh well,' Patricia said to Will, 'too late to change plans now. We'll have a feast of our own; there's plenty of food and wine to get through!' In fact, she concentrated more on the wine than the food and deliberately got Will drunk while staying sober herself. At that point, she started undressing him. Although he resisted a little, it was not enough to dissuade her. She had to take the lead throughout and ended up astride him. Afterwards he shuffled off to bed and she started clearing the table. He said nothing the next morning, and nor did she. The following night he started touching her, albeit nervously, and she helped him do the rest. From then on, sex did happen periodically and two years later the result was twins. After that, it ceased completely. Patricia was sorry, but no longer minded. Her sense of self-worth had been restored and the children she had wanted had materialised. If the rest of the marriage had not been good, it might well have made a difference, but she was content to sacrifice sex for the parts of the marriage that did work. Will continued to refuse to speak about it, and she gave up trying to fathom out the source of his inhibition. It remained a mystery, family life took precedence and sex became something that other people did.

Coming out

Rachel phoned me at home crying so much that I kept having to ask her to repeat what she was saying. It transpired that her husband Rick had been arrested. But that was not what had reduced a normally very strong and self-assured woman to a tearful wreck. As she haltingly tried to explain, various images flashed through my mind – he had been caught speeding, perhaps worse, had hit a pedestrian, or maybe had got into a fight at a bar and had hurt someone badly. It was none of these. He had been arrested in the public toilets having sex with another man. This occurred in the 1990s, when homosexuality was becoming more accepted but still subject to prejudice in many circles. But, for Rachel, the shock was much more personal. Was this the man whom she had married only two years earlier and by whom she was expecting a child? Was it a one-off or symptomatic of a hidden identity? How could she have not realised, or had she been deliberately deceived? What would it do to their future, or mean for their unborn child? After Rick was released, the three of us had a long conversation. He said he loved Rachel very much and wanted the marriage to continue, but that he was aware of also feeling attracted to men. He described it as an occasional feeling rather than a permanent situation, which is why he had always considered himself heterosexual and courted Rachel. Of course, as I mentioned to him, quite apart from the question of his sexual identity, one of the other issues was fidelity. If he had been attracted to another woman, hopefully he would have resisted, whereas he had not done so here. Just because it was a same-sex relationship did not mean it was any less of a betrayal of his marital vows.

Rachel and Rick stayed together, though I suspect he did have occasional gay relationships but made sure they were not discovered. However, subsequent years saw an increasing number of men and women who had been married for several years, if not decades, coming out and declaring they were gay or lesbian. When Samantha's husband of twenty-two years told her that he had fallen in love with another man, she was very upset at first but came to accept it completely within days. When I asked her why she was so phlegmatic about it, given that many others would be angry or distraught, she replied: 'If he'd fallen for another woman, I could have tried to win him back in some way – dressed better, altered my hairstyle, whatever – but how can I compete with another man? I knew I simply had to let go.'

The attractive father-in-law

Clive and his father had never been particularly close. There was no falling out or hostility, they just never had anything in common. He was at Clive's wedding, of course, as they were still family and he did get on well with Clive's wife, Claire. Unfortunately, he got on more than well with her. One day I had a call from Clive, who told me that Claire had left him. Before I had a chance to ask what the cause of the break-up was, he added: 'She and my father have gone off to live together.'

The usual platitudes about being sorry to hear the news are fairly weak when it is an ordinary split, but when it involves such a double betrayal, they are even more useless. I asked him if he had had any inkling of it in advance, but no, he had not seen any warning signs. I said he must feel devastated, to which he replied: 'More numb than devastated.' There are some splits, even those involving a third person, that can be healed, but I doubted that would be possible in this instance. They include, for instance, an affair that is discovered that neither party had seen as permanent and might have ended of its own accord; or a walk-out that takes place in a moment of frustration from which the person intended to return but the other partner misreads as final.

I did call Claire to see if she wanted to talk things over, but, as she put it: 'There's no turning back on this one.' They eventually moved to a part of the country where they would be unlikely to be known, and so would be seen by others as an older man with a trophy wife rather than be suspected as incestuous (albeit morally speaking, rather than legally). Clive had an especially difficult time, not only having to cope with an unexpected divorce, but facing those in the family who knew the full story. He told friends and work colleagues that 'Claire had gone off with another bloke', but never felt he benefited from the sympathy and support they offered as he knew it was based on incomplete knowledge, while he could never open up and express the true depth of his anger. He told me he was going to 'take a break' from the synagogue for a while as he feared he would either be physically sick or shout abuse if ever he heard the command about honouring your father read out. I did point out that it was not an absolute command, and quoted the rabbinic interpretation that it was conditional: yes, you should honour your father, but only if he acts like a father should; and if he does not do so, then he forfeits the honour due to him. But, while that made a lot of sense to me, to a hurt Clive it was no comfort and he duly left the community.

The virgin birth

D oris was an attractive divorcee, but at thirty-eight she was beginning to worry that she might never have children, something she desperately wanted. When she rang me to say she was pregnant, my first words were: 'That's great

– congratulations!' However, knowing that she did not have a steady partner at the time, I felt obliged to follow that up with the obvious question of: 'So tell me, who is the father?' (Incidentally, although that may seem intrusive, I have always taken the view that one of the rabbi's jobs is to ask the questions that other people do not like to ask. Such as that one. Or in hospital, to ask a terminally ill patient if they are afraid of death. Or a bereaved widow whose husband refused to quit smoking and died of lung cancer in his fifties: are you angry with him? Questions they can brush away if they so wish, but which they may wish to talk about, rage about or just have their silent nod acknowledged.)

In this case, Doris just said sweetly: 'There is no father.' Assuming she meant she did not want her custody of the child to be challenged by whoever was the father, I said, semi-jocularly: 'Hold on, the child may be yours and nowadays it is OK to be a single mum, but I presume you did sleep with someone?' 'No,' she replied. 'I did not sleep with anyone.' I gulped and was glad she could not see my facial expression: 'So are you saying it was a virgin birth?' 'Well, nobody else was involved, so I guess so,' was her verdict. I did press her on the matter when I saw her the following week, simply to prepare her for the onslaught of disbelief with which she would be greeted once she told others. Gently but firmly, I explained the logical unlikelihood, while also pointing out that its theological associations meant people would view her as claiming, at very least, some form of divine privilege. But it was all to no avail. She maintained her version of events for several months. A more plausible answer eventually came to light when her mother reminded her that, as a child, she used to be prone to sleep-walking and asked if there had been anyone else in the house around the time she got pregnant. In fact, there was – a student who was her lodger, while she had also had a male friend staying for a couple of nights. Doris was adamant that she had not had sex with them, while they dismissed the idea too. However, the odds on her sleep-walking down the corridor into either of their rooms, them willingly accepting an unexpected bed-mate, and her then returning to her own room afterwards, struck me as much more credible than the divine option.

The adultery that was justified

Ronnie and Celia had had a good marriage, but it was cut short when he had a brain haemorrhage in his mid-forties, which resulted in him going into a deep coma. Celia visited him in the local hospital daily, but never received the slightest response from him – which the doctors had warned her to expect, but which she had refused to accept. At first, she had spoken to him, told him what had happened to her that day at work and chatted about the news. After a while, she found this one-way conversation too depressing and just sat there in silence. After a few months, she cut the visits to twice weekly. After a year, she began to dread sitting alone with the man she still loved but with whom she could no longer communicate, something she found unbearable. She mentioned this to her neighbour while chatting to him one day when he asked after Ronnie. He offered to accompany her next time she went – 'it might help having someone else there' – which, after mulling it over for a couple of days, she accepted. Once there, they chatted about this and that, and Celia felt it was indeed much easier having company, both for her sake and just in case Ronnie could sense life going on around her. So when Henry – the neighbour – offered to come again, she readily agreed. In fact, she began to look forward to their weekly visits together.

As for Henry, he had only moved to the area three years earlier, after his divorce, hardly knew anyone locally and was glad to have one evening a week that he did not spend alone. When he happened to mention that his culinary skills were being tested to the limit after a year of cooking for himself, Celia suggested she'd make a meal for the two of them after their next visit and they could eat together. This duly happened, became more frequent, a relationship developed and the two of them 'became an item'. Celia came to see me about it. She was clearly a much happier person than before, and the haunted look she had acquired after her lonely visits to a comatose Ronnie had disappeared. Yet she also felt guilty that she was letting him down and betraying him. What should she do?

I felt enormously sympathetic towards her. It had been a good marriage, and she had been very dutiful ever since Ronnie had been in hospital. The doctors said he had no hope of recovery, but was it necessary for her to be entombed with him, or did she have a right to renew her life? Moreover, despite now living together, she and Henry both continued to go twice weekly to visit Ronnie, so, from a practical point of view, he was not being neglected as a result of their relationship. She had no intention of divorcing him, but did want to make her present and future with Henry. It was a limbo state of affairs, which he accepted, with the understanding being that, as and when Ronnie passed away, they would marry. From a Jewish point of view, this posed two problems. First, the obvious one of open adultery. Second, the fact that one cannot marry one's paramour, i.e. the person with whom one had committed adultery. I discussed both aspects with her. The rule about the paramour, I said, did not really apply to her situation, as it was aimed at adultery that caused a divorce and to discourage marrying the person who had been responsible for the break-up of one's previous marriage, whereas she was not jettisoning her marriage. As for the adultery itself: yes, technically it was wrong, but I reckoned that morally it was justifiable – both because she deserved some happiness and because Ronnie was not suffering because of it. I did point out that there were husbands and wives who would not countenance such behaviour and who would be horrified at having another relationship while their spouse was still alive. I told her that I would certainly admire their nobility and principles, but I could not find it in me to deny her practical happiness.

The story looked set to end well, but then had a strange twist to it. Celia and Henry continued living together – and visiting Ronnie – for the next three years, after which he died when he contracted pneumonia. After a respectable interval, they got married. Two years later, though, they got divorced. Was it just yet another break-up, so common in today's society, by a couple who were thrown together by chance – or did the death of the absent third party to the relationship somehow weaken it irrevocably?

The rise and decline of a mistress

Lottie was a vibrant lady, and still attractive in her early seventies. I was surprised she had never married, as she must have been the object of many proposals. I was right. She had refused them all, however, because of Kurt. Like her, he was from the Continent and they had both been fortunate enough to find refuge in England in the 1930s, before war slammed shut the gates of immigration and butchery descended upon Europe. They met after the war while working for the same textiles firm. By then, Kurt had married an English woman who was not Jewish. It was a reasonable marriage but not totally fulfilling. Not only was Lottie very attractive, she offered the familiar warmth of someone both Continental and Jewish. They became lovers, but Kurt always made it clear that he would not leave his wife because they already had children. Lottie regretted this, but understood and accepted it, for not only was it a sexual affair but based on a deep love for each other. For this reason, it continued for over forty years and it remained secret from the rest of the world. While they were both working it was relatively easy to meet privately, but retirement presented a challenge. It was solved by both buying dogs. Kurt's wife had no objection to a dog in the house, but was not particularly keen on having to walk it, so the understanding was that this was Kurt's daily task and part of keeping him fit. Every day, he walked the dog and at a discreet distance would meet up with Lottie, who would also, coincidentally, be walking her dog at the same time and place. By that stage in their lives, sex was no longer as important as it was during their earlier period together, and they were content to see each other daily, walk side by side and share a precious half-hour or so. To passing strangers, they were an elderly couple of dog-walkers deep in conversation, but they knew they were making love to each other. Much might have changed if Kurt's wife had pre-deceased him, but she outlived him. His death was doubly difficult for Lottie, for not only had she lost the man she had adored for most of her adult life, but she could not mourn in public. His widow received all the condolences, but no one offered Lottie any sympathy. His widow was allowed to break into tears with friends, but Lottie had to stifle hers. Only Lottie's dog knew, and in Kurt's honour they still took that same walk every day.

I had first met Lottie some two years after Kurt had died, and she did not mention anything about him, but I sensed there was a sadness inside her, somehow had an intuition as to what might be the cause and asked if she wanted to unburden herself. She did. The grief had become too much to hold alone. We also devised a discreet way of acknowledging his death and her pain, by me mentioning his name before the *kaddish*/memorial prayer every year at the Sabbath service immediately prior to the anniversary of his passing. I never looked in her direction when saying it, as I would normally do in the case of partners of other members, but hearing his name called out publicly in synagogue – her Kurt in her synagogue – helped her with what is probably the most difficult of all mourning processes, the loss of a love that could never be made known.

Professional sex

My father – generally a very astute man – made one major error of judgement when I told him that I wanted to become a rabbi. 'Why do you want to spend your days in an ivory tower studying ancient tomes and let life pass you by?' He could not have been more wrong – though maybe he was thinking of older models of rabbinic practice (sometimes cruelly typecast as 'invisible six days a week and incomprehensible on the seventh'). Far from being cut off from life, as a congregational rabbi, I am immersed in all its joys, sadnesses, bitter moments and sordid elements. This includes numerous sexual escapades in which various members have engaged, including professionals. Alice, an architect with a formidable reputation for eye-catching designs, added to her reputation in a less noteworthy way. She and a client had arranged a one-hour session together, but it proved inadequate and spilt over into dinner and then bed together. When he later checked the bill for that day's consultation, he found he had been charged not just for the one hour in the office, but four hours, including the time spent between the sheets. He had assumed that was not part of her professional services, but she obviously thought otherwise!

Meanwhile, Jolene was a barrister working in a prestigious set of chambers. She was defending a man accused of a serious breach of copyright resulting in profits he claimed were entirely legitimate but which the plaintiff thought amounted to corporate theft. When her client and his wife had met Jolene, the two women had seemed to click and agreed to meet socially. In fact, it was a lesbian tryst that continued throughout the court case. It meant that Jolene was having an affair with her client's wife while attempting to save him from prison. At least, my hope was that she was attempting to save him and not neglecting his case ... nor deliberately engineering matters so that he ended up being conveniently taken off the scene to Jolene's advantage. My trust in the goodness of human nature remains, but it has had to survive some ferocious battering.

Is it wrong or do all blokes do it?

Brian was an uncomplicated sort of person, for whom life was straightforward and who approached it in a very direct way, enjoying the ups and pushing himself through the downs. So I was not at all surprised when, during a chat about another matter, he suddenly changed topics and said: 'Can I ask you about something else? It's a question that's been bothering me for a while. My wife and I have a good marriage – genuinely – but when we make love I often find myself thinking about other women ... no one in particular, just women I've seen in the street or on TV, so no one I have a relationship with ... I guess because, after making love with the same person for over twenty years, it's more stimulating that way ... and I wanted to know if that's considered a sin in Judaism?'

I remember giving an involuntary laugh at the time, not, as I hastened to tell him at the time, because I was laughing at him, but because I was sure that it was a question common to virtually every other man in the community, but only Brian was the one who was uninhibited enough to actually ask it. Of course, it may also apply to women just as much. But as is so often the case, what is thought to be a daring, modern question had long been pre-empted by previous generations of rabbis. In this case, the great Egyptian scholar, Moses Maimonides, had tackled it as far back as the twelfth century. In his view, a man who thought of another woman while making love to his wife was committing adultery. When Brian's face fell at hearing this, I reminded him that we do not have the concept of infallible rabbis in Judaism. I had quoted Maimonides merely to show the issue had history and was not limited to his personal bedroom.

I also said that while Maimonides certainly needed to be taken seriously and was renowned for his pragmatic approach, here he was being uncharacteristically irrational. Judaism largely concentrates on what we should and should not do, but does not put nearly as much energy into seeking to control what we think. And for good reason, as it is almost impossible to edit one's thoughts, whereas what counts is what we do with them. Thus, we may envy someone else's wealth – sigh over their villa abroad or Lamborghini in the drive – yet we do not steal from them or vandalise their property, but try to work hard enough to achieve such possessions for ourselves too. It is similar with sex. Many a man would find it hard not to admire a beautiful woman or think about her afterwards, but that does not lead them to have an affair with her. Many would also find it impossible not to think of her while making love to their wife, but, providing it did not harm the relationship, there was no problem. Some sex therapists would argue that, on the contrary, it can help stimulate a sex life that has become formulaic and routine.

'So why did Maimonides object?' replied Brian. I told

him that my guess was that although he knew it was probably built into our sexual DNA and unalterable, he did not
want to encourage it. This might have been partly because
it can be seen as very uncomplimentary to one's partner –
'How would you feel', I asked him, 'if your wife thought of
George Clooney while making love to you?' – and partly lest
it eroded the boundary between thinking about an act and
doing it. I reckon Maimonides felt the closer we stuck to the
ideal position, when we departed away from it, it would not
be straying as far as we might otherwise go. I never asked if
Brian subsequently shared the conversation with his wife. I
suspect not – either because he thought that 'ignorance is
bliss' and he did not want to upset her, or, for exactly the same
principle, did not want to start a conversation that might end
up with her upsetting him if she admitted her fantasies!

Unholy sex

While in the ultra-Orthodox *yeshivah*/rabbinic seminary
in Jerusalem, I developed a friendship with an American called Frankie, who had also come from outside that
world. We had both gone to the Western Wall to pray there at
Kol Nidre, the night of *Yom Kippur*, and then made our separate ways back to the *yeshivah*, where we had accommodation.
The following morning, he woke me up and said we had to
talk, but insisted that it had to be outside the *yeshivah*.

He told me that, on leaving the Western Wall, he had
met up with a girl from his home state of Ohio, also around
twenty years old and who was at a women's *yeshivah*. He had

offered to walk her home, one thing had led to another, and they had ended up sleeping together. This was on *Kol Nidre*, usually considered the most sacred and awesome period in the entire year and when one of the five specific acts from which one should abstain is having sexual relations with one's wife. Having sex with someone who was not even his wife was an added sin and meant a doubling of his religious crimes. I told him that would have been bad enough any time of the year, but on the one night that sex was prohibited was breath-takingly wrong in that ultra-Orthodox setting. 'I know', said Frankie, 'but that's not the real problem I wanted to talk to you about.' I looked puzzled, wondering what could possibly be worse. 'I'm scared she might be pregnant,' he continued, 'as I didn't use a condom'. I gawped at him: 'Why on earth not?' 'You know as well as I do,' he replied, 'as it's strictly forbidden.' He was right, in that although contraception is permitted, Orthodoxy does not permit condoms. 'Hold on,' I responded, perplexed, 'condoms are banned, but so is sex on *Kol Nidre* and so is sex before marriage, so if you were going to break those two laws, then why didn't you break the third?' He looked sheepish and mumbled an incoherent excuse that did not alter the fact that he might have just become a dad. I advised that unless he wanted to marry the girl, or she wanted to keep the potential baby, he had better ask her to take a morning-after pill. 'But that's forbidden in Orthodox law!' he exclaimed. 'So was what you did, but that didn't seem to stop you!' was my practical but perhaps unsympathetic reply. As it happened, we were both leaving the *yeshivah* to go elsewhere, and in a time before mobile phones, emails and Facebook existed, it was easy to lose touch. So I never found out what happened, but my strong suspicion is that, just as lust had won over religious law the night before, so self-preservation would do so the following day.

No, don't tell your wife

When Richard came to my office at the time I had agreed to meet him, he sat down in the chair opposite me with a sigh. It was the sort of sigh that indicated he was gearing himself up to unload something that had been on his mind for a while and which had finally become too difficult to keep to himself. So I just waited until he was ready to tell his story. Essentially, he had had an affair with someone at work, kept it going for several months, felt increasingly guilty about cheating his wife and eventually brought it to an end without hurting the other person too much and before it became public knowledge. 'It was nothing deeply emotional, more the excitement of illicit sex, and although we liked each other, it was never going to go anywhere.' I nodded, said that these things happened and although it would have been better if he had never started it, he had done the right thing in extricating himself. But I was puzzled as to why he had wanted to see me. 'Do you feel you have not put it behind you fully?' I asked. 'Oh yes,' he replied, 'it's well and truly over, but I wanted to discuss with you how best to tell my wife.' Now it was my turn to sigh. 'Look, you may not expect me to say this, but my strong advice is not to tell her. Marriage is based on trust. If you tell her, you will not only upset her terribly, but endanger the relationship. If the situation were different and there was a strong likelihood of her reading about it in the papers, then I agree it would be far better for her to hear from you first and not from anyone else. But, assuming it is over and will stay in the past, then why make her live through it?' He started to protest, but I waved him silent and continued in an even more adamant tone: 'She is the innocent party in all this, so why make her suffer? What do you achieve? All you do is shift your feelings of guilt off yourself and do an emotional dump on her. The cliché "ignorance is bliss" is only a cliché because it is true. Save her a lot of pain and give your marriage a chance of recovering. And if you feel uncomfortable for a while, okay, that's your punishment, but don't punish her as well.'

He said he was surprised at my attitude and thought he ought to be honest with her. Resisting the inclination to yell at him for being self-obsessed, I replied: 'If you ended the affair so as to save the marriage, don't now wreck it by admitting the affair. Be thankful you still have her trust, and repay it by rebuilding your own trust in yourself to be a good husband. You've done the hard part already by finishing the affair, now concentrate on the marriage.' I could tell he was actually relieved that he did not have to tell his wife, but had psyched himself up into thinking it was his moral duty. I have no doubt that honesty is not always the best policy, and morality is much more complex than simply telling the truth. Fifteen years on, Richard and his wife are still married and, if asked, she would say how lucky she is to have such a wonderful husband.

The sexpert

There has been a remarkable progression in the socio-economic mobility of the Jewish community over the last century. Our great-grandparents – as a generalisation – were tailors and carpenters and boot-makers; the next generation went into business, and often ended up owning their own firm; their children went into the professions and became doctors, lawyers, dentists and accountants. The current generation has been much more diverse, but has tended to veer towards the caring industries, with many becoming teachers, therapists and social workers. But Maidenhead has seen a vast range of occupations among its members, including a milkman, a prize cattle-breeder, an army officer and an MP. One of the more intriguing jobs was that taken by Dorothy: a sex-caller. It was not her proudest moment, but it was a way of paying the bills when she had no other means of doing so. All she had to do was be at the end of a phone at certain times of the day, let men have verbal fantasies, respond appropriately and gurgle sounds that might excite them. At first, she took it very seriously, sitting at a desk in her front room. Then she realised it was quite easy to do while getting on with other tasks, particularly in the garden, and she would often talk into the phone in one hand and do the weeding with the other. Her clients, of course, had no idea that she was outside on her knees in overalls and no doubt imagined she was writhing between silken sheets. She also quickly found out that many callers did not actually want to talk dirty but just chat. It was not sexual frustration from which they suffered, but loneliness. When she told me, rather sheepishly, about her work, I told her not to worry: it was fine so long as no one was being harmed, including her, and for some people she may even have been doing a lot of good. I told her to think of herself as a social worker in disguise.

A marital mix-up

Gilly and Trevor were friends with Dennis and Evelyn, and the two couples had dinner together once a month. Unfortunately, Trevor came home one day to find Gilly in bed with Dennis. Divorce proceedings were initiated, during which time Trevor and Evelyn consoled each other and talked about how let down they both felt. After a while, they began to feel that they had much more in common than just being the victims of a betrayal. Within a year after the divorce, not only had Gilly and Dennis married, but so had Trevor and Evelyn. Although all four of them felt that, with hindsight, the spouse swap was more appropriate than the original marriages, there was still a lot of animosity over how the change came to be effected. Thankfully, there were no children involved and so the couples did not need to have any further contact with each other. The question that exercised me was: had the adultery had been for the best or not? On the one hand, it broke the marital vows. On the other hand, had it not happened – or had it not been discovered – it would not have led to the marriages breaking up and the repartnering, which everyone agreed was more suitable. It also highlights the fact that sometimes, second marriages can be the better marriages.

The overseas affair

I used to have a soft spot for Nicky until I realised what a cad he was. He came to see me after his wife and children had left for America, where the family were relocating. He was going to join them in three months' time, once he had sold the business. He told me he needed sex and women found him attractive. Would it be OK for him to have an affair for the next three months, providing it was strictly limited till his departure and that he was faithful to his wife once he rejoined her in the States? While I was surprised at his proposal, I was also surprised that he asked my opinion. Surely he would know that I would quote the Ten Commandments and tell him: 'Thou shalt not commit adultery.' It was clear that he was not looking for a moral response but wanted to discuss the practical aspects. Whereas there are many instances where the arguments are finely balanced either way, in Nicky's case they seemed overwhelmingly on the negative side.

I quickly listed six of them. First, it is impossible to predict that an affair will be short-term, and what would happen if he found that they had established a bond he did not want to abandon? Second, it would be enormously hurtful if his wife found out – did he want to risk that? Third, was it not being unfair to the woman concerned (I assumed he had someone in mind already), whom he was using merely as a three-month stop-gap? Would she know in advance or just find out when the time was up? Fourth, if he strayed now would that not create a pattern and make it more likely he strayed when in the States? Fifth, would it not affect his relationship with his wife, for even if she never knew, he would know he had been cheating on her? Sixth, what would it do to his own self-respect and the way he thought of himself?

The longer the list grew, the more I had the sinking feeling that Nicky was mentally ticking them off as 'yes, thought of that one, no problem'. I was just a sounding board to check that he had not missed anything before going ahead with his plan. Perhaps that should have been obvious the moment he revealed it, though part of me wondered whether he was still wrestling with himself on ethical lines. There was no doubt that he did love his wife, and was working hard to build a new future for his family, but he had compartmentalised the three-month separation as a time-out from the marriage. We parted amicably, but with a clear difference in approach. I strongly suspect he did pursue his affair, but he never saw his wife again. He was a keen horseman and died in a riding accident two months later.

Surviving an affair

Esther was distraught when she heard that Leonard had been having an affair with someone at work for the last month. The unusual feature was that Leonard had chosen to tell her after it was over, because he felt it was dreadfully wrong of him and he wanted to admit it and put it behind him. There is a strong argument that it might have been kinder for him not to have revealed the matter, especially if he was fairly sure Esther might not have discovered it, and he could have avoided inflicting her with such a sense of betrayal. If he felt guilty, then having to cope with it by himself would have been a penalty he would have had to pay. The other issue was how she would react. There were a variety of responses in other cases in the community where adultery was discovered. Sometimes the injured party would immediately sue for divorce. Sometimes there would be a long stand-off while the person expressed their pain; the marriage continued but always with a fault-line. Other times, the person opted to forgive their errant spouse, but primarily because they had also cheated in the past, and they could now feel more relaxed if it ever emerged, in which case they would say: 'Well, now we're on an equal par.'

Esther, though, had nothing to hide but also reined in her emotions, stood back and took a calculated decision. She decided that what was important was not the immediate hurt, but the long-term future. She was young enough to easily remarry, while her own career meant she would be able to look after herself financially if not. She felt that they were very suited to each other, had a lot in common, while their differences meant they complemented each other well. She decided, very rationally, that it would be wrong to let a regretted aberration destroy the decades they could still enjoy together. Of course, she never forgot, but she did not let it impede their relationship. She only alluded to it once, when she came to synagogue to celebrate their fortieth wedding anniversary, surrounded by children and grandchildren, after which she said to me in a whisper: 'I made the right decision, didn't I.' It was a statement, not a question.

2

Rabbinic follies and foibles

Kidnapped!

Islamic terrorists had just attacked various sites in Paris, including a left-wing bookshop and a *kosher* store. There had been other attacks in Rome and Brussels recently. Europe was on full alert for the next one. I had been asked to address a forum at the European Parliament on 'Freedom of Speech and the Right to Blasphemy'. It was being organised by political groups who wanted to rally support for secular liberties and oppose the attempt of religious extremists to impose their view on others. I had been invited because I had written various articles on the subject, arguing that no faith should be immune from criticism, and that if someone's God could be undermined by a cartoon, then that God was not a particularly stable one or worth subscribing to. I may be part of the religious spectrum, but am deeply committed to libertarian values. There is no contradiction here. I learnt that from an inter-faith conference in Germany, which brought together Jews, Christians and Muslims. The opening session was fine, albeit fairly predictable: everyone stated their own distinctive positions and their hopes for the future. The real eye-opener, however, was what happened at lunch and where everyone sat. I had assumed that there would be a natural division into three groups, with members of each faith gravitating towards each other. Wrong. There were two groups. The liberal Jews, Christians and Muslims all linked up, as did the orthodox Jews, Christians and Muslims. What united each group was the key question of the authority of scripture – whether it be the Hebrew Bible, New Testament or Koran – and to what extent one was bound by it or could depart from it. Whatever subject came up for discussion – abortion, role of women, mixed-faith marriage, cremation, gay rights – it was the right to change, or the inability to change, that guided the respective approaches of each group.

Back to the forum at the European Parliament. My plane landed and I was picked up from the airport by the designated taxi company that had been pre-arranged. It was my first time in Brussels, so rather than go over my speech one last time, I looked out of the window at the passing sights. I hardly saw any as my gaze was constantly distracted by the heavily armed police evident every 500 metres. Shoppers were making their way along the streets as normal, but there was clearly a heightened atmosphere and it was a city living on its nerves. Shortly afterwards I noticed we had left the built-up area and were going into the countryside. I was a little surprised as I had assumed the building was in the city centre, but did not worry too much as I did not know the area. That changed two minutes later. My phone buzzed and I saw a text from the taxi company apologising that the driver had reported in sick and advising that I go to the taxi rank at the airport, take the first one available and the fare would be reimbursed on my arrival at the parliamentary building. So who had picked me up? In whose car racing towards some woods was I in? Had I been targeted by those opposed to the forum, who had intercepted emails about my travel arrangements and hijacked me at the airport? I tried to innocently look at the driver's seat to see if there was any hint of a weapon stowed alongside or underneath. I also wondered about flinging open the passenger door (assuming it was not locked) and rolling out, with it being better to have some painful bruises than to end up as a hostage in a woodland hide-out, or even a bullet-riddled body later found by the police.

I decided that while those graphic images were far from fanciful, it was also possible that the taxi company had made a mistake and either sent the message to the wrong person or there had been a mix-up about the driver being ill. I did a quick calculation and decided that the likelihood was that I was not important enough to be kidnapped. Anyway, if I did roll out of the car and they were out to get me, the driver would just stop and shoot me. I might as well sit back and make the best of being part of either a dramatic adventure or an administrative cock-up. It was with some relief, therefore, that the woods turned out to be a small dividing area between one part of the city and another, and after a while we pulled up outside the Parliament. After that experience, everything else was comparatively inconsequential and I happily dealt with the more hostile questions that followed my talk. Rolling out of a speeding car was much more daunting.

Squeezing eternity into nine seconds

I t was the first time I was to be on the radio. The programme was due to start at 8 p.m. and I was told to arrive in plenty of time. So there I was at 7.30 p.m., ready and prepared. I was taken to a seating bay outside the studio and told to wait for the presenter, who would turn up shortly. 7.40 p.m. came but the presenter did not. The wait was agonising. I was psyched up to go, but nothing was happening. 7.45 p.m. and still nobody. 7.50 – I began to worry he had forgotten. 7.55 – was he stuck in a traffic jam? 7.56 – he arrives. Deep sigh of relief. He asks if I need the loo. I do, but don't want to delay getting into the studio, so I say no. 'OK,' he says, 'but I do,' and off he goes. I try to avoid watching the clock murderously kill what little time we have left. 7.58 – he returns and asks if I want a coffee or tea. 'Don't we have to be in the studio?' I half shriek. 'Nah – plenty of time,' and off he wanders to get himself a drink. I double-check the letter I had been sent – maybe I had mistaken the starting time and it is later on. Good grief no, it *does* state 8 p.m. and it is now 7.59 and ten seconds. He reappears. 'Perhaps we should go in now,' he suggests nonchalantly, 'and give ourselves time to settle in.' I resist saying that I had been ready to settle in thirty minutes ago and instead gurgle something affirmative. We sit down, he adjusts the microphones and then brings me to near collapse by saying: 'Just got to get a piece of paper I left in the office,' and disappears. I am alone with the microphone and millions of expectant people who are about to hear nothing. I wonder whether I should go over to his mike, pretend to be the announcer and declare that 'owing to technical difficulties beyond our control...' I

practise sounding official, give up and decide he can take the
rap for letting the nation down. He comes back, smiles and
says: 'We're on air in nine seconds, so we can relax for a while.'
Strangely enough, I do.

I had long admired the 'If' poem by Rudyard Kipling and,
in particular, its wonderful line about squeezing sixty seconds into every minute – but it was only after that radio programme that I truly understood the length of a few seconds,
and how to take control of time rather than it let control me.
The interview itself went fine, but much more valuable was
learning how the presenter used the time from 7.56 p.m. till
8 p.m. to go to the loo, have a cup of coffee, retrieve papers
from the office and still have nine seconds in which to relax.
My life has been immeasurably longer ever since.

The false arrest

I was the visiting Jewish chaplain to the local prison, which
had been immortalised in verse by one of its most famous
inmates, Oscar Wilde, in his *Ballad of Reading Gaol*. There was
a lengthy procedure for entry and exit so as to maintain security and prevent any escapes. One day I was doing my monthly
visit to the prison when, completely unbeknown to me, a distant cousin who was a solicitor with the same surname was
also there seeing a client. I finished my round and left. Ten
minutes later, he came to the exit gate. When the guard asked
his name, he said: 'Romain,' to which the guard replied: 'Good
try, but Romain has just left,' and ordered him to be taken to a
secure cell. Eventually he managed to prove his identity. Some

years later, we met and when he found out I was the Maid-enhead rabbi and used to visit the prison, he exclaimed: 'So you're the ***** who got me locked up!' Guilty, m'lord.

Mixing one's rabbis

I have occasionally suffered a professional disadvantage in being called Jonathan, for there is another rabbi of the same name. Moreover, he also has a doctorate, so we are both called Rabbi Dr Jonathan. This would not matter in the least, but for the fact that we both appear on BBC radio from time to time, although he more than I. I began to realise this was a problem when people occasionally came up to me and said how much they had enjoyed my 'Thought for the Day' earlier that morning, when in fact it was him, not me. Brilliant as he is, we have not always seen eye to eye on several issues, so these compliments were not appreciated, nor the time it took to explain that he was he, and I was me, and completely separate. Still, what cheered me up was the thought that the mistaken identity might also be happening in reverse. Per-haps every now and then people congratulate Rabbi Dr Jon-athan Sacks on his broadcast and for being so welcoming to Jews with non-Jewish partners, or on opposing faith schools because of the social division they cause, or for supporting the right of people to choose an assisted death if they so wish. I wonder if he politely nods and gnashes his teeth.

Still, at least such well-wishers know what a rabbi is. When I came to Maidenhead, I was the first full-time minister the congregation had employed and the first to be involved in the wider community. It meant that many locals were unfamiliar with my title and, when introduced, assumed my name was Robbie Romain. It even caused offence when someone once called out in the street 'Hi, Robbie', expecting me to turn round and greet them, whereas I heard it in the background and, because I did not think it applied to me, just walked on. I only realised my mistake when the person I was with asked why I had ignored the other man.

The challenge

I had been brought up in Orthodox synagogues, with Sephardi roots on my father's side and Ashkenazi roots on my mother's side. I am grateful that I had the experience of feeling at home in both worlds, even though I left them as I felt more comfortable with the principles of Reform Judaism and its attempt to marry tradition and change, combining the best of the wisdom of the past with the insights of modernity. I had always wanted to be a rabbi from the age of twelve or so, but there was a period when I was still unsure whether to become an Orthodox or Reform rabbi. I spent a summer in a very Orthodox *yeshivah* in Jerusalem as a way of trying to clarify the decision. On the first day there was a class led by the head of the *yeshivah* on the *Torah* portion of the week. We read a verse whose meaning was unclear but which he interpreted in a certain way on the basis that this was what the great eleventh-century scholar Rashi had explained. My hand went up. 'What if Rashi was mistaken? Were other interpretations not possible?'

It had seemed a reasonable question to me, but the room went deeply silent. The students who had been fiddling with their pens put them down in disbelief. The students who had been looking out of the window all stared at me. The person I had been chatting to on the way into the class shuffled his chair away from me. Rashi – wrong? A great sage impugned? Everyone then turned towards the head of the *yeshivah* expecting an explosion of curses and thunderbolts to spring forth. He was too wise a teacher to be angry, while he knew from the atmosphere of horror that had descended on everyone else that he did not need to make his point forcefully. He simply said: 'Rashi is never wrong,' and moved onto the next verse. Of course, he himself was wrong, as other great commentators have disagreed with Rashi over certain verses, although it is true to say that he reigns supreme as the lens through which much of Judaism is interpreted. But, to my mind, even great rabbis can make mistakes, while later rabbis can have deeper understandings. We may be pygmies compared to some of the giants of the past, but if you place a pygmy on a giant's shoulder, he can see further. The ability to question, challenge and differ from the past is one of the key reasons that made me certain that I would find Orthodoxy too stifling, while I also felt that being Reform would enable me to have the flexibility to be more responsive to the changing needs of Jewish people.

There is a well-known – almost certainly fictional – story along the same lines. A rabbi was appointed to a synagogue and was surprised to find that at a certain prayer half the community stood and half remained seated. Moreover, both sides tut-tutted at each other. It happened the following week too. The rabbi felt this was not decorous and there should be a unified policy. After the next service, he held an open debate on the matter. Those who preferred to stand during the prayer argued that this was the tradition of the community. Those who preferred to sit argued equally forcefully that this was the tradition. 'But that is ridiculous,' said the rabbi. 'How can both be the tradition? Surely it is one or the other, otherwise you will continue arguing over it constantly.' Everyone groaned and shouted out: 'That's the tradition!'

An urban legend

For many years, Maidenhead was renowned in British Jewry for its formidable outreach campaign. The idea was that any Jew in the area who was not already a member should be approached to join the community, both to boost our own numbers and because they would benefit from it. This was not an arrogant assumption, for it acknowledged that many Jews were agnostic and some were atheist and so would have no interest in the services, but they might still enjoy the social or cultural aspects of communal life, and benefit from the feeling of being 'linked in', even if they were not active participants. However, the many unaffiliated Jews in the area – who had largely moved there in the past ten to twenty years – tended to assume that Maidenhead was the same as the last synagogue they left: geared primarily to religious Judaism and so holding nothing of interest to them. Actually, we had repositioned the synagogue – in business terms, rebranded it – from a house of prayer to a community centre. I would often tell people that I genuinely did not care if they came every Saturday to services, every Monday to Jewish history classes, every Tuesday morning to Mothers and Toddlers, or once a month to the film club, or even if they just wanted to receive the monthly newsletter, know what was going on and feel connected from afar. The task was not just to achieve this more welcoming, user-friendly atmosphere, but to let all the hidden Jews know about it. So I gathered names from various sources and always asked members if they knew anyone else Jewish living locally (and also asked non-Jews, as well as Jews living in London or Glasgow whom I came across) and then knocked on their door. Of course, many were still not interested, but many were pleasantly surprised by this more accommodating form of 'Home Counties Judaism', which recognised that they were thoroughly integrated into the life of the area but still had a sense of Jewish roots.

My one golden rule was never to reveal my sources, lest it cause any embarrassment. Among the examples of our hyper-efficient intelligence system about Jews moving into the neighbourhood was the person I rang and who said: 'Yes, I wouldn't mind having contact, but do you realise I just moved in today after transferring from Blackburn – let me settle in for a week please!' Equally impressive, though with a less successful outcome, was the person I uncovered who said in a voice strangled with fury: 'Go away – even my wife does not know I'm Jewish – how the f*** did you find out?'

The urban legend concerns the tip-off that I received that one of the barmaids at a pub in Winkfield Row was Jewish. The trouble was, my informant could not remember her name, just that the topic had come up in conversation. The mythological version – about which a *Purim* spiel was performed one year – has it that I marched into the pub carrying a Scroll of the *Torah*, which astonished the regulars but which she recognised immediately and duly came over to identify herself. The true story on which this is based is that I did indeed go the pub, and looked for the most Jewish-looking of the barmaids. Holding in front me of a paperback edition of Golda Meir's autobiography *My Life* – which had a distinctive picture of her on the front cover with a large Star of David – I asked for a beer. I struck lucky, for as she drew the half-pint, she remarked on having read the book too. Bingo! I had enough time to obtain her phone number before she moved on to the next customer and, eventually, signed her up.

Arthur Scargill ruined my life

I had started to take an interest in using the media as a way of communicating with Jews living locally who were not members and therefore would not read the synagogue newsletter or *Jewish Chronicle*. They would, however, read the *Maidenhead Advertiser* or listen to BBC Radio Berkshire, and could be reached via those outlets. It quickly became obvious that it was even better to be in the national media, for that delivered a cachet that made non-members sit up, while members liked the prestige of seeing their community or rabbi mentioned in *The Times* or on BBC One. Each medium was targeted individually with a story that I felt sure its editor would feel was appropriate for its audience.

A programme that carried much weight and which I

had in my sights – but for which I had never had a relevant enough story to justify approaching – was Radio 4's *The World Tonight*. Then I went on one of my trips to the USSR to visit persecuted Soviet Jews and came back with some fascinating insights and personal testimonies. I called up the editor, he agreed that it was 'our sort of material' and invited me to come in that afternoon to pre-record an interview to go out that evening. He seemed pleased with it and said it would be the second item after the news summary. At six o'clock that evening, the then President of the National Union of Mineworkers, Arthur Scargill, called an all-out strike and launched a direct confrontation with the Thatcher government. Everything planned for the programme was cut to make way for the breaking news, including my interview. It took me several years before I found another suitable story for *The World Tonight*, which did get broadcast, and I have never forgiven Scargill for not waiting to announce his decision until the following morning.

Filming with Franco

From time to time, I am heard or seen on radio or television, but my 'media career' started with blockbuster films. Franco Zeffirelli had just finished shooting his about-to-be acclaimed *Jesus of Nazareth*, featuring Robert Powell. He was in London editing it and happened to know the Dean of the rabbinic college where I was studying at the time, Rabbi Albert Friedlander. Could Albert send along a couple of students to help provide some of the Hebrew voice-overs?

So off I went, and was surprised to find myself being told what was needed not by some assistant, but by the great man himself. Before we set to work, however, he wanted to discuss the subject in depth so that he had a better understanding of it. He asked me to do some Hebrew chanting, and then he himself sang some Gregorian chants, and compared notes (literally). Eventually the recording took place, and I thought nothing more of it other than an interesting experience – until I received a note inviting me to the premiere. If ever you see the film – often repeated on television around Easter – listen carefully when the High Priest is leading prayers and you can distinctly hear me for six seconds. Fame!

What do you mean – 'pray'?

I was in a studio doing a story on an early Sunday morning religious programme that is characteristic of most BBC local radio stations. I could see from the clock fast heading towards the hour mark that it was the last item and we were about to wrap up. At that point, without having mentioned it to me in advance, the presenter said: 'Many thanks, Jonathan, that was fascinating; perhaps you'd like to close the programme with a short prayer.' He was a full-time Christian minister – who happened to host the show as part of his extra duties – and, as befits his profession, was used to saying impromptu prayers several times a day with official groups or in private meetings. Rabbis do not do that. We have a set liturgy and, depending on our level of observance, say it three times a day or every Sabbath. But we rarely add anything new or say something specially geared to a particular situation. I was temporarily stunned. But I also knew that the one thing forbidden on radio is silence. God – or panic – came to my help, and I uttered the first line of a Hebrew prayer (so as to make it sound distinctively Jewish) and translated it in the most benign way possible (so as to make it acceptable for an early Sunday morning audience): 'God who creates all people, give us your blessing.' The presenter beamed at me and then said to the microphone: 'Which just proves how much we all have in common. Good morning and God bless.' I smiled weakly and resisted the temptation to cross myself.

A confession too far

I had been invited to address a weekend conference of Methodist members, the theme of which was family life, and they had thought it would be interesting to have a non-Christian perspective. The talk was well-received and the Q&A session went even better, with some good interchanges and humorous moments. Then I made the dreadful mistake of being too honest. Someone asked the question: 'What difference has being religious made to your own life and what would you have done if you were not religious?' I was a bit stumped, as it was such a hypothetical question. I told them that I had always been religiously inclined, and had not changed from being secular to being religious, so it was hard to imagine what that different life might have looked like. But, to hazard a guess, I said that, given male testosterone and given the availability of a lot of attractive

women, I may well have slept around a lot had I not had
a sense of religious discipline and values. The warm atmosphere froze, the women pulled their skirts down and their
menfolk looked hostile. I was taken aback. I had not said
what I did or what I wanted to do, but just speculated as to
what I might have done in the questioner's alternative imaginary world. But it was clearly a step too far. My status
had changed from an amiable rabbi to a sex fiend, whose
voracious lust was only just held in check by a dog-collar.
(Actually, rabbis do not wear them, so there was not even
that to keep me from being on the prowl in the pews.) Perhaps some of the audience might have thought the same, but
were embarrassed to admit it even to themselves. Thankfully,
the session was almost over, and after one more question and
a perfunctory vote of thanks, it came to an end, to the relief
of all concerned. Nobody said as I left: 'Lock up your wives
and daughters,' but I definitely sensed it was being thought.

Getting away with it

I have been struck over the years by the way in which some
rabbinic colleagues are harried by their congregants while
others have a wonderful relationship with them. Obviously
a large part is down to personalities and relationships, but I
also detect a professional technique that plays an important
part. What really matters to congregants is whether they feel
the rabbi is there for them, cares about them, knows their
names and those of their children, as well as their pet rabbit.
Do this and they will not mind too much if you give a bland

sermon, or a controversial one. 'Well, that wasn't his best sermon,' they'll say, 'but he's a good rabbi who looks after us.'

Conversely, that same sermon delivered by a rabbi with whom there is a bad relationship will elicit the response: 'Atrocious, typical of him, can't think why we have to put up with it all.' Not that a good rapport should be an excuse for bad sermons, but it does allow the rabbi to take stands and forge new projects that he/she might not otherwise be able to do. It is a simple rule: if your congregation feel you love them, they'll love you and let you take them in the direction you want to go; if not, it will end in tears.

Radio trauma

Over the years, I have done a considerable amount of broadcasting, partially on television but largely radio, some 1,500 appearances in all. Despite being a reticent person by nature, I have always enjoyed doing them. Invite me to a dinner party, and I am the boring guest who never says a word; put a microphone in front of me, and I am on fire. There was one broadcast that proved an abysmal disaster, and which I judge is more interesting to record than the stunning successes. I was invited by BBC Radio 3 to do a reading of a biblical text in English for which they had several pieces of music they were going to play before and after. What better, they must have thought, than to have a rabbi perform it? But what I did and what they had in mind did not match. I know that because I was in one studio and the producers were in another, but they had left their line open, so, unbeknown to them, I could hear in my headphones everything they were saying while I was recording the piece. After a couple of verses, I heard one of them say: 'This isn't going too well, is it?' After a few more verses, the other said: 'God, this is awful.' I kept going, albeit disheartened. As I approached the end, one of them added: 'We'll have to get someone else to redo it.' I finished, there was a pause the other end, and one of them said: 'Thanks, Jonathan, that was great, we'll let you know how it goes, bye for now.' I knew they would drop me an email saying that, for technical reasons, it did not quite work out and so they had had to find someone else as a last-minute replacement. I left the studio quickly, stopping only to deposit in the bin whatever shreds remained of my ego.

The bouncer

One of my first paid jobs was as a nightclub bouncer. It was not too arduous, just keeping a check on those coming in, with a restraining glare at anyone who looked likely to cause trouble. It turned out that the big lesson that I was going to learn that night was not in self-defence but humility. Because of the nature of the event, most clubbers were teenagers over sixteen. Halfway through the evening, a girl came out in floods of tears, accompanied by a friend. It seems she had run out very suddenly, and the friend had chased after her to see what was wrong. As I was on the door and they were hovering nearby, I heard her explain how upset she was because her boyfriend had split up with her the day before out of the blue, and now he had appeared at the event with a new girl under his arm. In between her tears, she explained how humiliated she felt and how much she had loved him and what he meant to her. She was remarkably eloquent about the depth of her feelings and how seeing him unexpectedly had devastated her.

I was amazed. I had recently discovered true love and, like any besotted young lover immersed in an all-consuming relationship for the first time, I had naively thought my feelings were unique, that no one but Romeo and Juliet had ever come close to feeling what I felt, and reckoned that poetry had not been invented until our romance had started. I was utterly astonished, therefore, to find this sixteen-year-old, badly spoken and wearing cheap perfume, expressing a depth of feeling and sensitivity for which I thought I had a worldwide monopoly. She had even used words that echoed exactly what I had said to my girlfriend the night before. How could anyone else, particularly someone like her, possibly understand the refined emotions to which I was privy? Despite my naivety, the lesson sank in at once, and never again did I make the mistake of thinking that my feelings were superior or even different to those of anyone else. So obvious, but it took a broken heart and cheap perfume to ram it home.

The postman

When a student at university, I did the then typical student job in the Christmas holidays of joining the Post Office to help sort and deliver the surge in extra post and parcels. After just two weeks of doing the rounds of 'my streets', you got to find out a lot about people without ever meeting them. There was Mr & Mrs Popular, who every day received a stack of what were obviously Christmas cards. Their neighbour was Mrs Sad, who never got anything personal but was inundated by catalogues and, from the number of parcels I delivered, clearly used them a lot. Nearby was Mr Broke, who only seemed to receive bills, some overdue with the tell-tale red letter warnings often visible. But the person who intrigued me the most was Mr Puzzle, who never ever received a single letter, even though he (or she) was clearly in residence. Each day I hoped that I would have something to put through the letterbox, which might indicate that someone else cared about their existence, but it never happened.

Fancifully, I even wondered about sending a card myself and signing it illegibly, but then dismissed it in case it caused more confusion to receive an anonymous card than the distress of no card at all. It also occurred to me that I was projecting wildly and they did not care at all at my lack of stops at their house, be it because they were happy being loners or, even better, had a wonderful set of friends who simply did not send cards. I decided to give up on being a social sleuth and stick to being a postman. Still, after I finished my last shift, I did send a card to an acquaintance to whom I normally did not write, but who I knew lived alone and had little family, so at least someone benefited from Mr Puzzle's empty box.

Chocolate cake

I have only (as far as I remember) made two resolutions in my life. One was while I was in the midst of giving a sermon during a *Rosh Hashannah* service, in which I talked about using the time to think about how we could best approach the coming new year. It was a chance to put into practice all the good intentions and high ambitions we had, but did not make happen. (Perhaps not all of them, as that would be unrealistic, but at least one or two of them.) Then it occurred to me that I should apply those words to myself and turn my own thoughts about a particular subject into action. I had long held that assisted dying was an option that should be available to those who were terminally ill, mentally competent and wished to end their life rather than continue to suffer for a few more weeks or months before dying. So I resolved to join the campaign to legalise it, called them the next day and became active in it. Sometimes it is good to listen to one's own sermons (…and act on them).

My other resolution was one I made on becoming a rabbi: not to eat cake. This was more for selfish reasons, but proved very wise. Each day I usually make two or more visits and am invariably offered a cup of tea and some cake. Had I had that slice in each household twice a day, six days a week, for forty-eight weeks of the year, every year… then I am sure my weight and size would now be deemed very unhealthy. It meant offending a few who had baked their own cake and were looking forward to telling their friends how delicious the rabbi had said it tasted, but, after a while, word got round that I was a cake-o-phobe, and puzzlement was replaced with looks of genuine sympathy at how much joy I was missing out on. I have no regrets, though, while my determination to stick to my resolution is often boosted when I see some of my more rotund fellow rabbis.

'I bet you don't remember who I am'

There is one group of people who tend to annoy rabbis most: people who you once met but have not seen for many years, and who then either visit the synagogue unexpectedly or who meet you in another venue... and who then try to catch you out by asking if you remember them. It is a cheap game. If you do recall them, then they feel very smug at being so memorable. If you cannot recall them, then they feel very smug at having caught you out. It is a win–win situation for them, while the rabbi is unfairly tested. Over the years, I have developed some techniques in response.

I bet you've forgotten who I am... 'Of course not, it's great to see you – how have you been keeping?' (Said warmly, this immediately puts them on the back foot, not entirely sure whether I have forgotten them or not, but unable to say so without seeming foolish, while the conversation has moved onto them and what they have been doing recently.)

You don't remember me, do you!... 'Of course I do, you're exactly the same person as you were when we last met.' (Said enthusiastically, this disorientates them as it is true but avoids their actual point.)

I bet you don't remember my name... 'How could I forget! It's lovely to see you ... tell me where you are living ... still in the same place or have you moved?' (This leaves open whether I do know their name or not, but seems very positive; asking about their address often helps remind me who they actually are, while it also takes the conversation to where they are living and away from whether I remember them.)

Conversely, I try never to put other people in the same

position, and whenever I meet someone at a general event who looks familiar but I cannot be sure I know, I always introduce and place myself: 'Hello, I'm Jonathan Romain, the rabbi of Maidenhead.' Usually it works very well, though it occasionally appears daft when it turns out the person and I have met and conversed not that long ago.

John Major's handshake

I had been invited to 10 Downing Street for a reception hosted by the then Prime Minister, John Major. As often happens on such occasions, guests are arranged in a line to be welcomed by the PM and then go into the drawing room for refreshments and speeches. The cruel reality is that everyone wants to speak to the PM, but he does not have the time (or inclination) to do so. I was very impressed by the way Major ensured the line moved quickly past him, by giving you a firm handshake but at the same time pulling you past him so that you just had time to say 'Good evening, how nice to be here' when you found yourself facing not him but the usher next to him, who gently showed you into the next room. It was a wonderful technique that meant he spent eight seconds with everyone, rather than the five minutes they intended. While it resulted in my time with him being limited, I was very grateful for the experience, for I have occasionally had to use it myself: at the end of a service at a crematorium, I normally say goodbye to all the mourners individually as they file out and say a word to everyone. But occasionally we have needed to clear the hall quickly because another funeral was waiting to take place, and so I have employed the Major handshake. Thanks, John.

So why did you do it, rabbi?

One of the more frequent questions I am asked is: 'What made you become a rabbi?' There is a latent assumption that it is a very strange choice of job, so there must be some rational reason behind it that I can divulge. Alternatively, they are intrigued to know if I had some mystic vision or dramatic, mountaintop experience. The latter is not the case, and when I tell that to people, the disappointment on their face is clear to see. In fact, I have often toyed with the idea of making up some wondrous tale of a voice from heaven to stop them feeling so let down. Still, at least they are impressed that I have always wanted to be a rabbi since childhood, and it was not a later idea after other careers proved unsuccessful. The reason is partly the influence of my maternal grandfather, who took his Judaism very seriously, and partly that I had three excellent teachers at Religion School – Gordon Smith, Sidney Fenton and Abe Simons – who inspired a love of Judaism, particularly Jewish history and ethics. That led to me wanting to pursue Jewish knowledge and one of the few ways of doing so then was by becoming a rabbi. In fact, I had intended to be an academic, but the rabbinic training at Leo Baeck College not only involved studying midweek, but also spending weekends doing congregational work. To my surprise, I found I loved it. Life is with the people. Although I have always made time to write books, I reckon they would be sterile if they were not rooted in the issues that arise in everyday life; conversely, just doing pastoral work without any time for research into causes and trends would be too shallow. Contrary to the popular saying, being a rabbi is a wonderful job for a Jewish boy (or girl). My other surprise is what has become one of my main rabbinic tasks – not debating the nature of God with conflicted congregants, nor called upon to check if a chicken was kosher, but being asked to sign passport application forms. Over the years, I have only periodically done the first, never done the second, but have done hundreds of the third. It is clear what people value me the most for...

The challenge to my faith

When I went to visit Hannah – who I was told was Jewish and living in the area – she was pleased to have a conversation with me but adamant that she would not join the synagogue. 'After the Holocaust, I simply cannot believe in God.' She is not alone. Personally, I have never found the Holocaust to be a theological problem. The questions it begs – why do innocent people suffer? How could God allow this to happen? Why did not God intervene? – apply just as much to a drunk driver who kills a mother pushing a pram. The only difference is the scale of numbers. I agree that if you believe in an interventionist God, then both cases pose enormous problems; but if you believe in a God who has set the world up and left it in our control, then God is not to blame and religion has a powerful role in helping to better that world.

What I have found much more challenging is inter-faith

dialogue. The more I have learnt about other faiths, and the more I have seen such different beliefs and traditions – which are all held to be based on revelation by God and communicated via holy texts – the more obvious it becomes that they cannot all be right and it is likely that most are wrong. I can accept, though, that even if they do not have divine origins, they have become sanctified by time. Keeping *kosher* or fasting during Ramadan or abstaining during Lent, for instance, may not be the express will of God, but have gained both communal and personal meaning because so many members of the faith have observed them for so long. That is why it does not matter how strange some rituals are, or how irrational are some beliefs; what counts in any faith is the ethics it promotes. How we conceptualise God is interesting but largely limited to our thoughts, whereas how we treat fellow human beings is crucial and affects our actions. The test of whether a religion has any validity is not its belief system but its moral code. Hannah did not formally join the synagogue, as that would have offended her anti-religious principles, but she did become an 'associate' because she wanted to support the work we do, socially and culturally. That is fine by me, especially as she has identified our most important task.

Jewish doppelgangers

When I had a period of Sabbatical leave some time ago, I decided to visit other synagogues throughout the UK to see the different practices that occurred at them and to bring back any good ideas to Maidenhead. It turned out to be an eerie experience as, to my astonishment, I found that many of the members with whom I was familiar back home seemed to be present at every synagogue I attended. Was I being followed around the country? It was not actually them in person, but other people bearing an uncanny resemblance to the roles they played.

There was the stalwart you can depend upon when something needs doing. I noticed the rabbi groupies who swarmed around him or her. Very obvious was the person who barges in and wants to make a particular point irrelevant to the conversation you are in the midst of having with others. I spotted the shy individual who lurks and then slinks off without saying what he/she wanted to say. Equally evident was the person who you sense is heading towards you wilfully even though he/she is at the opposite end of the room. I identified the quiet, reliable getter-on-with-it, who does not wait to be asked. Was I projecting my assumptions, or does every community have their own version of certain characters without whom life would be dull and the world would not spin around?

3

At the end of our lives (and afterwards)

The widow who still fed her husband every day

Ian died in early August after only three years of marriage to Lilly. It was one of those relationships where to say 'they were devoted to each other' was utterly true and not just a compensatory cliché. I called Lilly a month after the funeral to check up on her, as that is the time when life is usually the most unbearable. There is a protective numbness at the time of the death, the next week or so is spent rushing around making arrangements, while friends and neighbours are often very solicitous for a while longer. Then the visits tail off, people expecting you to return to normal, forgetting that 'normal' will never return again. It is when the sense of despair and bleakness can become most acute.

When I asked how she was coping, Lilly was surprisingly cheerful. She had gone back to work in her estate agency firm, but had developed a particular routine: 'Ian also worked in the High Street, so we often met for lunch. So now I go to the cemetery every day in my lunch hour and take a plate of food for Ian. I leave it on the grave and have a chat. When I come back the following day, it's always gone. He loves his food!'

I was sure Ian had been an appreciative eater while alive, but equally certain that it was the rabbits and squirrels who were now benefiting from her cooking. Still, I kept that to myself, as the thought of him still tucking in obviously gave her comfort. I wondered whether she truly believed her own story or if, deep down, she knew how absurd it was. Perhaps she chose to ignore reality and enjoy the sense of satisfaction? It also gave her something to do every day – both in terms of structuring her time and having a sense of purpose.

But I did wonder how healthy it would be for this to continue. If it carried on too long, the harmless myth might turn into an obsessive compulsion. She could end up feeling guilty for stopping and no longer 'feeding him'. It might also delay the grieving process, prevent her 'letting go' and accepting that he was dead, which included not having any more to eat. How to help without being brutal?

So I said how nice that was, but added that while it was good to visit the grave, it was also important not to spend too much time at the cemetery. I suggested it might be an idea to set a time limit, such as carrying on for another month, and then calling a halt. After that, the weather would change and it would be a good time for her to start doing other activities. She agreed immediately. I suspect she knew it would have to stop, but didn't know how to end it. Sometimes, people need permission to take steps they are perfectly capable of doing themselves, but still need that nudge to make happen.

Next time I was at the cemetery, there were some very hungry-looking rabbits and squirrels.

Suicide – always sad, sometimes selfish

When Selma threw herself under a train, she felt that life was not worth living and that ending it was the most positive thing she could do. Such was the depth of the bleakness in which she lived. To her, suicide was not a desperate action but a logical necessity. She also saw her decision purely in terms of her life and totally ignored any consequences it would have for others. If she did give a passing thought to anyone else, be it family or passers-by, then it was more about how to avoid them stopping her and not about how they might feel. I was so angry with her. Angry that she had wasted her own life. Yes, I knew she had problems, but others have them and cope. Yes, I knew that the depression had taken control of her, held her mind in a vice-like grip and that she was its victim. But I was also angry for what she had done to others. To the driver, who could not sleep for weeks without the scene replaying itself in his dreams. To others on the platform, who were traumatised by what they saw. To the emergency services, who had to pick up pieces of her body strewn across the track. To the policeman who had to inform her parents and see them collapse in a howl of agony. To the two of them, who had invested so much of themselves in her upbringing and nurture and now had years of 'if onlys', question marks and self-induced guilt ahead of them. To the people on that train, whose journey was delayed along with several hundred others while their trains were stopped or rerouted and who therefore missed business meetings, seeing friends, giving a lecture, catching planes, picking up the children, watching a play, performing an operation and countless other human activities that never happened because of Selma. Of course, she never intended all this, and it was part of the black cloud that surrounded her and that made her impervious to anyone else's feelings. Part of me knew I could not blame her, but part of me wished she had quietly taken an overdose at home and had not died in a way that hurt or disrupted so many people she did not know.

The funeral was doubly horrendous. First, along with the sadness that is natural upon any death, there was the guilt that everyone felt: why had we not spotted the signs earlier? Why had we not done something to stop her? What if I had phoned up for a chat or taken her out to lunch – might that have helped? Where did I go wrong? She may well have deliberately hidden the signs, or not have responded to offers of help, but that did not stop everyone feeling personally responsible for her death in some way. The second aspect was the number of people present: over a hundred. She was not alone – she had many colleagues, friends, relatives – but the tragedy was she *felt* alone, *felt* isolated, and had not been able to see the love and support that had been around her if she had had the ability to reach out or had they realised how close to the brink she was. Somehow, it would have felt more fitting if there had just been a lonely coffin and a handful of indifferent mourners. Having so many caring faces at the cemetery was a much more powerful indictment of the dark forces that impelled her to leap than any words could express.

In another case, Gary, a retired optician, found life too much and hanged himself in the garage, tying a rope to a beam in the roof, standing on the car and then jumping off. He genuinely thought he was being kind to his wife and that she would be better off without him. He could not have been more wrong, as she loved him dearly and would have been happy to help him through his bleak patch. Now she is alone and grieving and missing him and feeling guilty for not having pre-empted the situation. She also had a terrible practical problem. She lived in the countryside, with no access to public transport, but after finding him swinging from the roof she could not bear to open the garage doors again, let alone get in that car. She was physically trapped, reliant on friends to drive her around. She did not want to move, so sold the car, bought a new one and kept it in the driveway. Gary had never thought of that – one of many unintended consequences of the darkness that descended on him and likewise on others.

How to say sorry to a dead man

Stephen was not Jewish but had come to see me because he used to listen to my Sunday evening stint on LBC Radio for a religious agony aunt programme. People would ring up with issues or crises, except that instead of a counsellor, they were speaking to a vicar or rabbi. But he wanted to speak to me face to face. The problem with which he was wrestling went back many years. He had been running a sportswear firm with Jerry, an older man. It was a venture that Jerry had founded, but he needed someone to help develop it and made Stephen an equal partner. Although they were not, as he put it, 'close buddies', they worked together well and business thrived. Unfortunately, Stephen had run up some debts, gambling beyond his means. His solution was to take money out of the business without Jerry realising. It was a typical story of a downward spiral in which he genuinely intended to pay it back, gambled more to acquire sufficient funds, kept losing and stole more. Eventually, the business went into liquidation and Jerry – who had relied on selling it one day to pay for his retirement – was left too depressed to work again, and was forced into an impoverished existence. Stephen had spent a period in prison for his monetary theft, but although he felt he had paid for his crime, he did not feel he had atoned for the personal hurt he had done to Jerry. It had been bothering him more and more, and he now wanted to act on it.

'So why not contact him and apologise?' I suggested. 'And even if he refuses to accept it, at least you will have made the effort.' 'That's the problem,' he replied. 'When I tried to discover where he was living, I was told he had died two years earlier. I feel stuck with permanent guilt and no way out.' I told him there was an option still open to him. It would seem strange but it might work. He should find out where he was buried, or where his ashes had been scattered, go to that place and say out aloud what he would have said had he been alive. True, Jerry would not be able to respond, but Stephen would have made the effort of physically going there and uttering words of contrition. He could never be directly forgiven – for that can only be granted by the victim of a crime or hurt – but he could find atonement, which is a form of self-release and can be just as important. It would allow him to 'move on' and not let the past be an albatross around his neck for all time. Stephen stared at me blankly, and then smiled. He could see a way forward and although he declared, 'I'm going to feel a right idiot talking to the air,' it was clear that he could see himself doing it successfully. I told him to let me know how it went. He never did. Being optimistic, I like to think that is because all went well and the graveside chat meant he put it all behind him, including me.

The teddy bear in the coffin

Any minister will tell you that among the worst funerals are those of children. A person who dies in ripe age may be much missed, but relatives can accept the inevitable cycle of life. Much harder is the person who dies tragically in their forties, leaving behind a young family. Amid the devastating pain, at least there are achievements to speak of and a legacy that has been left behind. But a young child who passes away has not even started to develop their potential, while the parents – who, unlike past generations, nowadays have every reason to expect their offspring to grow into adulthood – feel that the natural order of life and death has been overturned.

However, I was taken aback by a phenomenon that was very unusual when I first came across it, but has since become much more commonplace. It was when Chloe died, aged four. I visited the family and we talked about her, and also their feelings: a mix of grief and incomprehension, which sometimes lapsed into anger, raging against a world in which such deaths could occur. We also spoke about the funeral itself. As the visit drew to a close, I asked if there was anything else we needed to talk about that had not been covered so far. Chloe's mum hesitated and then said: 'What goes in the coffin?' I explained that some people liked to put their *tallit* in it, but, apart from that, nothing else. 'We'd like to put in her teddy bear,' she responded. 'Is that OK?' I remember feeling very torn. Part of me felt uncomfortable, that it was pagan, reminding me of the Egyptians putting spears and armour in the pyramids, to be used by the dead Pharaoh in the next world. Did they think Chloe would play with her teddy bear wherever she was heading? But the greater part of me had a warm feeling. The teddy bear was not for Chloe; it was for the parents. It would give them the comforting image of her lying with her teddy next to her, just as she did when asleep in her bed. It may also have carried a latent sense of teddy being able to look after her now she was going to a place where they could not join her. He would be their emissary, a part of them keeping watch over her. 'Of course,' I replied, 'it's a lovely idea,' and was aware that some of the tension in her face dissipated when I said that.

Other parents who have lost young children have made similar requests for a favourite toy to be in the coffin, no doubt for the same reasons. But it is a growing trend with adults too. A ninety-year-old woman stipulated in her will that she be buried in her wedding dress. (Some might marvel that she still had it, and that she could still fit in it.)

It reflected the fact that it was one of her happiest moments and determined the course of the rest of her life. It was a request that she had lodged many years beforehand, perhaps after becoming a widow. It gave her comfort to think that her marriage was not over, so to speak, and would live on after death. Many widows might feel that emotionally, but she wanted to give physical expression to it in this way. And her wish was granted.

But should certain limits be drawn? This was my immediate thought when another member of the community asked if it was possible for him to be buried with his cricket bat. My eyebrows obviously spoke volumes, for he followed it up by saying that he had played since he was eleven, was still doing so periodically in his sixty-second year and it had been one of the few constants in his life. On the one hand, Egyptian artefacts came to mind again; on the other hand, if this was meaningful for him, why should he not have the right to choose what happened at his own funeral? After all, we only have one, and if the main object is honouring the person who has just died, who are we to disregard his or her last wishes?

Of course, once you say yes to one person's favourite item, then it becomes very hard to use any objective criteria in considering those of other people. The person who had been devoted to her cat, and vice-versa, for many years, had kept the cat's ashes and requested they be buried with her when her time came. Here was a clear emotional attachment that was easy to understand, and the fact that it had been agreed in advance had been a source of comfort to her for several years. In another instance, at which I did not officiate but with which I was involved, a man who had been a generous host and known for his appreciation of fine food and wine requested that a bottle of champagne be put in the grave alongside his coffin. The rabbi permitted it, though I am sure others would have been less accommodating. Still, I know some mourners objected because they felt it was a waste of a good bottle, while others wondered whether the groundsmen who filled in the grave after the mourners had left might have rescued it for themselves. Hopefully, they at least toasted his memory.

No, you can't speak to Mum – she's buried in the garden

Sharon rang up to say that her mother had just died. She had been living with Sharon and her family for the last two years, becoming progressively frailer, so her death was not unexpected. When I went over the following day to see them about arrangements, Sharon opened the door but said she needed to show me something before I came inside. Taking me round the back to their long garden, she halted at a particular spot and said: 'This is where I'd like Mum buried.' It is possible to have a burial in one's garden provided one satisfies various legal requirements. In fact, Sharon had already investigated the matter and done the paperwork to gain permission in advance.

'So, is that OK by you?' she asked once we had sat down indoors. I said it would be only after I had alerted her to the reasons for not doing so. One was that there was a danger of not letting go. Her mother had died. Taking her mother out of the house and putting her in a cemetery some distance away was a physical acknowledgement that her mother had passed away and left her. Being down the garden, rather than upstairs, might be a form of denial and impede the grieving process. Even if that was not the case, would she feel obliged to go and visit her mother every day, and feel guilty if she did not do so? Then there was the issue of what would happen when she eventually moved from the house. Would she feel she was abandoning her mother? Would the buyer feel comfortable with a dead body next to the rose bushes? Might it affect the sale price? Sharon was adamant that she had already thought about all these questions and wanted to go ahead. The funeral duly took place in the normal way and afterwards we went inside for some tea. While still there, a distant relative who had not heard the news rang up to see how Sharon's mother was and asked if she could have a word with her. Sharon's reply, 'No, you can't speak to Mum – she's buried in the garden', may have been perfectly accurate, but was a little too concise. The arrangement may have worked for her, but I would not advocate it as best practice.

God had taken her daughter

Roberta – who was a widow – and her two teenage daughters were members of the community whom I saw from time to time, but more often in the High Street than the synagogue, as they were not 'regulars'. One night I had a tearful phone call from her saying that one of the girls, Melissa, had died in a road accident, having driven her car into a tree. It was a heart-rending funeral, a young life cut off just as it was about to express itself in the wider world and flex its muscles. There was also the puzzle as to what had caused the accident. The weather conditions were good, no other car had been involved, she was not under the influence of any substances. After detailed investigations, all the police could say was that it happened: cause unknown. The week after the funeral, Roberta came to synagogue. After the service, I went over to chat to her and before I could even say hello, she blurted out: 'I know why Melissa died. God was punishing me for not coming to synagogue.' I replied that I had no idea why she had died but was certain that was not one of the explanations. I did not believe in a God that would punish one person because of the faults of another person. That was a very unjust God. Nor was the sin of not coming to synagogue so great that it merited a death sentence. That was a very cruel God. But she was adamant that this was the reason. The following Sabbath she returned. Afterwards we had a repeat conversation, with me emphasising that God did not use the lives of innocent teenagers as a divine blackboard to communicate messages. Roberta chose to disagree.

Every week the same scenario would reoccur: she religiously attended and we discussed (better: argued) over whether God was punishing her for her non-attendance in the past. It did not matter how many times I said I found the thinking behind such a notion un-Jewish and distasteful, she resolutely argued the case. Then, one day, I realised what was going on. She had found a reason for the accident. It did not matter whether it was a good reason or a bad reason: it was a reason. The one thing she could not cope with was the lack of a reason, along with the thought that her precious Melissa had died by chance. God punishing her may be theologically dubious but it answered a deep emotional need. There was a cause, and whether she liked it or not, she could rest from pursuing that most impossible of searches: why?

There was also an even subtler dimension. She had another daughter, and she wanted to protect her. By coming to synagogue every week, she was lessening the chances of a similar fate befalling her. It was not just a matter of atoning for the past, but protecting the future. So, from then on, I did not disagree when she told me God was punishing her – I stayed silent and nodded in acknowledgement. And she would nod back, caught between pleased that I had let her win but missing the opportunity for a verbal fight to prove her case. She carried on attending for the rest of her life, although by then she had become a familiar face and a regular part of the community. Whether or not her attendance had any beneficial effect on her surviving daughter, she had inadvertently found a new home for herself.

Grave humour

Something that many congregants do not know – be they Jewish or Christian – and may even be shocked at, is that a lot of ministers prefer taking funerals to conducting marriages. This is not because we are a morose lot, but because of the differing dynamics of the two situations. Marriages may be wonderfully upbeat occasions, but the minister has little role other than reading from the service booklet. The couple are going to be happy whether we mess up the lines or not, and everyone else will be jolly whether we utter some insights or are mind-numbingly boring. Anyway, the attention is usually on what follows next, with the reception, dinner, speeches and dancing all being religion-free zones. At a funeral, though, the minister's role is not decorative but crucial in turning it into either a dire experience (dreary, nothing of comfort, no sense of the deceased, no healing of family splits) or a deeply meaningful one (where the deceased is celebrated, the mourners are helped, family tensions are acknowledged and reconciled).

Of course, some rabbis are prone to mishaps. My favourite stories are those my teacher Rabbi Lionel Blue tells about himself. Such as the time he stood too near the grave while officiating and slipped in. As he arose from the grave, he quipped: 'Now I know what Jesus felt like.' Another time he had some rose petals in his right-hand pocket, which he had put there to throw over the coffin as it was being lowered. Unfortunately, he put his hand in his left pocket and threw out some Green Shield stamps instead. On the positive side, I do remember a piece of good advice for students: do not put your prayer book on the coffin during a cremation. I can only assume he once did… and then watched it head towards the flames.

Another of my teachers, Rabbi Hugo Gryn, used to tell the story of a man he was asked to bury whom nobody liked and about whom no one had a good word to utter. After speaking to several members of the family, he at last found something positive to say: 'Compared to his brother, he was a saint.' The murmurs of approval with which this was greeted indicated that he had struck the right note! Personally, I have always found it best to be as honest as possible, albeit in a gentle way, so that mourners can feel they are saying goodbye to someone they know rather than a person they do not recognise. At Carl's funeral, for instance, I said: 'I think it's fair to say that a lot of us thought the word "stubborn" had been invented for him.' It was true, and the, till then, impassive faces lit up and nodded in agreement.

One of the great changes in the conduct of cremations in recent years has been much greater variety in the musical pieces that are chosen for the service. Mournful dirges or classical pieces have often been replaced by songs that the person enjoyed (be it classical, blues or jazz) or by titles that reflected their name ('Danny Boy') or life (such as Frank Sinatra's 'My Way'), or that were a commentary on the event (Led Zeppelin's 'Stairway to Heaven'). Occasionally, faulty technology or human error means that the wrong track is played. The most apocryphal story is that of the woman who requested 'Somewhere Over the Rainbow' from *The Wizard of Oz*. However, on the day, something went wrong with the CD and out came 'Follow the Yellow Brick Road'. Realising his mistake, the person in charge quickly moved to the next track and the result was 'Ding, Dong, The Witch is Dead'.

A good death

It is the continual dilemma: how best to go? A sudden heart attack out of the blue in old age – quick, painless, free of worry – or a gentle decline that allows one to say goodbyes and finalise arrangements? Still, either one is far better than the myriad of other deaths that people experience at younger ages, through accidents or after debilitating illnesses. But there is one factor that I have noticed cuts across all ages and situations. Those who have had a satisfying life up to that point, be it in terms of relationships or personal achievements, fear death less than others. They feel they have got out of it the best they could and, like an appreciative theatre-goer, although they would like the show to continue, they accept the curtain coming down. Conversely, those who have had unhappy or unfulfilled lives feel cheated by it and tend to resent the end of life more. It is as if they are losing a present that they were never able to unwrap and enjoy properly, and is now being taken away from them for ever.

The afterlife

If there is one question that, over the years, I have been asked more than any other, it is about the afterlife, both by members of the synagogue and non-Jews interested in the Jewish view. It crosses all age groups, as well as levels of belief and disbelief. It is the one thing totally beyond our control and, whether worried by it or not, most people would like to know: what happens next?

I am always pleased to be able to say that, unlike some faiths, which have a definite map of the hereafter – varying from heaven and hell to cycles of reincarnation – Judaism has largely been content to say 'we don't know' and leave it at that. That has not stopped individual rabbis speculating,

but the official position is that we will find out when the
time comes, that it is God's domain, and in the meantime
we should concentrate on this world and how we lead our
lives right now. However, while this makes perfect sense to
many, others are disappointed. They want to know. They
cannot cope with no image in the mind as to what to expect.
Some would even prefer a ridiculous projection to no idea
at all. There are also those who want the comfort of being
reassured that they will meet up with loved ones again. It
does not matter that they knew their bodies were riddled
with cancer or that they may be smashed to pieces in a car
accident, they still have a deep hope of seeing them whole
again, feeling the warmth of their hug, hearing the familiar
voice that meant so much to them. I know they feel I am
letting them down emotionally by not saying the words they
want to hear – 'yes, you will be reunited' – and instead saying
that we will all find out one day, but till then our gaze should
be on the here and now.

When I am pressed by a person desperate for some cer-
tainty, I refer to three rabbinic stories about the afterlife that
do not give the desired answers, but are instructive in a different way. One comes from the *Talmud*, compiled in the fifth
century. Rabbi Baruka was standing in a marketplace when
the prophet Elijah appeared to him. He asked the prophet if
anyone there was destined for heaven, and when the latter
pointed to two men, he rushed over to them to find out what
they did that made them so deserving. They replied: 'We are
merry-makers. When we see a person who is downcast, we
cheer him up; when we see two people quarrelling with one
another, we make peace between them.' The second is a tale

from the Middle Ages, which envisages us standing outside the gates of heaven, but points out that, perhaps contrary to expectation, the questions we will face at the entry point will not be: 'How many prayers did you say each day?' or 'How many candles did you light?' Instead they will be: 'Were you honest in your business dealings?' and 'Did you keep faith with those who trusted you?' In more modern times, a Hasidic story has it that when we are queuing up at that same place, we will not be asked: 'Were you another Moses?' or 'Were you an exceptional human being?', but 'Were you yourself? Did you make the best of the abilities and opportunities you had?'

In all three cases, no details are given as to the nature of the afterlife; instead they reflect on how we spent our time on earth, be it our relationships with others, the ethical standards we kept and whether we fulfilled our own self-potential. Once again, the emphasis is thrown back to what happens today, with the future being left as a question mark. When asked my own personal view, I explain that the following image is just a guess, without any basis in fact, but it works for me: that when rain falls and it hits a tree, you can see the course of the individual raindrop as it slides down the bark. That is the course of our life (complete with smooth bits, bumps, twists and turns). Then, at the foot of the tree, it disappears into a puddle. The raindrop has lost its individuality, we can no longer see it or identify it, but it still exists in another form, and will eventually evaporate or seep into the earth. Still, to be honest, I do not care whether that image is brilliantly correct or abysmally wrong, because all that is important is how well or badly I conduct myself the rest of today.

His wife's ghost

Archie and Tammy had been married for fifty-six years. There were no children, and while that may have been a sadness for them, they were very happy together and considered themselves very fortunate. After she died, knowing that he had no family and his friends were of an age when they were becoming equally house-bound, I called on him whenever I was in the area. During a chat around three months later, he said: 'Have I told you about Tammy's visits?' He proceeded to tell me that his wife would visit him two or three times a week. She never said anything, just sat in a chair opposite him. It was not her full body, but her outline. Each visit would last a few moments and then she would slowly disappear. He was not asking for my view, just letting me know, so I refrained from giving an opinion. Personally, I am sure it was some kind of projection or auto-suggestion, though I would not dismiss it entirely as I am prepared to accept that things happen that defy explanation and there is much that we do not understand. Still, he clearly derived enormous comfort from it and I would not have wished to detract from the pleasure it gave him. If asked, I would have said that I accepted what he told me and hoped she kept on visiting him for a long time to come.

The painful death

When I went to visit Gareth in the Royal Berkshire Hospital, he was doubled up in agony. That was not a turn of phrase but a literal description. He was kneeling on his bed, with his face down, and gripping his body with his arms. He said it helped with the pain. His wife had died some years beforehand, and he was being looked after by his sister, who was distraught at the hospital's inability to control his pain. To be fair, they had offered him morphine, but he had not wanted to take anything that would dull his mind. Unfortunately, whatever would be strong enough to ease the pain would also sedate him. Although I have seen many people die, Gareth's death was particularly significant because it started my conversion from opposing assisted dying to supporting it as an option for those who so wish it.

Prior to that moment, I had always taken the traditional line that 'God gives and God takes', and that we should not shorten life in any way. After Gareth, I began to wonder: if a person is terminally ill, fully competent, suffering pain or distress, and wishes to end their life rather than carry on for a few more weeks or months, why should they not have the right to do so? For whose benefit are we forcing them to stay alive? Is it not more religious to let them slide away gently rather than grimly continue? Obviously, there would have to be legal safeguards to ensure that vulnerable people were not pressurised and that it was the free decision of the person concerned. Those are technical details that can be discussed and amended, but the principle is what counts. Gareth and others convinced me that there is nothing sacred about suffering, and those already dying who wish to avoid it should be given that ability. The Book of Ecclesiastes famously talks about there being 'a time to be born and a time to die' – but it does not say who chooses the latter time. In certain, tightly regulated circumstances, it should be the individual facing

the onset of their death and they should have the choice of
carrying on till their last breath or letting go earlier.

False grief

I knew Margaret and Reggie well enough to say hello and
chat generally about them and what their children were
doing, but not well enough to know their true situation. In
fact, Margaret had kept it secret from the rest of the world,
and it only came out into the open now that he was dying
of cancer. She told me that although everyone assumed they
were a loving couple, in reality he had behaved brutally towards her for many years and had made her life a misery.
She was not telling me all this so as to rake over the past –
her worry was what to do now. Although she would do her
duty to make his final weeks as comfortable as possible, she
was looking forward to his death and the release it would
bring her. At fifty years of age, she still had many years ahead
and, whether or not someone else appeared on the scene, she
would live her days free of constant humiliation. She wanted
to know whether to go through the usual mourning rituals,
as it would be totally hypocritical to pretend she was grief-
struck and she did not want to face the avalanche of sympathy
she knew would descend upon her. What should she do?

My first reaction was to be appalled that she had suffered
in silence for so long. Judaism believes in being loyal to one's
husband or wife, provided they act like a responsible husband or wife. If they do not do so – such as through physical violence or verbal bullying – then they have broken the

marriage contract and the other person is freed from their obligations to it. Marriage should not be a licence to oppress. If she had told me her story when Reggie was in good health, I would have urged her to consider a divorce. Now that he was about to die, my gut reaction was that, having kept her secret for so long, there was no point in revealing it now and it might well be counter-productive. It would antagonise family and friends who might not believe her, or who would resent being forced into thinking ill of him at the time of his death. In addition, she might then feel guilty for causing so much emotional upheaval at such a sensitive point when she had kept it secret for so long beforehand. I told her she would be better off having a simple funeral, dealing politely with the phone calls and cards and, even if it meant doing so through gritted teeth, getting through the initial period after the funeral. By signing off the past with dignity, she would feel better equipped to then make a fresh start. She could also use the funeral itself to mourn not him, but the sterile relationship, unfulfilled hopes and wasted years.

I also suggested that she should find someone to speak with about the real situation – be it a friend or professional counsellor – so as to be able to express the anger, resentment and hurt that she must have been storing up inside her for so long. Repressing it would mean carrying the pain with her and stop her from enjoying the new life she deserved. Still, I had no real worries about her, as she seemed like someone who had been lost in underground caves and was now confidently climbing toward the light. My concern was for all the other Margarets leading secret unhappy lives and feeling totally trapped without any hope of release.

The séance

Jean was heartbroken when Danny died. It had been a good marriage and they had been together many years. As I often have to tell widows or widowers, there are no shortcuts with grief, and they have to go through the seven different stages that accompany a bereavement: initial numbness and feeling of disbelief; tears and pain when the reality becomes clear; guilt (often unjustified) when thinking about what they could have done better for the deceased; anxiety over having to manage by oneself, whether it be the garden, cooking or financially; anger at the deceased for dying and leaving the person alone; depression because of the bleakness the person feels; eventual acceptance of the death and adjusting to one's new circumstances. The stages may vary in length and in the order they are experienced, while one also has to go through at least a year's worth of 'firsts': their own first birthday alone, their spouse's first birthday, their first wedding anniversary, or *Rosh Hashannah* or *seder* or Christmas holidays. Each one is painful and cannot be avoided, and will gradually become easier. The cliché 'time is a great healer' is only a cliché because it is generally true. It is the case that some people never recover from the loss of their partner, but most people learn to adjust, and some people go on to develop new friendships, including second marriages, even when their first one had been idyllic.

But Jean felt she could not bear to live without Danny. Six weeks after his death, when I called her for a general chat, she informed me that she had gone to a séance session. The person leading it had apparently made contact with Danny, identified certain characteristics about him, and Danny had sent Jean a message saying he was alright. I was appalled and tried to tell Jean that as gently as I could. It may be that some people have special gifts and can either make contact with someone who has died or know details about their life to which no one else would normally be privy. However, for every such person there are dozens of charlatans who are manipulating such events and taking advantage of people when they are at their most vulnerable. But, what is worse is that such activities impede the mourning process, for they effectively deny that the person is beyond reach and attempt to keep the relationship going. It stops the bereaved person 'moving on', prolongs the grief and prevents them from gradually re-entering the flow of everyday life. The present may be hard, but living in the past is much worse.

Those who are plagued by 'if onlys', or regret matters that were unresolved, are far better accepting that not everything goes right in life and instead determining not to make those same mistakes again with others. As for Jean, she did go several more times to the séance, but eventually realised it was not helping her and stopped. I cannot say for sure that the medium was a fraudster, but I am certain Jean would have been better not to have gone in the first place.

Jackie Collins was wrong

When the novelist Jackie Collins died of cancer in 2015, her family were shocked. She had kept her illness a secret from them – and I reckon she made the wrong choice.

It was, of course, *her* life and *her* cancer and *her* impending death. She owned all three of those. Like any other person in that situation, whether a celebrity or the person living next door, every individual has the right to decide who and when to tell according to what they feel are their own needs and the best interests of those around them.

I can understand why she or others may wish to keep a terminal illness a secret. There could be a misplaced sense of shame at having a disease. Or not wanting to be an object of pity. They may not want to be inundated with constant demands for medical updates. Or they might feel that they would cope better if they were allowed to get on with ordinary life, whereas they would go into meltdown if they were surrounded by sympathy. Or that family members would be distraught, so why share out the pain when they could keep it to themselves? It might be that the person did not have the energy to deal with non-coping relatives.

But, while these are all considerations, there are other, in my opinion more powerful, arguments against such secrecy. It would save the family the shock of finding out about the cancer shortly before the person's death and give them time to come to terms with it. It would save them the embarrassment of hearing from strangers if, as is quite possible, news should slip out. It would save them the distress of feeling that the person did not value or trust them enough to share their condition with them. Of course, that may well not have been the sufferer's reason at all, but it would still be hard for others not to feel slighted by the decision.

It would allow them the chance to help the person in various ways, be it practical, such as giving lifts to appointments and collecting prescriptions, or providing emotional support, which they would have been happy to do and from which the person could have benefited. It would give them the chance to tell the person things that they can now never say. It might be an apology for some hurt in the past, or an expression of love, or a promise to look after a relative who was vulnerable. Such words could be enormously enriching for both the person and those concerned. It would help them grieve better after the death rather than have anger and confusion mixed in with their sadness and taking over from it.

It begs the question of whether we own ourselves totally or if others have a share in us. We are social creatures who bond and interact with others, so their lives are affected by our lives, including our illness and our demise. Jackie Collins chose a route that may have been appropriate for her, but, in most cases, secrecy is unhelpful, if not hurtful, for family and friends. Illness is not shameful and usually brings out the best in those around the person. Loss and grief cannot be avoided and are much better anticipated and shared.

But where's the body?

Marjorie's death was greeted with widespread sadness, as she had been a stalwart of many local groups and societies, always got on with other people and no one ever had a bad word to say about her. Not surprisingly, there was a huge turnout at her funeral. The only person missing was Marjorie herself. She had elected to donate her body to science – as she put it: 'I might as well be useful once I've gone'

– and although not all offers are accepted because of the condition of the body at the time of death, hers was. As she had requested, it was a normal funeral service, but just without a coffin. The only other difference was the venue. As there was no point being in a cemetery or crematorium, it was held in a communal hall. While this did give the ceremony a slightly different feel, it was the absence of the coffin that was the most significant aspect. Everyone spoke movingly about Marjorie's life and her contribution to all she touched, but the lack of a focal point gave it an element of unreality. It is hard to know whether that was just because of habit and not being used to a coffin-less funeral, or whether it was because we had no one to address when we said 'We will miss you' or 'We will always remember your kindness'.

There is a trend in some secular circles, even when there is a body, for mourners not to be present at the actual burial or cremation, leaving the funeral directors to do the disposing and everyone gathering afterwards for a 'celebration' of the person's life with speeches and music. While this can be no less sincere than if done at the funeral, or as well as the funeral, it is dangerously close to denying the death, along with the grief and tears that are an essential part of mourning a loss, and coming to terms with it. Death hurts, creates a gap in people's lives, and a good gutsy funeral can both acknowledge it and help people deal with it. Trying to sanitise death away in a sugary celebration without going through the painful part may be doing ourselves a disservice.

Funeral fashions

The one area of religious life where there have been the most dramatic changes in recent years is funerals. In fact, almost every aspect has options that were not considered twenty years ago. The venue may now be a woodland cemetery rather than the standard one. The coffin might be wicker rather than wooden. There are also specially shaped coffins that are available, such as that of a motorbike. The service may include poems and prose passages that are taken from outside the formal liturgy, because they hold meaning for the family or the deceased. The eulogy itself, once the preserve of the minister, is now often given by those close to the person. The music is not necessarily a religious composition or sombre in tone, but includes modern songs and is often upbeat. The ashes may be scattered in the rose garden, but are just as likely to be taken to a place that was special to the deceased, such as a woodland through which they often walked. I always warn those intending to scatter the ashes that, if it is a windy day, they should do so down-wind, lest some of the deceased go home with them. There are also cases of the ashes being carbonised to form a ring, or sent up in a firework display so that the person 'goes out with a bang'. Yet another recent custom is to divide the ashes, as Heather did, stipulating that hers be equally divided among her three daughters so that each of them could keep a bit of her. She would not have dreamt of dividing her body into three, or giving each a mini-coffin, but ashes lend themselves to innovations. If there is a burial and a gravestone, a photograph of the person is now sometimes embedded in it (although usually looking at their best!).

The changes are partly because people who have grown used to controlling their lives are now controlling what happens at death. It is also due to a democratisation of death, no longer being willing to simply follow what religious institutions have laid down as the set rites, but wanting a much wider interpretation of what is possible. Some ministers raise their eyebrows at the choice of music or the more raucous eulogies, but the changes should be welcomed. It engages the family much more closely in planning the funeral, and encourages them to think what would be most appropriate and how best to express the person's essence. The result is that the ceremony is usually more true to the life of the deceased and more meaningful for those who have come to mourn.

Shall I bring the kids to the funeral?

When Mandy's mother died, I went over to discuss the funeral arrangements. One of the points that came up was her close relationship with the grandchildren, Mandy's six- and eight-year-olds. 'What do you think about me bringing them along?' she asked. There was a period when children were never brought to funerals, as it was thought it would be too upsetting for them, either to see a death or to see parents cry. I recall the shock when, as a young child at a memorial service in synagogue, I saw my grandfather cry. At that time, my grandfather was everything to me, almost god-like, and the shock of seeing God cry was traumatic. In recent decades, though, there has been a change in attitude and a feeling that it is good to involve the children and let them see the cycle of life unfold. That is certainly true, but much depends on the context: will it be a helpful way of saying goodbye to a loved relative in a supportive environment, or will they find it frightening or confusing? Parents also have to be prepared for very direct questions, such as 'What if Grandpa doesn't like being in the box and wants to get out?' or 'What happens when it rains and Grandma gets wet?' I also pointed out to Mandy that, if the children came, it would change her own role from being that of a mourning daughter to a protective mother. If she brought them, therefore, it might be an idea to allocate someone else in the family to look after them, otherwise she would concentrate on their feelings and not her own.

So, when I am asked what I think about bringing children to a funeral, I never give a stock 'yes' or 'no', but discuss the options with the parents. Ultimately, it is the parents' choice, but I urge them to consider two matters. First, if they bring the children, to explain in advance exactly what is going to happen, so that when the coffin is lowered or the crematorium curtain closes, it is expected and not scary. Second, if they do not bring them, it is important that the children do not feel excluded or neglected, so a role can be given to them to make them feel included, for example picking some flowers to be put on the grave at the funeral (or doing it themselves a week later), or being 'in charge' at home and taking everyone's coat when people come back to the house afterwards. In the end, that was the course that Mandy adopted, but others choose differently, Frankly, I do not think there is a right or wrong decision, just whether it is a decision handled well or badly. Ideally, going to the funeral of someone whom the children knew but to whom they were not very close – an uncle seen only occasionally – can be a gentle introduction to loss and a good preparation for more difficult occasions. Perhaps parents should consider it as much part of the children's education as taking them to a museum?

Mummy is not in heaven

When Pippa died of cancer aged thirty-two, she left Howard with two children aged six and nine. He and I had met up a week before she died, as she was obviously going downhill, and he wanted to discuss options for funeral arrangements in advance, so as to be prepared for when she died. One of the questions I asked him was: 'Have you thought about what to tell the children?' He said that his mother had suggested that they be told that 'It was the will of God'. I do not usually react sharply, but did on that occasion. 'There is no way you should say that!' I explained that all it would achieve was that the children would resent God. The same applies to other lines that are meant well, but are counter-productive. If you say: 'God wanted Mummy to be with him so that He could look after her,' they will wonder why the doctors could not continue to do so and ask God to give her back to them. Inform them that 'Mummy has gone to sleep', and you may make them terrified of going to bed at night, lest they do not wake up in the morning either. Telling a child that Mummy is in heaven will just lead to more questions, such as 'Where is heaven?', 'Why did she go there?', 'What is she doing there?' and 'Can I go there and see her?'

Children are very literal and want concrete answers rather than obfuscations. Our difficulty in explaining death to children is often not to do with finding the right words for them, but because we ourselves do not know, or because we are uncomfortable thinking about it too much.

When Howard responded: 'So what should I say?', I suggested he stick to the truth and simply say that she had died. Children see death all the time and take it for granted. They notice leaves turning brown and falling away, flowers in the house drooping and decaying, hedgehogs and squirrels lying dead by the roadside, perhaps pet animals passing away. I told him to be very matter of fact: 'Dead is the opposite of being alive. When we are alive we breathe and think and do things. When we are dead, we do not breathe or think or do things. That is why we put people away in a box at a funeral and say goodbye, even though we are often very upset at having to say goodbye.' If the child asks where they have gone, it is best to avoid contortions and either admit you are not sure too (which puts you on the same side) – 'I don't know. All I know is she is no longer with us,' – or to say that she has not gone anywhere but is just dead (which reinforces the notion of 'dead' being a fact that we have to accept). I also told him not to be afraid of talking about Pippa in front of the children or shedding a tear; that way he would not make her death a taboo subject, while they learn it is permissible to express emotions and to cry. Howard scribbled some notes down. 'It's going to be tough for them,' he said. I agreed, but reminded him that it was going to be tough for him too, and that the fewer denials and euphemisms we build around death, the better adults and children alike can cope with it.

The funeral from which I was asked to stay away

When Ros fell pregnant, she and Daniel were delighted. They had been married five years, had enjoyed life with each other and now felt it was time to start a family. Like most couples, they assumed all would go well; they decorated a nursery and talked about schools. Whereas their great-grandparents might have expected to have had at least six children, and for two not to survive infancy, the vast improvements in domestic conditions and medical care since then have meant that most pregnancies today are successful. It was desperately sad, therefore, when Ros's baby was a still-birth. Their reaction was very much conditioned by their parents, both sets of which belonged to Orthodox synagogues. Their tradition was not to have a proper funeral for a child that survives less than thirty days, for it to be buried in an unmarked plot, no family to be present, and no mourning rites to take place. The thinking was – especially in an earlier age, when deaths within a month of birth were common – that it was kinder to the parents to treat the child as if it never existed and quickly move on to a new pregnancy and, hopefully, a sustainable life.

I was aghast. Of course the child existed. It may never have breathed, but Ros had talked to it for nine months, Daniel had patted it, both had based their life around it, and, in a very meaningful sense, it had a living presence. Even if it had never looked at them, I felt they should mourn the child, as well as the loss of all their hopes and plans. But they were adamant that they wanted to follow the path of a non-funeral. I never found out whether this was out of respect for the Orthodox tradition, or because they were too grief-struck to think and were just happy to be told what to do by their parents. In most other cases of baby deaths, we have had a full funeral and mourning rituals so as to acknowledge the parents' pain. To be fair, Ros and Daniel do not regret their decision and it highlights how there is no 'right way' to deal with grief, but there are different options for different people. Happily, Ros did conceive again, and this time had a pair of very healthy twins.

The cremation mystery

Whereas some Jews shy away from talk of death – super-stitiously fearing that talking about it will somehow bring it closer – others are keen to make it known in advance that they want a burial or cremation for very definite reasons. Interestingly, it is not so much because they positively prefer one method to the other, but because they dislike the other so much. Some hate the idea of 'being burnt' or there being no place for their family to visit, while others are repelled by 'being cooped up in a box' or 'left to rot'. It is a very personal matter and, as far as I am concerned, neither is right or wrong and whatever the person had stipulated should be followed. I was puzzled, though, by a particular pattern. We had a number of Continental members who had come over from Germany and Austria in the mid-to-late 1930s to escape the Nazis. By the 1980s and 1990s, many of them had reached old age and started to pass away. In every single case, they opted for cremation. Given the fact that many of the six million Jews murdered by the Nazis had ended up in crematoria, I had expected such dreadful associations would lead those that had survived to veer away from them. The fact that 100 per cent of my German and Austrian members were nevertheless opting for cremation – whereas for other members it was an even split – meant it could not be chance. Surely there must be a specific reason. Maybe there was an inverse connection? Maybe they felt a sense of guilt at having survived and now wanted to identify with murdered family and friends by sharing the same end? I did not want to ask an insensitive question, but after yet another German Jew died and was cremated, I decided to approach one of the few remaining ones before it was too late and find out what impelled them all to choose it. Far from being embarrassed at my query, Heinrich burst out laughing: 'It's simple. We German Jews – certainly the more integrated ones – already had a tradition of cremation long before Hitler came on the scene. Once in England, we just carried that on!' It meant that, indirectly, there was a connection with the Nazis, in that by continuing to opt for cremation they were effectively defying Hitler and refusing to let his usage of crematoria change their own pattern of behaviour.

Shall we tell him he's dying?

Elliot had been having persistent pains that had defied the doctors. The tests showed nothing and there was no explanation. But he was clearly getting worse. His wife Phoebe approached a different consultant and Elliot went in for more tests. The consultant rang her the next day to say it was not good news. Elliot had an aggressive form of pancreatic cancer from which he would not recover. A few minutes later, she rang me to ask whether she should tell him. For me, it is not a moral decision but a practical one and so I asked her the obvious question: 'How would he take the news?' I have seen some people fall to pieces. Even though they were told they should have at least six good months left before deteriorating, they wasted them entirely by constantly worrying about what would happen afterwards. In effect, they died six months early. Others, though, have used the knowledge of their limited time to full effect, either pursuing long-held dreams or putting their affairs in order. It also allows family to be more open with them, as well as to start coming to terms with their own emotions at the impending loss. 'But doesn't Elliot have a right to know?' she asked. That is a powerful point, especially if one cannot be sure how the person would react. In many cases, though, they often give a signal. People who want to know will ask if they are dying or how long they have got. Those who do not want to know (even if they suspect they are facing the end) will not ask. I advised Phoebe that if Elliot did ask, she should tell him the truth, but if he did not do so, then she could just tell him he was in a serious condition and the doctors were working on it. That would then lead to him asking more questions or dropping the matter, and she should follow his lead either way. As it happened, he accepted the analysis of 'a serious condition' and did not probe any further. It corresponded to what his body was telling him and he was content to be looked after without thinking about the future, or a lack of future. Eighteen years later, Phoebe herself developed cancer, a different form but equally terminal. When I visited her in hospital, her first words were 'I want to know'. So I told her.

The bereavement strategy

Frances had always been an immensely practical person and so she came to see me a week after her husband died and gave me a blunt challenge: 'This is my first experience at losing a husband, but you must see it happen all the time – what's the best way for people in my situation to cope?' I had to start with the obvious caveat that everyone mourns in their own manner and at a different pace. There are no rules and no right way, while much depends on what support they had. But I also told her that there are two particular guidelines that many people will find useful. One is to never turn down an invitation, especially in the immediate aftermath of a death, when they tend to be more frequent than later on. Even if the person feels they would prefer to curl up and be alone, it is good to get out and about. There is plenty of time at night to howl alone. Of course, you then have to reciprocate, and it means you keep relationships going so that they are still there when you do feel ready for them. What is more, one invite leads to another, whereas if you regularly turn them down they start to tail off. So get into the habit of saying 'Yes, that would be great'. The second strategy is not to repeat everything one did with one's spouse as if on autopilot, be it the annual weekend in Devon or visiting the Chelsea Flower Show. It will only make you conscious of your loss and reinforce how alone you are. Instead, try new activities, take up new hobbies and visit new places. That way you gradually create a way of life that is centred around you as a person, not you as the remaining half of a former couple. You will also meet new people, while they will respond to you as you are now, rather than as you once were.

Frances sat back and thought for a while. 'Yes,' she said. 'I'm not sure about all the new stuff, but certainly the first idea makes sense to me.' Actually, I think the second part makes sense too, but much depends on one's temperament, and some people will find doing exactly what they had done previously has a comforting familiarity to it. Before she left, I gave her one final piece of advice: 'Be gentle on yourself. You have just received one of the worst blows possible. You may want to show the world you can cope, and you certainly will do so, but you should also allow yourself to have wobbly moments and weepy times. It proves you're normal.' Frances looked as if she was about to make some piercing repartee, but then changed her mind, blew her nose and nodded.

4

Tall tales (but true)

Weddings that go wrong

Sometimes good ideas simply do not work. One couple looked at large hotels with scenic gardens, but wanted exclusive use so as not to have other guests wander into the proceedings. This proved to be far too expensive, so they opted for a small hotel, which they effectively took over, whose small garden backed onto the River Thames. The absence of acres of rose beds in full bloom, they figured, would be compensated by the still waters making a perfect backdrop to their ceremony. The wedding duly took place on a glorious Sunday afternoon in July in the hotel garden. What they had not bargained for, however, was the river traffic! A succession of pleasure boats went past and when the occupants realised a wedding was in process, those lying on sunbeds raised themselves up to shout greetings – usually celebratory, but occasionally suggestive – while the person at the steering wheel invariably honked his horn. It was the noisiest and most interrupted wedding at which I have ever officiated. It would be nice to end by saying that the couple was so in love with each other that they did not notice. Unfortunately, though, they did notice and fumed throughout. My intended remarks – about the day being a wonderful start to what we hoped would be a lifetime of happiness – had to be rapidly changed, and I think I muttered something about it being so memorable that even passers-by wanted to join in. I also made a private note never to use that venue again unless the ceremony took place indoors on a freezing winter's day, when nobody was on the river.

Another mishap also occurred during a river wedding. This time the couple had the bright idea of everyone being at the waterside and the bride arriving by boat. At first, all went well. As her boat came into view, with her standing on the foredeck, shimmering in white, a mighty cheer went up. Another arose when the boat moored at the jetty. That is when the problem occurred. It was a tightly fitting dress, with little width around the ankles, akin to a hobble dress. The problem was that it left her unable to step from the boat onto the jetty, as they had not taken account of the fact that the boat rested against fenders, leaving a gap too wide for her to cross. After some half-hearted attempts at manoeuvring across, the bride decided that she was beginning to look somewhat indecorous in front of the hundred or so invited guests. Eventually, two of the ushers came forward, stood either side of her and lifted her across the fifteen-centimetre chasm and she was safely ashore. One of the sniggering guests received divine punishment. He had a camera with him, which was in a leather case whose straps were around his neck. It seemed safe enough until he bent over for some reason, and the actual camera popped out of the case and into the river. Splash! The water there was far too deep to rescue it and, anyway, the camera would have been ruined by the time they did. It happened in a matter of seconds, but I suspect he was cursing his misfortune for the rest of the week.

Another couple also suffered a major disruption despite being miles inland, in a lovely garden at the home of the groom's parents deep in the countryside. What they had not expected was that, in the adjoining field, a massive combine harvester was chugging up and down, not only making a tremendous noise but covering the guests in dust. Urgent phone calls to the owner got him to call a halt for half an hour to let the wedding proceed audibly, but by then everyone had bits of chaff in their hair. I suggested we rebrand it as confetti and so all was well.

The worst possible wedding was one at which I was not present, but about which a friend who was there told me afterwards. The ceremony went well and the reception was great. The bride's father duly made a speech, as did the best man. Then it was the groom's turn. He said he would not speak for long as everything he wanted to say could be seen by the guests themselves, at which point he asked everyone to stand up. He asked them to turn their chairs upside down. The cries of 'why?' and 'what's all this about' soon turned to gasps and then stunned silence. Under each chair was attached a photo of the bride in bed with the best man. 'This was something I took secretly last week', he said, 'and I wanted to share it with you.' He then walked out of the hall, leaving the guests in shock and the two families about to break into warfare. When I heard the tale, I was caught between admiration and horror. Admiration at having emotions of steel to carry out such a plan, keeping up the appearance of jollity until the moment of his speech, attaching the photos to over a hundred chairs the night before, taking the risk that nobody would tip over the chair by mistake and notice. The horror was at what it did to the two families. By all means give a black eye to the best man and call his fiancée four-lettered names, but why punish everyone else? I suspect everyone at that wedding left feeling soiled, having been made party to an infidelity they did not condone but would have preferred not to know about.

Thou shalt not go to the toilet in the dark

In the days of yore, when *bar/batmitzvah* pupils did not simply download their portion from the internet, they learnt it from a tape that was individually recorded for them by their teacher, Alec Belkin. This included the Ten Commandments, which they also recited. Roy's son was coming up to his big day in a few weeks' time and, having got off to a slow start, was now practising whenever he had a moment. A few days beforehand, Roy went to the toilet in the middle of the night. Half-asleep, he did not want to wake up properly and so did not put the light on, so stubbed his toe on something as he sat down on the loo-seat. After a few seconds, he nearly had a heart attack when he heard a voice booming out of the dark at him: 'I AM THE LORD YOUR GOD WHO TOOK YOU OUT OF EGYPT, OUT OF THE HOUSE OF SLAVERY.' His first thought was that a new revelation was taking place. Then, perhaps more realistically, he reckoned he was about to be punished for some misdemeanour. Finally, he realised that he had stubbed his toe on the cassette-player that his son had left in the toilet and thereby turned it on. It was Mr Belkin, not God, addressing him. I must ask him whether he was relieved, or disappointed.

The groom who couldn't get off the speeding train

Whenever a couple approach me about officiating at their wedding, a conflict of interest always arises. Whereas they want to talk about the five or six hours of the wedding day, I want to talk about the fifty or sixty years that come after it. So, we have two meetings: one between the three of us to discuss the particular arrangements, and the second with everyone else getting married that year to look at relationships. On the one hand, it is simple stuff: asking them how much they really know about each other, questioning if they have the same goals, looking at their aspirations for career, children and home life. On the other hand, I warn them that although they think it is all totally obvious, one in three couples who reckoned they were the perfect match end in divorce. As I count out the figure and point at every third couple in the room, a look of consternation flickers across their faces and they begin to realise they might have some homework to do apart from sorting the guest list and choosing the band. Some of the questions I throw out are factual (what is his/her favourite way of relaxing?), others produce giggles (what do you do that annoys him/her the most?), but several make them pause for thought (what is his/her greatest regret? Where does he/she want to be in twenty years' time?). The object is not to get them to call off the wedding, but to think through the difficult bits that lie ahead as much as the fun side. This includes being sensitive to the other person's needs, and being aware of the compromises both of them might need to make to achieve overall harmony. That way they might be among the two in three that do succeed.

There was one couple, though, for which all the excitement of new love could not mask the underlying tensions. The way Ryan and Jenny spoke to each other was so worrying that I arranged a private session with them a week later. We went over a few issues and alarm bells kept ringing. I said very directly: 'Look, it's your feelings and your marriage, and it's very hard for me to judge, but I have to tell you I'm picking up all sorts of negative signals and wonder if you feel something is not right between the two of you?' They looked at me in astonishment. It was as if I had told them to adopt a kangaroo and make it the best man. So I said that as long as they were sure, that was fine, and we chatted amiably about other matters. But I was still bothered. Maybe they were inhibiting each other from speaking honestly? I phoned both of them individually 'just to check everything's okay'. Both assured me life was perfect and although it was kind of me to ask, there was nothing to worry about. The wedding duly went ahead... and three months later they applied for divorce. I met with them both, albeit separately.

Jenny said she knew Ryan had major issues about the marriage, but she really wanted to make it succeed and had gone ahead on that basis. Ryan said that he had realised that the relationship was wrong and would end in tears, but that he could not bring himself to tell anyone. It was not so much a matter of hurting Jenny's feelings but of not knowing how to halt the wedding train which was speeding ahead: the hotel and flights that had been booked, the guests that had been informed, the flowers that had been ordered, the music that had been selected, the wines that had been chosen, the suits and dresses that had been tailored, the honeymoon that had been pre-paid. The train was hurtling too fast to stop it or for him to jump off. It would be easier, he felt, to go ahead with the wedding and then get quietly divorced shortly afterwards. Part of me was relieved that my marriage antennae had not been at fault, but the greater part of me was saddened for each of them, not to mention their horrified families. There was a certain logic to Ryan's decision, in that although the wedding train crashed, it was with less people watching. Still, it would have been far better if he had had the courage to be honest, sat down with Jenny to explain why he was calling it off, relay it to both sets of families and then let friends know. No doubt he would have received criticism from some people, but hopefully support from most others. I also wondered how much Jenny had unconsciously colluded with the deceit, whether deep down she knew what was happening and preferred to be a young divorcee rather than a jilted bride. Both for her and others, the former might have a higher status than the latter, and be seen as less wounding. Over the years, there have been other couples who contributed to the 'one-in-three-break-up' statistic, despite protesting that it would never happen to them, but none quite so quickly.

The royal cup of tea

Princess Margaret did not always receive a good press, but when she came to Maidenhead Synagogue on official business, she performed her duties well. It was me who upset royal etiquette. It was 1990 and, as the community had been founded in 1940, we held various events to mark our Golden Jubilee, including a special service at which she was the guest of honour. We had asked her officially because we were the only synagogue in the Royal Borough of Windsor and Maidenhead, but primarily because we wanted the excitement that came from a royal visit. There was also a personal connection, for the community was founded by Jews coming out of London to escape the Blitz, and that same year Princess Margaret, along with Princess Elizabeth, had left Buckingham Palace to live in Windsor Castle during the war years. The Jewish evacuation from the capital and new life along the Thames reflected her life too.

Of course, whereas all our members were a little nervous at how to behave, what to say, and whether to bow, shake hands or curtsy, she was well used to dealing with such events. It also helped put people at ease when, immediately after the service and before the official tea, she asked: 'Is there time for a fag?' At the tea, she commented on the fact that we had said a prayer for the royal family during the service. When I told her that it was a long-standing Jewish tradition and that we did it not just because she was present but every Saturday morning, she replied: 'That's nice, they don't do that in church for us each week. I'll tell my sister.' We never got to hear what was the royal reaction.

At that point, we were seated at a table, along with other guests. The conversation moved on, and someone started talking about changes in local life since the war. I lifted up my cup of tea and was about to drink from it, when I felt a royal finger tapping on my hand: 'That's my cup of tea!' Princess Margaret said with mock sternness. Somewhat embarrassed, I returned it to its rightful owner and located my own cup. In previous eras, the Tower of London might have been my next stop, but thankfully these were more relaxed times. And I had let her have her fag.

The bigamist

I had married Pete and Bryonie three years earlier and whenever I had seen them since then, they had seemed very together and it appeared the marriage was fulfilling all their hopes in each other. That is also what Bryonie had thought. Then she received the phone call that totally traumatised her. When they had their wedding, Pete was already married to someone else. Not only that, but he was still seeing his other wife – along with their child – very regularly. The reason he was able to do that so frequently and without Bryonie realising what was happening was that she lived in a village only a few miles away. In fact, it was the proximity of the other wife that Bryonie initially found herself fixating on more than the deception itself. She felt it would have been more bearable if she was living in a different part of the country, but being so close made it feel much worse. As she put it: 'How could I have been such a fool not to notice what was going on right under my nose?' She phoned her parents to tell them the news, and they came over immediately.

When Pete came home later that evening, the three of them confronted him. He admitted the truth almost immediately, saying that he genuinely loved Bryonie but that he had got into a situation from which he felt he could not extricate himself. His 'pathetic explanation', according to Bryonie's father, was that he found her attractive, started going out with her, not telling her about his existing marriage, and matters escalated from there. Nor did his wife know the situation. He simply told both women that he had business trips or conferences elsewhere in the country when in fact he was spending time with the other one. Naturally, his wife was furious when she was informed, although after a period of anger, she decided to dismiss it as the equivalent of an affair, put it behind her and move on together. This was helped by the fact that he faced a short prison sentence for bigamy, after which they continued with their marriage. But, for Bryonie, the emotional consequences were much deeper. Her marriage had to be annulled and she did not have the option of whether to take him back or not. At the same time, the deception was much greater than an ordinary affair – they happen and are hurtful, but do not compare to the level of deceit involved in going through a false ceremony, planned months in advance and conducted in front of dozens of guests. She was left wondering how she would ever be able to trust anyone again.

The prisoner's wives

One of the permissions granted to Jewish prisoners is to be allowed the special foods required for Passover. As Reading prison only had three or four Jewish inmates at any one time, and not all of whom wanted them anyway, there was no official ordering system for the festive foods and they were brought in on an individual basis by an approved person. Doing my chaplaincy rounds shortly before the Passover, a prisoner in his late forties called Darren asked whether, if his wife was to purchase the products, she could drop them into the synagogue for me to bring in to him. At the appointed time, a very curvaceous lady in her late twenties, dressed very fashionably, came by with a box for 'my Darren'. I duly put it aside for my next visit. Two hours later, another lady, fairly drab-looking and in her mid-forties, turned up saying that she was Darren's wife and that she had his Passover order. He was obviously playing the field! I decided not to tell her about the previous delivery, though I did point out to Darren when I saw him that it would only end in tears and he was already in enough trouble without adding domestic strife. I also warned him that he might have got away with double rations that Passover, but I would not be his mistress's delivery boy next year, even if it was in a religious cause.

The poltergeist

Beth was a very down-to-earth woman and immensely practical. When her husband was ill, she took over his business affairs until he recovered. When her children had problems, she was the one that sorted them out. I was very surprised, therefore, to receive a phone call asking me to come round to say a prayer to get rid of the bad spirit in the house. I listened to her tale without interrupting lest she think that I did not believe her. She said that a strange atmosphere had recently developed, as if there was something negative in the air. She had heard noises, felt cold and hot winds, lost items that turned up in strange places. Personally, I reckon that in nearly all such cases there are rational explanations. Moreover, once the person thinks there is a poltergeist, then anything unusual that happens is seen as reinforcement of that fact, rather than chance, coincidence or a perfectly natural cause. Still, as I told her, Judaism does not claim to know everything and there are things that occur which we simply cannot explain. It may be there is a spirit realm, and although I do not think it controls our lives, it may be that on rare occasions we encounter it. I am sure we should not try to delve into it – partly because we do not know how real it is, partly because it deflects us from everyday life, and partly because it is easy to be misled by charlatans who claim to know this realm.

Still, I did recognise that although Beth's angst was a subjective matter in my eyes, for her it was an objective reality. So, I duly went off and composed a benign prayer – nothing mystical or involving black candles at midnight – and recited it in the house in her presence. The noises stopped, the gusts disappeared and objects stayed where they should be. Was it due to me? I strongly doubt it, and am much more inclined to put it down to Miriam's powers of auto-suggestion. However, ask her what happened, and she will tell you a very different story as to why the poltergeist left her home.

What shall I call my child?

Most parents take the names of their children seriously and spend considerable time debating the options depending on whether it is a boy or a girl. One mother took it to another level, though, by not opting for names that reflected family members whose memory she wanted to recall, nor ones she liked because of good associations with them. Instead, she decided on the aspects of nature that she wanted them to cherish. She called her first son Sunray and her second son Lightshaft. But, when it came to her third son, she found herself in a quandary. She had already expressed her two favourite natural phenomena, and did not want to choose a lesser one for the baby. Yet, with two siblings called Sunray and Lightshaft, he could not possibly be given an ordinary name such as Charles or Barry. It would make introducing the three of them together very strange. For nine months she wrestled with the problem and still had not solved it four weeks after his birth. It might seem something relatively simple for others to decide, but she had got into such a mental stress over it for the better part of a year that she simply could not think straight anymore. The deadline for naming a child – within the first six weeks – was fast looming. So, when the synagogue held a barn dance the following Sunday, she devised a novel fund-raising idea. Instead of a raffle, she stood up on the stage and invited everyone there to think of a name they would suggest for the still anonymous child, write it on a ten-pound note and put it in a box. If she chose one of the names, the person would get fifty pounds in return, the synagogue would have the rest and she received a name. It was also a unique opportunity to name a child that most people never have offered to them. It was a brilliant idea and people in the hall warmed to it, though it was hard to know whether out of sympathy at her plight or incredulity at her methodology. In the event, she chose a name that nobody suggested – Moonswimmer – and on the very last day before the legal deadline. Nobody minded about their lost ten pounds because, apart from the money going to a good cause, they all sensed they had taken part in an event that would probably never ever happen again.

Let's steal a sacred scroll!

I faced a very unnerving first council meeting after I was appointed as the synagogue's first full-time minister. It was not that the council members were hostile to me, just that I had to assert my authority somewhat more dramatically than I had expected. The problem was that the two Scrolls of the Law that the synagogue possessed were not actually ours – they had been on a long-term loan from an east London congregation that had a declining membership and so were surplus to its needs. However, after some twenty-five years, it was assumed that the loan was permanent, and the council reacted with shock when a letter unexpectedly arrived from the congregation asking for its scrolls back. How would we survive without them? How could we afford the thousands of pounds to purchase new ones to replace them? The Senior Warden presented his plan of action to the meeting: we would say that we would love to help, but that we had lost them and could not oblige. What could be simpler?! A few other members nodded in agreement. It was at this point that I decided to intervene, pointing out that not only was this lying and not only was it theft, but it was lying about and stealing the very codes that told us not to lie and steal! The other members glumly felt duty-bound to agree, and the scrolls were duly returned after agreeing a six-month extension in order to allow us time to fund-raise for two replacement scrolls.

This may not be true

When I first came to Maidenhead, I found that a few older members who had been very involved in past years had resigned even though they were still living in the area. The reason was that they had fallen out over this or that incident. The most notorious was that of the Christmas crackers. After the Second World War, the country may have been victorious militarily but it was impoverished economically. Rationing had to be kept in place until the early 1950s. A year or so after it ended, the Ladies Guild decided that, having put on enjoyable but meagre *Hanukkah* parties every year for the children, this year they would make it truly festive. One of the ways of doing this was, after the fun and games, when they sat down for a tea, on each child's plate was not only a piece of cake and some jelly but a Christmas cracker to pull. Many had never seen such an item. What fun! However, a certain member was incensed. How dare they bring a symbol of Christianity into the sacred interior of the synagogue hall? This was sacrilege! (Or heresy or blasphemy or whatever it was that we had and they did not...) His rage was such that he reported the community – which was then run under the auspices of the Orthodox religious authorities – to the *Beth Din*, the rabbinic court. That much is known to be true. The version of what happened next is less authenticated.

Apparently, the learned judges, steeped in Jewish law in a world of their own and cut off from everyday realities, said: 'What are Christmas crackers?' They were greatly relieved to discover that they were pulled, not eaten. Once they realised there was no worry about the crackers being made from non-*kosher* ingredients, they dismissed the case. The power of the story was such that it was told and retold, and handed down for almost thirty years until my arrival.

The sermon that he thought he heard

I was walking down Maidenhead High Street when I saw a member of the synagogue... and my jaw dropped. He was around thirty-five years old, tall, good-looking and had thick black hair. Or, rather, he *had* thick black hair when I had seen him a few weeks ago at a service. Now he was completely grey. I do not normally comment on personal appearances, but the difference was so dramatic that I had to do so.

'I can't help noticing your hair colour has changed very rapidly,' I said, as tactfully as I could. 'Is that a family trait?'

'No,' he replied, 'it was your sermon, rabbi! You spoke about the pretences we build up and hide behind, and that instead we should be honest both about ourselves and about our relationships with others. I went grey when I was in my twenties, and was so ashamed that I've been dyeing it ever since. But after your words, I decided to accept who I am and what I look like … and I feel much better for it.'

I had been completely unaware of that. It shows that people listen to sermons in ways that preachers can never anticipate. It also explains why I – and other clergy – can feel we have given a below-par sermon, and are then surprised when someone says how much it meant to them. A chance sentence can inadvertently address a pressing concern that had been gnawing at them. Conversely, a brilliant sermon can fall flat for congregants who are too bound up with issues of their own to listen properly.

Note to clergy when they get despondent: giving a sermon is like fly-fishing: however skilfully done, it still needs someone to pick it up; but carry on, for unless you keep throwing your line out, there's no hope of it succeeding.

Multiple murders

It seemed like an ordinary visit. Bert was in his forties and invited me round for tea with his wife. After the usual generalities, he said: 'I've got a little problem I'd like to discuss with you.' He wanted my help in resisting extradition to France. Offering me a biscuit, he explained: 'I've been accused of multiple homicide – there was an incident I was connected with in which six men died – but I never carry guns and am entirely innocent. It's a classic stitch-up.' The intense stare which accompanied the remark made the biscuit take a little longer to go down my throat than might have been considered usual. I recalled countless conversations with those I visited in prison as part of my duties as a chaplain. It was very rare to meet a guilty person, with most claiming they had been victims of a mistake, miscarriage of justice or just happened to be in the wrong place at the wrong time. All of them. Bert went on to explain that he had helped the French police at the time with their enquiries and had actually shown them where the men had been buried in shallow graves. But he felt he had now fulfilled his duty and it was not right to make him face trial.

In my mind I quickly went over the course on Practical Rabbinics I had done in my last year at rabbinic college. Conducting a baby blessing and doing a hospital visit were on the syllabus, but I was fairly sure that advising a possible mass killer was definitely not something we had covered. We talked around the issue. I made suggestions about legal options and also tried to be of some help to his wife, who was clearly distraught both by his involvement and what the future might hold. There was the added complication that some of the dead men's friends also held him responsible and had promised to track him down. I decided my role was not to be prosecutor or judge, but minister, and give whatever comfort I could. I kept in touch, but was not entirely surprised when, after a big piece about him in a national newspaper a few weeks later, he and his wife disappeared and could not be traced.

He was a very naughty boy

When I visited new members Helen and Mick, they seemed a very amiable couple in their sixties, who had been married for almost forty years. He seemed particularly charming. We chatted generally for a while and then I asked what Mick had done before retirement. 'I was a bank robber,' came the reply. I must admit it was not what I was expecting, but it made an interesting variation from the usual answers. At that point, Helen jumped in with an apologetic 'Yes, but he never hurt nobody, the guns was just to scare them … though he was a naughty boy,' looking at him affectionately. In fact, he had not been a particularly successful bank robber, which is why they were living in a council house, and also why he had spent long spells inside prison. Helen had been used to living large chunks of the marriage alone, but was clearly as much in love with him as when they first met. As she put it later on in the conversation: 'Whatever happened outside the house, he was always a right gentleman at home. When he was living here, he would always bring me a nice cup of tea in bed every morning.' What might have been laughable naivety was genuinely touching, though I suspect those who met him in banks had a less rosy view.

Approaching the end of the world

I was somewhat bemused when I was approached by an intensely devout Christian who was convinced that the Rapture was about to occur, in which all true believers – which included her – would be transported to heaven. This was based, she assured me, on her reading of I Thessalonians 4:17. But it was not this expectation that bemused me, as I was used to periodically being told this by those who have exclusive access to the Truth (which always has a capital 'T'). Instead, it was her request for me to recommend a Jewish lawyer – which she obviously considered as a sign of efficiency – with whom she could arrange the disposal of her worldly goods. If she was going to heaven and everyone else was doomed, I thought, what did it matter what happened to her premium bond certificates and her collection of signed Hollywood photographs?

In similar vein, I was non-plussed when I heard about a local church who were proclaiming that all should repent because the world was about to come to an end. Yet, at the same time, they were seeking a 25-year mortgage for their new building. Whatever happened to faith?

The gay sauna sacking

I had always had a soft spot for Alexander. He was a senior executive for a major company who had a heavy workload, yet always made sure he was there for the children when they had school plays or football matches where it was important for them that Dad was watching on admiringly. He liked to come to services from time to time, though he always positioned himself at the rear because he had a bad back and preferred standing, doing so without disturbing others. One day he rang to say he was moving away from the area as he had been sacked and was having to downsize. 'You'll read about it in the papers fairly soon,' he said grimly. It turned out that he had been accused of visiting a gay sauna for up to three hours at a time during the working week. His boss had become suspicious of his absences and hired a firm of private detectives, who tailed him to the sauna. However, contrary to the saying, there can be smoke without fire. Six months later, he was awarded £450,000 in damages (a hefty sum back in the early 2000s) for unfair dismissal. The judge backed Alexander's assertion that he had gone to the sauna purely because of his back problems and had no idea of its reputation for gay liaisons. Moreover, he had an agreement for flexible working hours in his contract, and had always made up for the hours that he took off. As the judge said in his summing up: 'The claimant has produced photographic evidence to show that there are times of the day when a casual observer would be wholly unaware what the true nature of these premises might be. I am not persuaded that the claimant did attend these premises other than for therapeutic purposes.'

Still, the large pay-out was no compensation for the loss of his job, home and reputation.

Three weddings and a stone-setting

If this heading sounds suspiciously like a well-known film, that is because truth is often stranger than fiction, as so many of these other anecdotes prove. It also represented a single Sunday's work for me one September. It started with a stone-setting, but it was the three weddings that I conducted one after the other – and all in different venues – that, in hindsight, proved the most memorable. They all ended badly. The first led to a divorce after only a few years; in the second, the husband succumbed to a fatal illness not long afterwards; the third turned out to involve bigamy and was declared void. It was a disastrous afternoon's work and I always shudder when I think of it. Had the stone-setting been found to have the wrong name engraved on it, or the stone been placed over someone else's grave, it would have completed a miserable day, but at least that went off without any hitches. In terms of attendance, marriages are obviously much happier ceremonies to be at than funerals – but in terms of what happens afterwards, the former are much harder to predict than the latter.

Kosher cock-up

The *barmitzvah* went fine, the boy did well and everyone was pleased with the event. The lunch afterwards went less smoothly. It was at a local hotel and the family had given strict instructions to the manager that no meat was to be served. It was not that the immediate family were that observant, but they knew that some relatives objected to non-*kosher* meat and so thought it best to stick to a fish meal. They realised their mistake when the waiters placed a large salmon on each table, decorated with prawns. I knew I had to step in before the gasps turned to recriminations and simply stood up and said: 'Maybe we should ask the waiter to take the dish away and remove the prawns.' The chorus of approval meant that a major family *broigus* was avoided, although I felt sure there was an unusual tang to the salmon they brought back.

There was also a time when I accidentally ate pork as part of my rabbinic duties. Raphael's wife had died and everyone was invited back to his house after the funeral for the *shivah* (prayers and refreshments). A caterer had been hired to provide nibbles, and as I was chatting to someone a waitress came round with them. I took something casually, without paying much attention, as I was concentrating on the conversation. It was only when I was distracted by an unusual flavour in my mouth that I looked down and realised I had a mini pork sausage on a stick... or, rather, that I had half a mini pork sausage on a stick. The other person had not noticed and carried on chatting, as did I, though I was bemused to think that the only place I had ever been offered a pork sausage was at a *shivah* at a congregant's home.

5

The astonishing things people get up to

The eternal silence

I was leading a residential youth weekend, a mix of boister-ous fun and serious content cunningly slipped in. It was the tradition to do a sung grace after each meal, which was a rowdy, tub-thumping exercise that even those who thought it cool to look bored quite enjoyed. The theme of the weekend was different faiths in the UK. As the evening speaker, a Bud-dhist monk, joined us for dinner, I thought it would be an idea to invite him to do his grace and experience his tradition at first hand, so I handed over to him. It turned out to be a silent grace, though that was not surprising. The only problem was that it went on for a long time. The sixty teenagers were not good at sitting still. At first, his bowed head and flowing robes commanded their respect. After four minutes a few whispers occurred, which I managed to silence with a glare. After an-other two minutes, a few titters broke out, this time curtailed with a pointed finger. I knew I could not hold the line for much longer, yet the monk seemed deeply immersed in his silence. I heard a few drumming fingers. When we hit the ten-minute mark, I decided I had to intervene to save the occasion while there was still some decorum left, so I interrupted the silence with a loud Amen and told the kids to go to the lounge. The monk turned to me and said: 'Thank you, that was lovely, though I have to tell you that our grace is much shorter.'

Here's some gossip

I was brought up on the saying 'Sticks and stones may break my bones, but names can never hurt me.' I quickly learnt that it was not true and that the reverse can be the case: a physical wound usually heals, but a verbal insult can fester away and damage us for years. Yet, what we do not like others doing to us we often do to others, particularly the way we spread gossip, often disguising it as innocent chatter so that we do not feel guilty for its insidious effect. How often have you come across lines such as:

I don't know if it's true, but I heard that... (Nonsense, you are assuming it is true, otherwise you would not be passing it on.)

There's a thing or two I could tell you about... (Which immediately casts aspersion that person.)

I'd hate you to think I meant ill of her, but I know that... (Which really means: don't think ill of me despite the nasty things I am about to say.)

Don't get me wrong, I like the fellow a lot, but I heard... (Of course you do not like him, otherwise you would not enjoy spreading the dirt.)

The rabbis are spot on when they say that gossip actually hurts three different types of people: not just the person being talked about, but the person doing the gossiping (because they demean themselves) and the person listening to it (because their view of the person being discussed is permanently poisoned, however untrue the statements). Of course, the problem is we like hearing gossip, so it takes an effort to walk away from conversations in which we know we should not be participating. Maybe it is worth bearing in mind that you often hear people saying 'Don't speak ill of the dead' – so why let our scruples stop there and speak ill of the living?

The throwaway line that can slice others to bits

We were having an open discussion in synagogue during the Saturday morning service. I had long established the custom that once a month they could do without a sermon and instead I would take a topical issue and open it up to general debate. It was their chance to answer back. We were talking about children, and a parent present said, 'You know, they are so much trouble, you wonder whether they are worth it!' It is one of those remarks one casually throws out and never gives a thought as to where it will end up. This one landed badly, for although most people laughed, one woman burst into tears. She had been trying for a child for several years and was only too willing to put up with all the trouble that having a child entails. Certainly, the Bible has numerous examples of women who could not conceive, either initially or permanently, or who died in childbirth. We tend to forget what a privilege it is to be able to give birth, and what an amazing sequence of developments occurs from the act of sexual intercourse to a sentient being emerging nine months later. I have never witnessed a miracle in the biblical sense of divine intervention, but by my own definition, I have seen four miracles: four children tumble into the world when a few seconds earlier they had not existed outside the womb. Just as incredible is that this process happens whether the sex is done lovingly, drunkenly, adulterously or even without one partner's consent. It is probably best we do not know how we were conceived and just get on with using the remarkable gift of life as best we can. As for the woman who cried: most throwaway lines are harmless most of the time, so we should not be too over-neurotic about them, but a slight pause before deciding to utter them might save a few broken hearts.

When lightning struck… and never went away

Derek had never been the easiest of people. He had issues with others, he had issues with himself, there were periods of depression and it culminated in a failed attempt at suicide. It was while he was recovering at the clinic that his experience happened. There was a storm raging outside and he opened the window, perhaps as a distraction from the boredom indoors, perhaps because he felt it mirrored his own inner turmoil. He says that he was struck by lightning, but, rather than leave him hurt, he was physically unharmed and spiritually uplifted. Clearly – or at least it was clear to him – God had touched him, chosen him, opened his eyes to the wonder of the world and tasked him with sharing God's light. It would be easy, of course, to say that this was imaginary, resulting from hallucination due to the drugs he had been prescribed, or arising out of some auto-suggestion that helped him re-establish a sense of purpose for himself. Even if he was actually struck by lightning, it was Derek's interpretation that turned it into a divine post-it note. Still, when he told me the story, I did not suggest any of these (to my mind, likely) explanations, for whatever occurred had helped him and he was now coping, working and interacting with others. As far as he was concerned, he was in a state of grace and life was now worth living.

He had not been to synagogue much in previous years, but now he started attending services every week, finding it a way of maintaining his newly discovered sense of God. In fact, he always occupied a seat in the very front row, so as to be as near as possible to the Ark and the scrolls inside containing God's word. The downside was that he felt certain that God had given him the right to point out to others when they were departing from the divine path. He would regularly criticise others in synagogue – out loud – if he thought that they were erring in some way. It put me in a difficult position. Knowing Derek's troubled past meant that I was keen to make him feel at home in a stable environment, but that could not be at the cost of antagonising others who had an equal right to be there. We had periodic chats about his behaviour and the needs of others.

He never accepted either point; God had chosen him, so

why should he change his ways? He regarded me as sadly lacking in true religiosity, obviously inferior to his heightened vision, but humoured me by ameliorating his behaviour – until the next time he felt God's honour had been slighted by a congregant. Moreover, he would always justify his infinite rectitude by sending me cards with an appropriate quotation, imploring me to open my eyes to what God wanted, and never failing to sign off: yours gracefully. I usually felt that signing off 'yours arrogantly' would have been more accurate.

I always knew it would end in tears. You cannot be so utterly convinced of your own uprightness and everyone else's blindness for it not to end in a mini-Armageddon. It came when someone approached the Ark, whom I had asked to open it during a service, but who Derek did not reckon was worthy of doing so. He deliberately stuck out his foot, tripping up the person in an attempt to stop him reaching the Ark. That was it. I could cope with him emitting hostile glares and vituperative words – and the continual job of me having to mop up other people's hurt feelings by explaining that 'Derek is little bit different from the rest of us, so don't be upset by anything he says'. But tripping up people – and acting as self-appointed gatekeeper of who could be called to the Ark – that was unacceptable.

Derek was told to leave the synagogue and banned from future attendance. Life was much more peaceful without him. I was wonderfully relieved that he had gone and that the weekly trauma of trying to second-guess 'what would happen this week?' was over, but also a little guilty that I was pleased he had taken a step too far which had forced me to get rid of him. Similarly, I was pleased that we had stretched our tolerance for some three years to keep him among us, but also sad that we had not been able to give him a home for longer. In the end, though, the fault lay with him rather than us. What is more, he was not a one-off, but typical of those who are so full of God's light that everyone else is trapped in darkness and unable to find the path to Paradise that only they can tread. Every congregation has its Derek, and it is just a matter of when they leave and how much mayhem they cause before then.

Hidden love waiting to be found

One of the sadnesses that bothers me is why some people never manage to find a marriage partner, even though they would make wonderfully loving companions and have so much to offer. It is not because there is anything wrong with them, and is instead to do with chance and meeting the right person at the right time. It is also very obvious how many people's social horizons shrink once they leave college and become straitjacketed into just mixing with those they see at work or meet at the gym. In recent decades, the internet has meant that the opportunities for social dating have exploded beyond recognition, but not everyone wants to expose themselves so publicly (even if they hide behind false names), while others are worried about being duped by strangers. It is the same reaction that used to occur in pre-internet days when the main option was dating agencies. I often heard: 'Oh, it's only for losers', or 'No, my friends say it's useless.'

My response was always to tell them about Brandon and

Julia – both in their late twenties, both good-looking, talented, outgoing and personable and both very lonely. Somehow, the right relationship had not happened for either of them. Luckily, they both had the gumption to register with a dating agency, were 'matched', went out and eighteen months later I officiated at their wedding. In fact, they were so good-looking that the dating agency obtained their permission to use them for their adverts and for the next two years I was frequently faced by them on London Underground adverts. I suspect most other commuters thought they were professional actors posing for the advert – but they were for real. They were certainly not losers, but did need help meeting.

There is no shame in being alone, but there is no merit in thinking that that has to remain the case. Whenever people tell me: 'I'd love to meet someone but it doesn't look likely to happen,' I reply: 'I am sure there are lots of people who'd love to meet you, but first you have to let them know you exist.' And I tell them about Brandon and Julia, who could not find each other until they realised they needed help doing so.

A Christmas puzzle

It was extraordinary. Attendance at services is modest but respectable, but one particular weekend it shot up. Why? Because the Friday was Christmas Eve and the Saturday was Christmas Day. These, of course, are Christian festivals and so should not have any bearing on synagogue life. Yet exactly the same thing happened a few years later when the dates coincided. There were several possible explanations.

One was guilt. They were enjoying Christmas: not going to church, but having the parties and presents and festive atmosphere at large. Yet they also felt they had betrayed their Jewishness in some way, and so had better come to synagogue to atone, or at least reassure themselves of their Jewish roots.

A second was not worries about their conscience, but the children's identity. They had succumbed even more to the seasonal jollity and were probably more familiar with 'Away in a manger' than Jewish songs. It was time to give them a lesson in Jewish awareness.

A third was the heightened sense of nobility in coming to synagogue over Christmas, sacrificing invitations to a neighbour's drinks party or a friend's brunch. The inner glow that came from such martyrdom for one's faith was a powerful compensation.

A fourth was to teach the rabbi a lesson. He would not normally expect you to appear on an ordinary Sabbath, even less so on such a special day with so many competing calls for your time, so it was worth reminding him that his low opinion of you was totally unjustified and misguided.

A fifth was the complete opposite: to keep the rabbi company. The assumption was that the rest of the irreligious congregation would not turn up and it would be appalling for the rabbi to be alone, so you had better go along.

A sixth was more to do with domestic chores. Given a choice between going off to synagogue or staying at home, clearing the main room, preparing tables and chairs for the lunch-time guests, divine worship suddenly became very attractive.

A final reason – the most charitable – is that those who genuinely wanted to come to services but found themselves overwhelmed with tasks most weekends, now had the leisure to attend.

From my point of view, I never question people's motives in coming to services. I know that on most Sabbaths there is an unholy mix of reasons: some due to sense of duty, others because they want to, yet others because they need to. Frankly, I do not care why they come; instead I see the rabbi's task as to make it sufficiently interesting, enriching or sociable that when they leave they feel they have benefited from it in some way.

I also know that it does not mean they will come again – for there are so many competing calls on one's time – so attendance rates are not necessarily a reflection on satisfaction levels. Every minister wants a bumper crowd, but we may have to settle for the warm thoughts of those who are not present.

Convict converts

Something that puzzled me initially about Reading prison when I became a chaplain was the number of requests I had to see non-Jewish prisoners who wanted to convert to Judaism. After speaking to other Jewish chaplains, I realised this was common elsewhere too. The reason had nothing to do with a religious experience, but was entirely practical. Studying would help pass the time away (boredom is a major problem for many prisoners), while they also reckoned they would gain various privileges, such as special foods. For others, the attraction was that it would enable them to take time off on Jewish Sabbaths and festivals if they did not like the work schedule for that day. There is a general rule observed by Jewish chaplains that people cannot convert inside prison. They can read books about Judaism, but can only join conversion courses once they have been released. This is because being part of a local Jewish community is seen as a vital part of the conversion process. It also helps to dissuade prisoners seeking conversion for opportunistic reasons. Still, it is amusing to note the contrast between those in prison who see it as a privilege to take time off for Sabbaths and festivals, and congregants outside prison who do not always share that enthusiasm.

Till faith us do part

One of the issues in which I have specialised is mixed-faith marriages. My mantra has always been that it involves issues rather than problems, as common sense and goodwill can solve a very high percentage of the situations that arise. Sometimes, though, people score unexpected own goals. When Mary (nominal Christian) and Harvey (nominal Jew) married, it was a great ceremony and they had a lovely honeymoon. But their first day home proved difficult. She thought she would give him a nice surprise by bringing him breakfast in bed, except that it involved bacon and eggs, at which he went berserk. Why had she not known this would be his reaction? Because, like many Jews, he had never minded eating pork products outside the house but baulked at having them at home. They simply had not discussed the food aspects of the domestic life together. They had talked about joint bank accounts, life insurance, future schools for the children – all very sensible – but had forgotten about what could and could not go in the fridge. Communication! It also highlights the great shock that many non-Jewish partners have when they realise that a lapsed Jew is still Jewish. They may not be religiously involved, but care about certain rituals, resent criticism of Israel by non-Jews (by Jews is alright) and often have a very different attitude to family (as one person put it to me: my non-Jewish wife phones her mother once a week and thinks she is a good daughter; I speak to my mother twice a day and think I'm a bad son). A lapsed Jew is always much more Jewish than a lapsed Christian is Christian. It is to do with roots and culture, and so whereas Mary plaintively said afterwards: 'But I thought you were not religious,' she had misunderstood the situation entirely. The same happened with Dora and Joseph. They survived their first day back and everything was fine until that December. On a whim, after work, she brought home a small Christmas tree, which she (being lapsed Christian) thought would be a pretty decoration for the front living room. However, he (being lapsed Jewish) saw it as a declaration of religious war. Homework: talk more!

Cathy and David had a different problem (and theirs was indeed a major problem). They lived next door to each other in Liverpool, grew up together and got on well. When they were in their late teens and started dating each other, her Catholic parents and his Jewish parents both decided this had to stop. The couple were deeply in love, but it was at a time when parental commands held sway. David was sent to London to work with a family member, eventually married but got divorced three years later. One day, on a business trip to Liverpool, he realised he was driving very near to his old home (his parents had moved elsewhere by then). Out of a mixture of curiosity and nostalgia, he knocked on the door where Cathy's family had lived, intending to ask what happened to them and maybe get a glimpse of their familiar hallway. To his immense surprise, Cathy opened the door. They got chatting, she invited him in, and he made sure he was on another business trip to Liverpool shortly afterwards. The relationship resumed, and they are now happily married with two children. Their only regret is the heartache of the separation and the years they spent apart.

Jane had a unique situation that is the butt of many a joke, but was not funny when it happened to her in real life. Her parents did not mind her marrying Rob, who was totally secular, liked him and considered him a good match. It was her grandmother who objected, so much so that she refused to attend the wedding. It was not just that Rob was not Jewish, it was his occupation. He was a pig farmer. How could she tell her friends what he did for a living? 'My son the doctor' has a familiar ring about it, but 'my grandson-in-law the pig farmer' was definitely not *kosher*. She has also refused to see them since, and so has never met her great-grandchildren or bounced them on her knee. It still upsets Jane a lot, but I cannot help feeling that her grandmother is the one who has missed out most.

That isn't to say mixed-faith marriages are issues for the Jewish community alone. The worries and concerns behind them (including 'Will it work or end in tears? Even if it survives, the faith will be abandoned'; 'We won't have anything in common with the grandchildren'; 'It's not right'; 'Forget religion, he is not part of our tribe') are common across all religions. I remember speaking to a tearful Paula, a Catholic, whose lapsed Anglican in-laws refused to attend the wedding if it was held in her church. They had not been to their own church for years, but they were certainly not going to steep inside a Catholic one. Principle or prejudice?

Sometimes the parents confuse matters by giving mixed signals. Mark's Jewish parents had no problem welcoming Jackie into their home when they were dating, but the moment he announced they were getting engaged, they said she was no longer welcome in the house. Did they not know that the only cause of mixed-faith marriage is mixed-faith dating? In contrast, Annette's mother made it clear from the start that she did not want her to continue her relationship with Dean. It was because he was Jewish, but not out of any sense of prejudice. She liked him and had many Jewish friends herself. Instead, it was because she had lived through the war in Holland, seen what the Nazis had done to Jews, and did not want her grandchildren to be potentially open to the same persecution should another right-wing dictatorship arise. She did accept the relationship once they got engaged, but still harboured latent worries about what the future might bring.

What about the children?

Most mixed-faith couples manage to negotiate the courtship and wedding reasonably well. The issues become more complicated when children arise and decisions have to be made about them. I usually advise couples to clarify their thinking by separating three distinct aspects: religious education (what they know), religious status (how they are classified by the faith groups) and religious identity (what they think of themselves as being). It is possible to have several different computations of these three depending on what the couple think best. The most common tends to be education in both faiths and being brought up in one of them. That way they can relate to the different traditions of both sides of the family, but be rooted in one particular identity. But it is a totally personal decision and the key is what works for that particular couple. For instance, I thought it was somewhat eccentric of Rudi and Janice – who had two children – to bring up their son Jewish, like his dad, and their daughter Catholic, like her mum. In a mixed-faith household, why consciously divide the children? But they put a lot of thought and effort into it, the children grew up well-adjusted and respectful of both faiths, and it worked.

Some decisions have to be made much more quickly. If it is a baby boy, then the question of circumcision arises, which often throws up a major cultural gap. Many non-Jews object (unless they are dads who have been circumcised themselves and so see no problem), regarding it as either unnecessary or harmful. The terms 'mutilation' or 'barbaric' are often used. In vain does the Jewish partner point out that Jews are neurotic about their children's health and if it had been proved to be dangerous, either physically or psychologically, then it would have been abandoned centuries ago. Not all Jews particularly enjoy the circumcision ceremony, but they have 3,000 years' worth of tradition pushing them along. Some mixed-faith couples agonise about it from the moment of conception, others put off discussion till the birth – in case it is a discussion in vain, but then face intense debate at a time when they are both exhausted and emotional if it turns out to be a boy. Some do a compromise – 'you dunk him and I'll slice him' – even though they are not equivalents to be swapped, for baptism is an act of religious commitment whereas circumcision is just a ritual observance. Still, if it keeps the domestic peace, or placates competing family demands, then maybe it is worth it.

What is often forgotten is that a mixed-faith couple is for life, and managing the end period is just as important as the beginning part. Until recently, Jewish cemeteries had by-laws forbidding non-Jews to be buried in them. Given both the antipathy to cremation – changing now, but once very strong – and that most Jews still want to die Jewish even if they never lived Jewish, it meant that the couple were buried in separate cemeteries and their children had to visit their parents in different locations. Attitudes changed, and more and more mixed-faith couples opted for cremation, so that at least the ceremony could be in the same place and their ashes scattered under the same non-denominational rose-bush. Nowadays, some Jewish cemeteries, including the Maidenhead one, do permit mixed-faith burials. It may not be traditional, but the justification is simple: who am I to separate in death a couple who have been happily together in life for forty or more years? Still, it does produce some odd situations. Several times I have officiated at a funeral of a Jewish person with fifty or sixty people present, but only two Jews: me and the corpse; and I have ended up tailoring the service to non-Jewish mourners.

Having worked in this field for over thirty years, I have developed two golden rules – both of which may seem obvious but are remarkably often ignored by individual couples. The first is to discuss everything in advance – not just the wedding day, honeymoon and mortgage, but all the little things that come after it. The wedding day may last five or six hours, but it is the next fifty or sixty years that need planning, including what to do at Christmas and Passover, whether any children will have a *bar/batmitzvah* and putting up a *mezuzah* or not. Whereas Jewish–Jewish couples may take them for granted and sail on unthinkingly, mixed-faith couples need to work them out so that there are no sudden hiccups or running sores. The second is to keep the channels of communication open with family, even if relations are difficult at times. One day the couples' parents will become their children's grandparents and they should ensure that there is no severance between the generations. Conversely, I always advise the parents that however much they might object to the marriage, once it is definitely going ahead they should accept it and be present at the wedding. The one thing you cannot do years later is put yourself back in the wedding photo where you are missing.

One oddity that has arisen is the disproportionately high number of Jews who marry Catholics. There are not that many Jews in the UK, while Catholics are relatively limited in number too, so the odds on them marrying is low, yet up to 26 per cent of Jews marry Catholics. This is doubly strange given the bloody history in previous centuries of relationships between the two faiths, characterised by burnings at the stake and expulsions. Clearly there is some underlying attraction between Jews and Catholics that defies the statistical odds against such unions. One explanation may be that both have a powerful set of shared values underneath the surface differences: individuals may not be that regular service-attenders but believe in family, home life and ethical values. When they meet, therefore, they find they have much in common. Another cause may be that both are minorities and so have a slightly different worldview from the vast CofE-ness of everyone else, are used to being seen as a little odd and may have experienced anti-Catholic or anti-Jewish bullying. This, too, can lead to a click-factor. Moreover, both being minorities means that they do not challenge each other's separate identity as much, whereas a minority faith person marrying a majority faith one can feel taken over and swamped by the dominant faith.

Over the years, I have noticed two unexpected curiosities emerge. One is that many couples say they have a stronger marriage because it is a mixed-faith one, as they have had to discuss in advance issues about home life and family prac- tices that they would otherwise not have done. As George and Henrietta put it: 'We've done marriage guidance in ad- vance, and understand each other's needs and red lines much better.' The other curiosity is that the Jewish partners often say they feel more Jewish because they are in a mixed-faith marriage. Vicky explained: 'If I as a lapsed Jew had married another lapsed Jew, then we'd have both stayed lapsed. But because I'm the only Jew in the marriage, I feel I have to fly the flag and keep up ceremonies, like Friday night *kiddush* or *Hanukkah*, that I would not have normally bothered with. Because if I drop them, then they die completely and no one else is going to continue them.'

Oops, the rabbi has noticed

I had arranged to visit a new member. I duly rang the doorbell. They were obviously busy doing some last-minute tidying, and did not answer immediately. So, as one normally does while waiting on a doorstep, I casually looked around. At that point, the wife opened the door, saw me absent-mindedly gazing around but totally misinterpreted what I was doing. 'Ah,' she said with embarrassed haste, 'you noticed we don't have our *mezuzah* up. We do actually have one, rabbi. In fact, we only took it down last week because a friend of ours up the road was having an Orthodox visitor last weekend, didn't have one and asked to borrow ours. So we lent it to him. Sorry if we have offended you. We should have got it back by now.' In fact, I was not offended at all and had not even noticed. But I was bemused at her story – which I am still not sure if it was bizarrely true or ingeniously fabricated – while I was very grateful for the lead about someone Jewish in the area that I did not know about.

Much more common are the guilty apologies I receive whenever visiting members in December and finding an enormous Christmas tree in the hall. 'It's just for the kids,' they say imploringly, as if they had no control over it being there. Still, I am genuinely not bothered. It is their house and I have no desire to legislate as to how they fill it. My mission is to make them feel at home when they come to the synagogue. 'That's fine,' I usually respond. 'I'm here to see you, not your hallway.'

Spreading the risk

There was a two-year period in which synagogues in Europe came under attack, necessitating armed guards being stationed outside them. Although no such terrorism had happened in the UK, some Jews were afraid it would occur here at some point. Most synagogues stepped up their security arrangements, partly to pre-empt any attacks and partly to reassure members that it was still safe to attend. Individual responses varied greatly: some did stay away; others who did not normally come made a point of participating so as to defy the terrorists and emphasise that they would not be cowed; others came out of a desire for a sense of solidarity at such a tense time. One family at Maidenhead decided to hedge their bets. Reg had two sons whom he normally brought to the Religion School every Sunday. But, from that point on, he brought each of them on alternate weeks. As he explained to me: 'This way, if one gets caught in an attack, at least the other will be at home and OK.' I was torn between admiration for his determination to keep coming and puzzlement at his willingness to take a weekly gamble, in his own eyes, with the life of one son.

Definitely not coping

Pauline had issues. That was obvious when she started coming to services, but part of being a community means giving a safe space to those who are vulnerable and who cannot cope so well in society at large. We were able to provide that support for several weeks, but then she suddenly disappeared. Then I heard what had happened. She had gone up to Oxford Street, one of the busiest shopping areas in central London, stripped off her clothes and ran naked down its long stretch. She was sectioned and disappeared from view. Synagogues, and other religious institutions, attract a higher than average number of people who are disturbed in some way. I have never quite worked out whether that is because we are expected to be kinder than others, or because religious inclinations are part of their psyche. Many such cases need a level of professional help that we cannot provide, but others do find a home with us, because kindness may not heal everything but can make many problems more bearable.

Is that what you are really called?

Judaism is no longer a missionary faith. It was in biblical times, when the religious opposition was largely pagan religions, with their human sacrifices and sacred prostitutes, to which Judaism saw itself as superior. This extended to the first century and the description in the Gospels of how the Pharisees 'travel over sea and land just to make one convert' (Matthew 23:15), which is seen as a complaint but which I have always taken as a compliment. But once other monotheistic faiths arose, Judaism drew back, asserting it had a distinctive route to God but not the only one.

This attitude still holds today, in that those who wish to become Jewish can do so, but no energy is expended in attracting converts. Those who do adopt the faith are then regarded as fully equal to born Jews.

Although it is sometimes said that one Jew can always tell another Jew, actually that is complete nonsense as there are so many varying racial or cultural influences that while some Jews can appear very Jewish, others go totally unnoticed. However, there can be one give-away sign for those who have converted: if they are called Christine or Christopher. There is nothing wrong with the name, but it is so identified with the church that nobody Jewish would give their child that name, and so they must have been born to non-Jewish parents. But, while this may hold true as a generalisation, it cannot be universally applied. When Gerry and Kate, both of whom were Jewish, moved to the area, they brought their young son Christopher with them. When I visited them and asked about the origin on the name, Gerry looked a bit sheepish and Kate explained for him: 'We couldn't agree on a name and left it really late. When we went to register him and were asked what we had chosen, Gerry said we were still debating but he wanted to name him after his father Chaim and asked what names began with "Ch". The registrar said Christopher and we said OK. It was only later that we realised we could have gone for Charles.' 'Mary' is also unusual for Jewish children, but has been used by one or two who chose Miriam as the girl's Hebrew name and then looked for an everyday equivalent.

That's strange, it doesn't feel like spring

Marty was an American member who had come to England with his wife on a two-year business contract and had ended up staying here for many years. With retirement looming, they decided to return to the States and planned their move for mid-November. I visited them both shortly before they were about to leave and was surprised to find several boxes of *matzah* and tins of horseradish piled up in the dining room. 'How come all these?' I asked. 'Ah,' he said with a smile, 'I was going to tell you about this, rabbi. As you know, we don't have family here, so every year I've always invited my local non-Jewish friends for a Passover *seder*; we have fifteen or so around the table, and they absolutely love it. This year, it falls in early April, but we won't be here anymore, so I thought I'd bring Passover forward a few months and we're having a farewell *seder* next week!' I was not sure whether to despair at his cavalier attitude to the Jewish calendar or be lost in admiration at his religiosity.

In court

Monique was, to the outside world, a vivacious Belgian woman, who used to work in a local pet shop and was married to a highly successful stockbroker. What was not generally known was that she had been convicted of shoplifting five times. As they were relatively minor instances of theft, she had been given fines but the courts were now beginning to lose patience at the repeated offences and on the last occasion she was given a three-month prison sentence suspended for two years. Six months later, she was again caught and now faced imprisonment. I was asked to attend as a character witness. It was an almost textbook case of dysfunctionality. The problem was that her husband had a dominating personality that had manifested itself in constant criticism – over her cooking, her looks, her friends – that had worn down her sense of self-worth. She hardly went out and had started drinking at home. Her despair was compounded by the fact that her two daughters – previously the one joy of her life – were now away at university.

The shoplifting was never for financial reasons as it always involved petty items, but was a complex psychological response: it was partly an act of defiance against her 'respect-able' husband and to show him that she had a will of her own; partly a cry for help, wanting to be caught and for the outside world to know that all was not well with her; and it was also a convoluted means of gaining affection, for her husband went through an initial period of being much more considerate to her after each incident, presumably recognis-ing that he bore some responsibility for her unhappiness. Monique was very fortunate that she had a probation officer who looked beneath the surface thefts and recognised that they were symptomatic of the underlying personal prob-lems. She suggested that a community service order would be a more constructive alternative to prison, as it would take Monique out of the house, bring her into contact with others and hopefully begin to restore her self-esteem. The judge concurred. It proved a wake-up call for both Monique and her husband, and although the domestic situation was never ideal, it became more bearable. The drinking and shoplifting came to an end, and the misery that some couples inflict on themselves lessened.

THE ASTONISHING THINGS PEOPLE GET UP TO   149

Kabbalah

It is one of those phone calls I dread. It comes from Jews and non-Jews alike, who ring up because they want to learn some *kabbalah* and want to know if we have classes. I have trained myself not to follow my instinct and say tartly down the line: 'It is not suitable for you. Try yoga or speed-dating.' Instead, I take a deep breath and say: 'Why do you want to learn *kabbalah*?' In doing so, I am attempting to distinguish between those who are looking to engage with Jewish study and are prepared to invest a lot of time in it, and those who are bored, going through a bad patch or are looking for some meaning in life and have heard that *kabbalah* is the solution to everything.

Personally, I blame Madonna for that. When she, and other celebrities such as Jerry Hall, Britney Spears and Gwyneth Paltrow, had contact with an organisation known as the Kabbalah Centre, it thrust into the media a barely known and esoteric Jewish form of learning. Unfortunately, there is a big difference between real *kabbalah* and the pop-*kabbalah* to which they were introduced. Real *kabbalah* is often referred to as 'Jewish mysticism', but does not entail incantations or bizarre rituals. In reality, it is a method of studying biblical and other texts through a more poetic lens, trying to understand the nature of God and our role in the universe. Thus, the Sabbath is not just a period of rest with a long list of what is and is not permissible during that time, but is seen as a marriage between heaven and earth and a union between God and Israel, with the Sabbath being 'the bride'. For those immersed in Jewish knowledge it can be deeply enriching.

Traditionally, it was only learned scholars that studied *kabbalah*, and there was a rule that it was only open to those who were over forty, had a beard and at least two children. In other words, they had to be thoroughly grounded in reality and used to the demands of everyday life. It was not for the footloose or spiritual wanderers.

The pop-*kabbalah* that Madonna and others were served was not based on them having a deep knowledge of the Bible and Jewish law, nor was it predicated on them being actively involved in Jewish life and practice. What they were given was a superficial layer of Jewish ethics and lore, designed to encourage a feel-good factor that did not greatly differ in essence from Zen Buddhism or Transcendental Meditation. Some rabbis objected that this was not the real thing, and it fell foul of the Trades Descriptions Act. Others voiced concerns that that it was a much more inward-looking version of *kabbalah*, concentrating on the individual's personal spirituality and ignoring a sense of communal involvement and wider responsibilities. There is nothing wrong with this, and if some people found it meaningful, even though it is far removed from real *kabbalah*, then that is for the good. The greater worry that I and other rabbis felt was that those seeking *kabbalah* are often in a vulnerable state and if the teachers are less than scrupulous, they can take advantage of them, be it emotionally or financially. Most of the celebrities have now tired of the Kabbalah Centre and moved on to whatever is the most recent religious fashion, but the lure of *kabbalah* still remains and the phone calls keep coming. The simple act of asking if the person can read the Bible in Hebrew, and would they like to learn how to do so if not, is often sufficient for many to decide that yoga or speed-dating might be better after all.

Playing games

One of the characteristics of the Jewish world – but equally true of most other faiths – is the divisions within it, with different groupings such as Liberal, Masorti, Orthodox and Reform. Whereas most have a working relationship with each other, there has often been animosity between the Orthodox and the other groups, with the former considering themselves 'true Judaism' and everyone else heretics or pseudo-Jews. The fact that today's Orthodox Judaism was a later development within Judaism, and is very different from the practices of the original Judaism of the Bible, does not bother them. They are right and everyone else is wrong. It is one of the frustrating ironies of more liberal forms of Judaism that we tolerate those who do not tolerate us. Still, more moderate voices within Orthodoxy have begun to develop in recent decades, and they are willing to work together on issues of common concern, such as Israel or anti-Semitism, even if there is no meeting of minds on religious matters. As a gentle way of fostering links with our local Orthodox synagogue, we suggested that we play an annual cricket match together (in fact twice a year, home and away). Their leadership welcomed the idea and it took place for four years, not only battling each other on the pitch but enjoying each other's company at the tea afterwards.

Unfortunately, a new rabbi was then appointed to their synagogue. He decided that although cricket was a religion-free zone, such contact was a slippery slope that might lead to religious interchange and was therefore a dangerous liaison that had to be stopped. So, sadly, the matches came to an end. As for the difference between the Orthodox and the Progressives (a generic term for most other groups), it centres around the right to change. Orthodoxy regards Jewish beliefs and practices as stemming from the revelation at Mount Sinai, where they were given by God, have divine imprimatur and cannot be changed. Reform sees Judaism as a marriage between the wisdom of the past and the insights of modernity, a mix of tradition and change. Thus, within Reform synagogues, women have full equality in religious life, are not segregated at services and can be rabbis. Still, our cricket team was men only, so there was no need for the Orthodox to fear that the matches might have led to inter-dating between our two congregations.

Helping the police with their enquiries

From time to time the police phone. Sometimes it concerns a member of the community who has broken the law and cited me as a character witness, no doubt to attest that they are the most saintly person in the world and couldn't possibly have done whatever it was they have been accused of. On other occasions, it is for advice, for example, when someone had cut some mysterious shapes in a public garden, including a Star of David, I was asked whether I had any idea why. It was eventually decided that it was some form of black magic rather than anything Jewish.

Another call came from a lawyer who said he had a client who had been arrested for harming her child. In her defence, she had claimed that the act of cutting herself, cutting her child and then mingling their blood together was an ancient Jewish custom that she was obliged to follow. 'Is it?' they asked. The answer was simple: no, it was just an act of cruelty by a mother who was either mad or malicious.

Pregnant schoolgirls

Shortly after Lizzie entered the sixth form at school, she accidentally fell pregnant. I never found out whether it was him or her that had failed to take the contraceptive, but once she had conceived, it was irrelevant. The key question was: what happened next? As the pregnancy was discovered at an early stage, I had expected her to have a termination. The pregnancy was not intended, there was no question of her marrying the father, she was studying for her A Levels and planned to go to university afterwards. Abortion should not be seen as a casual form of contraception for those who cannot be bothered to take precautions beforehand, but nor do I believe in bringing unwanted children into a world in which they may not be cared for properly. But Lizzie felt very strongly that a life was already being nurtured inside her and that she did not have the right to kill it. Her parents both supported her decision and said they would help look after the child as much as possible while Lizzie was at school, and later on at university, though it would mean she would have to go to one that was relatively near so that she could come home at weekends.

It was a principled decision by all three of them, as an act of folly lasting a few seconds had meant the course of their lives was dramatically changed. The child itself was lucky in that it would be born into a household that would give it much greater love and care than many other babies that had been unplanned and would lack such a supportive environment. I knew there was another teenager in the community who had taken the opposite decision and had gone for an abortion. She had her career mapped out and intended to have children in her early thirties, not when she was sixteen years old. She put 'the mistake' behind her and did exactly that. I am not convinced that there is a simple right or wrong response, and that much must depend on individual situations. My only definite view was that if a child is to be brought into the world, it should be wanted and it should be assured of having the love it needs for a happy childhood.

The 'living together' puzzle

One of the social changes in recent decades has been the number of couples living together before deciding to get married. What is puzzling is that it has not affected the divorce rate. In theory, couples who live together before getting wed should have a good knowledge of each other and should have established a way of co-existing relatively harmoniously. This should mean that marriages take place between those who are known to be suited to each other and so should have greater chance of success. Yet around one in three couples continue to divorce, including those who had these 'trial marriages'. Having witnessed this transition and puzzled over it, I reckon there may be some cogent reasons why living together before marriage is no guarantee of success after it. One is that the marriage often takes place shortly before or after the arrival of children, when the couple decided 'it is time to settle down'. But children can not only be a wonderful occurrence, but can also have an unsettling effect on marriage. The partner giving up work can feel a loss of identity. The financial income can dip and cause tensions. The transfer of the mother's attention away from her husband to her children can cause resentment. Lack of sleep and lack of the previous freedom to organise one's time how one wanted can also add pressures.

Another issue is that some couples who live together but who are not necessarily best suited just get used to being with each other and assume that marriage is the obvious next step, when actually it is not and just adds to the divorce statistics. Even those who suspect that all is not well find the idea of splitting and undoing joint possessions – from CDs to furniture to mortgage – too difficult to contemplate and so stay in a relationship which is bearable but not ideal, and which will eventually fall apart. Yet another issue is that some couples living together but experiencing problems in their relationship think that getting married and having a public act of commitment might be the solution to their difficulties. In reality, though, they may have a splendid day, but the underlying fault-lines still remain and so the split is merely postponed. But whatever one's approach to marriage, it is probably one of the biggest gambles we ever make in our lives: the promise to feel the same about someone in several decades' time, the assumption that we will be as compatible then as we are now, the hope that our relationship will not be derailed by the enormous amount of changes we will encounter. Like all other gambles we make, preparation and foreknowledge are vital, but are still no guarantee of success. It is equally the case that those looking on can be just as surprised at the marriages that work as they are by those that fail.

Caught by a cult

June phoned to say that she had just got back from India and needed to talk to me about it. A 62-year-old stalwart of the Mothers' Union, I had not anticipated what she was about to tell me. She had gone to an ashram, a guru's commune, and had totally fallen under his spell. The woman, whose home was immaculate and which had a separate entrance for tradesmen, had been happy roughing it in a dormitory of ten other women of various ages and backgrounds. She had listened to his talks every day, spent hours in meditation and had helped with jobs that needed doing.

June also mentioned how she had been told she had special skills that could be of great use. Obviously it was a release from her regimented, and perhaps suppressed, lifestyle in Maidenhead, and I was happy for her new-found sense of self. However, I was worried by her totally uncritical endorsement of the ashram. According to her, it was heaven, it was utopia, it was the answer to everything in life. It may well have a lot to offer, but that level of expectation would be impossible to fulfil long-term and, when it came crashing down, would leave her feeling desolate and betrayed. She would also have lost her former identity and might find it very hard re-establishing her life. June brushed aside my concerns, albeit very graciously, saying that if I met the guru and spent time at the ashram, then I would realise how wonderful it was. She also teasingly asked if I was jealous: 'After all,' she said, 'you never got me to come to synagogue very often, so maybe you feel piqued about my religious discovery!' Nothing was further from the truth, for although I do want people to be part of the community, I never stipulate how – whether through services, social events, cultural activities or whatever. I was genuinely worried that such an intense religious high could result in a major depressive fall. Unfortunately, I was right; the ashram was caught up in a series of financial and sexual scandals, leaving numerous adherents, including June, physically homeless and spiritually devastated.

But it would be wrong just to concentrate on June's naivety. The fact that cults, including many based in this country, flourish and attract people is also an indictment of more established religions. Clearly they are offering religious goods that, however flawed, initially appeal to those who have not found a religious home in church or synagogue. It might be community or spirituality or feelings of self-worth or personal identity or sense of direction, and while all of these are present in mainstream faiths, they are not perceived as being available. Of course, that is also because mainstream faiths tend not make false claims about instant religious gratification. Religious satisfaction, they say, comes from personal effort, needs patience and often involves interacting with others. Moreover, they stress that religion is not just about the self but the individual as part of the wider community. Religion is not just about the ego but about bettering society as a whole, and any faith group that is totally self-centred or that isolates the select few from the wider world is suspect.

This can also apply to Jewish cults, although they may resist that label. The most obvious are Lubavitch, though some would include Aish HaTorah, who operate solely within the Jewish world and have a clear agenda to get Jews to be more observant. While this in itself is not a problem, difficulties arise when their level of observance means that 'born again' Jews can no longer eat in their parents' home. This can mean them moving out, or, if already living elsewhere, visiting home less often. Keeping *kosher* and observing the Sabbath can be very enriching, but are less beautiful when they cause family break-ups. In addition, the stark binary worldview that is engendered – God's truth and falsehood, observant Jews and non-observant Jews, Jews and non-Jews – can lead to isolationist tendencies as much as other cults. Just because the Jewish ones have a familiar *Fiddler on the Roof* surface feel to them does not make them any less willing to engage in love-bombing and mind-control techniques.

6

Dilemmas

You have one minute to decide

It looked set to be a normal wedding. It would, of course, be special for them, but would largely follow the pattern of most ceremonies in its format. There was a slight complication we had discussed at the planning stage, but it was not expected to alter the overall shape of the day. This was the fact that the bride would not have any immediate family present. Her mother had died a while ago, she was not inviting her father – with whom there had been a fall-out on some matter in recent years – and she was an only child. But there were uncles, aunts, cousins and friends galore, quite apart from the groom's side of the family, so it would still be a much-shared occasion.

The wedding was about to begin when a relative rushed up to me and said that the bride's father had turned up. He had heard about the date and venue through a family source and was demanding to be let into the synagogue. I asked the couple what they wanted to do. The bride was furious and the happy smile of a few seconds ago was replaced with a venomous look that was chillingly quick in its arrival. She was adamant that he was not invited, not wanted and should not be allowed to attend. I did suggest that, although that had been her intention, now that he was here and others would soon find out, it might be kinder to let him in. I also said that it was far better to err on the side of generosity. In later years, she would be much more likely to regret excluding him than rue including him. There was also the question of what message it gave to other family members, not to mention the in-laws. She stood her ground: 'If he is allowed in, I am leaving. It's your synagogue – please sort it out.' This was not the time for a technical debate over who actually owned the synagogue – the rabbi or the Board of Trustees or the membership at large. The message was clear and I had to act either way.

I felt torn. On the one hand, it seemed cruel to exclude a father from his daughter's wedding, to shame him in front of the rest of the family. If relationships improved in the future, he could never be put back into the wedding photos, and banning him now might guarantee that the rift remained a permanent one. On the other hand, I did not know what lay behind the hostility and whether she had just cause in reject-ing him. The very fact that he had arrived knowing he was uninvited might hint at a certain insensitivity, if not much worse. On top of all this, I only had a minute to decide. He was banging at the door, the guests were waiting, the couple were ready to walk out. I felt I had no choice but to exclude him. Sabbath services may be a public occasion open to everyone, but weddings were a private event by invitation only. The bride had the right to determine whom she wanted to be present on the most special day of her life. I went outside to explain this to him in person. It is not easy telling a father his daughter hates him, nor rushing such a conversation. Perhaps it helped that I was wearing a gown and looked official. Put on a peaked cap – or any other badge of office – and people will often do what they would not do if you had told them exactly the same thing without wearing it. With her, he would have argued; with me, he accepted it with genuine puzzlement.

When I went back into the synagogue, told the couple he had gone and alerted the choir that the wedding was about to start, I thought the worst was over. It was not. What was much harder was delivering the wedding address ten minutes later, telling the couple the thoughts I had prepared about the value of family and the importance of domestic harmony. It was hard not to wonder what had gone so wrong in their lives, or to speculate whether divine retribution would come about in two or three decades when their children rejected them. Curiously enough, as sometimes happens, when the couple did have children, she re-established contact with her father. Perhaps she suddenly understood what it must have felt like for him, or maybe she felt it important for her children to have a grandfather. But one day they will see the wedding photos and wonder why he was not there.

To my horror, I had to deal with a repeat scenario eight years later: a much-loathed uncle turning up uninvited to a Saturday morning *barmitzvah*. I was asked by the boy's parents to exclude him from the building. This time, though, because it was a public service, I felt I could not do so. Instead, I ensured that he sat well away from the family and gave a member of council who was present the task of 'minding him' and checking that he did not disturb anyone at the *kiddush* afterwards.

When some secrets need to be told

Bob and Eve were a decent couple, and had been involved in the community both religiously and socially. They were popular and were often invited for dinner by others and reciprocated generously. It came as a surprise, therefore, when Eve rang to ask me to come round as soon as possible. She told me that she had asked Bob to leave after she had come home early one day to find him in bed with a neighbour. After listening for a while, I asked whether this was the first time he had been unfaithful. She confirmed that, to the best of her knowledge, it was. So I mentioned that, shocking as this must have been for her, people have lapses and later regret them. If that applied to Bob, would she take him back? It was then that the truth emerged. No, she said, she was glad to be rid of him, for beneath the genial exterior he had bullied her throughout their married life. He had been considerate in public, but constantly demeaned her in private. It all poured out in a rush, the first time she had ever spoken of it, unloading decades of resentment. She paused a while, I thought to catch her breath, but in fact to unleash another revelation. He had abused her physically too. She had never had the courage to speak out, becoming more and more submissive over the years, but having been shocked into action by the sexual betrayal, she was certainly not going to let him take control over her again.

So Eve applied for a divorce. When they sold the house, Eve moved away to be nearer her family, but Bob stayed locally and remained part of the community. Bob knew I was aware of the affair, and we had talked about it, but not that I had been told about the abuse. After a couple of years, he began dating another member, and my dilemma began. She was a strong-minded woman, had been divorced for a while and I knew she was looking for a permanent partner. From what I could tell about both of them, it seemed a good match. But should I tell her about his past behaviour? It might be that the nature of the new relationship was such that he would not dream of treating her the way he treated Eve. Would it be wrong of me to prejudice what might be a good second marriage for both of them? Or was it irresponsible to withhold information about a serious character defect that she might only discover once it was too late? Yes, people could change, but often they did not do so, and a man who abused one woman was likely to abuse another.

I decided that the greater harm would come from silence. It is not easy telling someone that the person with whom they are besotted and on whom they are pinning great hopes for the future is not all he seems. It can lead to them either collapsing in floods of tears, distraught at the truth they never suspected, or angrily denying the information and haranguing the messenger for daring to spread such hurtful lies. In the event, she took it very calmly, and said she was aware he had a past. I felt there was an element of denial in her reaction, as if Bob may have done wrong but was provoked by Eve and so could be forgiven. Still, I had given her the facts and she had the right as to how to interpret them. Some months later, the relationship ended. I did not hear it from her directly, and she never spoke about the break-up to me even though we continued to see each other regularly for several years. With most other people I would have found a way of gently asking, but with her I did not. I reckoned I had

invaded her privacy enough already, and if she ever wanted
to talk about it with me, she knew she could.

The secret that stayed secret

Jenna and Steve were at a service and afterwards said, very
nonchalantly: 'Do you have five minutes for a brief chat?'
Their casual attitude hardened the moment we sat down and
I asked: 'So, how can I help?' Steve looked at me and said: 'I'd
like to stay out of prison.' It turned out that Jenna had an elderly aunt they used to visit from time to time. When she felt
she was unable to look after her own affairs, she asked them
to take out power of attorney over her. All was well at first.
Then Steve's business began to run into difficulties and suffer
losses. Without telling anyone, he siphoned off some of the
aunt's money to help with the cash flow. Over the next two
years, the initial £5,000 became £72,000. He said he knew
it was wrong, but the aunt was in a home by then, all her
bills were paid for and her day-to-day life was not affected by
the borrowings. When I corrected his terminology and said:
'You mean theft', he replied that it was always his intention to
repay the money.

Jenna had found out a few days ago, but had agreed to
let the situation continue so long as her aunt's care home
expenses could be maintained and he came to see me and
confessed. I am not sure if she wanted him to feel remorse
or needed a witness to the facts in case matters ended badly.
What was clear was that she felt very conflicted: she was
horrified when she discovered what had happened and the

deception involved, but was also aware that the business was their sole means of support and they needed it to survive. They both wanted to talk through what might lie ahead.

We discussed the options. One was that he went to the police, admitted the crime and would no doubt go to prison. Steve knew he deserved it, but also knew the business would crash, Jenna and the children would be left homeless and the aunt would not benefit. His plan was that, now that the business had stabilised, he would repay the money in instalments over the next two years. If there was still an outstanding amount, they would sell the house and downsize so as to release some capital. The only problem might be if she died in the meantime, in which case the missing funds might become apparent when probate took effect, but that was a risk he would have to take. 'What do you think of that?' asked Jenna. I was torn. On the one hand, it meant that he would 'get away with it' and, providing the plan worked, escape any punishment for a major breach of trust and a large theft. On the other hand, it would restore the aunt's estate and keep a roof over the family. A wrong would have been righted and no damage would have been done. It was also possible that if Steve had told his aunt about his financial difficulties, she might have loaned the money to him in the first place.

Still, even if Steve was reluctant to go to the police, or Jenna to report him, I could do so. There was a strong argument that it was both my civic and religious duty. I do not believe in the 'secrets of the confessional'. If someone does wrong, telling a priest or rabbi should not lessen their need to face justice. Why should a victim – in this case an aunt who had been cheated, in other cases it might be a child who had been abused or a woman who was raped – remain unprotected simply because the victim had told a minister of religion rather than a police officer? However, in this particular case, the aunt had no idea she had been wronged and the loss might be rectified. It seemed a rare opportunity to turn the clock back. I reckoned that a practical solution was preferable to a morally correct one and agreed to Steve's plan. The downside for me was that I was now complicit to a crime and, by agreeing to a way of restoring the original situation, I was effectively condoning it. They left, relieved that they had found a way out. I felt tainted. I also wondered what the odds were that Steve was being over-optimistic about his ability to repay the money and whether the marriage would survive if he did not.

I never found out. Seven weeks later, they disappeared. Steve, Jenna and the children moved away, and both their home and business phones were disconnected. Had the business proved unable to cope? Had Jenna gone off with the children or had she decided to stick with Steve and leave the aunt to the care home staff? And what had been their real motive in coming to see me? Had Steve known the likelihood of this happening and just gone through the motions of contrition to win round Jenna? Had Jenna been a partner in crime all along and was seeking some form of atonement? And, of course, the other obvious question: had I been duped? I was not too worried about that, for I would prefer to trust and be taken advantage of occasionally than be permanently suspicious and let that discolour my relations with people. As for the aunt, I had no idea of her name or where she was living, so no means of enquiring after her welfare.

But I know that if another couple came to see me with the identical problem, I would probably give the same response.

You will always be my only love

When Peter died in his mid-thirties from a heart attack for which there was no medical history or prior warning, Charlotte was devastated. They had been married for three blissfully happy years, were hoping to have a family and now the love of her life and the future they had planned together were ripped away from her. It was a difficult funeral and I made sure I kept in regular touch with her afterwards. But a serious problem arose when we came to discuss the stone-setting. She showed me the design she intended giving to the stonemason, which had at the top the words: 'You will always be my only love'. 'Is that alright?' she said, clearly expecting me to reply along the lines of how appropriate it was. I felt obliged to say no. Trying to put it as gently as I could, I said: 'Look, normally I am very happy to let people choose their own words – it's your husband and your ceremony, and you will be the one who visits it and draws comfort from it. But I have concerns about the future. I know he is your only love now, but, unimaginable as it may feel at this moment, one day you will meet someone else, feel ready to start a new relationship and fall in love again. It won't mean that you have betrayed Peter, nor that your love for your new partner is false, for both will be genuine. That's what humans do and it's the way things happen. But if, every time you come here you see those words, then you will feel guilty and feel as if you have broken your word. How about something that is equally loving but less of a hostage to fortune, such as 'I will always love you'?

I could see immediately from her face that this was totally unacceptable to her. It was partly because she was – inevitably – too immersed in her grief to consider loving anew (though I was adamant that it was my responsibility to share the long view with her, however insensitive she might think I was being). It was also because he had given her a ring engraved with those words, 'You will always be my only love'. She felt she had no choice but to put it on the stone. We agreed to chat about it again in a month's time, but her resolve had not wavered and the stone duly went up with the wording she had stipulated.

Some three years later, Charlotte rang to tell me about her engagement.

The funeral fall-out

Louise and Vivienne had been given the same religious upbringing and education by their parents, but in later life took very different paths. Louise became very Orthodox and fully practising, whereas Vivienne joined a Reform synagogue in which she participated actively on the cultural side but avoided services. It did not stop the two sisters getting on well, but a serious rupture did arise when their father died, leaving instructions that he wished to be cremated. Vivienne saw no reason not to go ahead as requested, while Louise was horrified, declaring that cremation was against Jewish law and demanding he be buried instead. Reform Judaism sees no problem with cremation, and the objection that it is not traditional is not sufficiently strong to deny it to those who opt for it today. I also hold that a person's last wishes are a very powerful statement and should normally be honoured. Those who object can do differently at their own funeral, but should not edit what happens at someone else's funeral. There is also a certain comfort in knowing we have carried out a person's last wishes and, whether we approve or not, have done what they had considered and decided upon. Even if we do not want to physically make the arrangements ourselves, because of personal discomfort, we can ask someone else to carry them out. In this case, because Vivienne was the more relaxed of the two and did not want to fall out with her sister, she allowed Louise to go ahead and arrange a burial. It may have been a pragmatic decision, but I am not sure it was the right one.

The wedding I refused to conduct

A young Jewish couple moved into the area and called me. They wanted to get married. We met up, talked about them and discussed options for the ceremony. All seemed fine till the very end, when I asked if there was anything else they wanted to mention that had not been covered so far. 'Actually, yes,' they replied. 'Could we include the "Our Father" prayer in the service?' 'But that's a Christian prayer,' I replied. 'So why have it in a Jewish ceremony?' They looked at each other, hesitated for a moment, and then said: 'We are Jews for Jesus and so we'd like to have it.' I do not know what my face displayed, but my heart sank. I have no problem with people believing in Jesus if that gives them religious fulfilment. I also have no problem with Jews believing in Jesus if they feel it is right for them. But then they are no longer Jewish. With Judaism and Christianity having so many ethical teachings in common, it is the person of Jesus that is the critical dividing line between the two faiths. Regarding him as a gifted individual and fine teacher means you are Jewish; regarding him as the Son of God and Saviour of the World means you are Christian. This couple may have been Jews who then adopted Jesus, but that meant they were now Christian. As such, I could not marry them, partly because it would have been hypocritical and they would be better off with a sympathetic vicar, but mainly because it would have been illegal as rabbis are only empowered by the state to officiate at marriages between two people 'both professing the Jewish faith'. They seemed very disappointed, but I had no option but to tell them I could no longer help. Still, they obtained their Jewish marriage in the end, for I later discovered that they had approached the local Orthodox rabbi and he had gone ahead with the ceremony. He did realise they were Jews for Jesus, but he took the attitude that '*meshuggene* [mad] beliefs' did not count and that, being born of Jewish mothers, they were legally Jewish. In an unusual role reversal, it meant that I had been holier than the Pope (to mix religious metaphors) and he had been much more liberal than me.

The uncomfortable wedding

There was a wedding I agreed to conduct with which I felt uncomfortable throughout. He was Australian and she was Welsh, but they had met while skiing in the same resort one winter. It made me marvel at how chance can play such a major role in so many people's lives, as epitomised by them. Had one of them chosen a different ski resort, or the same ski resort but different dates, or the same ski resort and the same dates but gone on a different route that day, or set off ten minutes later, they would never have met or be standing under the marriage canopy in front of me. How many other marriages have occurred because the two partners just so happened to be at the same place at the same time when they could so easily not have been? And how many children or business ventures or artistic endeavours owe their existence to that chance chain of events? (This applied to my own life too. When asked to select one of five congregations I would like to go to as a student rabbi at weekends for a year, I chose Maidenhead simply because I once had a girlfriend here and so had romantic associations with the town. It turned out to be a perfect choice professionally, but only because of a teenage girl called Catharine!)

But this was not what bothered me about the wedding. The problem was that the bride was twenty-five and the groom was forty-nine. There was no question of him taking advantage of her, or vice-versa. Both were sensible, both were strong characters and it seemed a very good relationship. However, I did worry what would happen in twenty years' time, when she was forty-five and he was sixty-nine, and whether their needs, interests, energy levels and health would still match so well. There was also the question of children – if they had a son the following year, by the time he was ten, his father would be sixty. Of course, a sixty-year-old dad can be very loving and caring – and perhaps have the advantage of having more time to spend with the child – but he will not be running along the beach with him or climbing up trees. I had felt obliged to raise the issue when we met to plan the wedding, in case everyone else had felt too embarrassed to mention it and they had never had a chance to discuss it openly. But they said they were aware of the age gap and not bothered by it. I did not offer any judgements, but did suggest practical steps, such as taking out life insurance and other protections. As it happens, my fears were unfounded and twenty years later they were still happily married… and still taking the children skiing. It proves that it is impossible to tell which marriages will last and which collapse. Of the many weddings at which I have officiated and that have ended in divorce, very few could have been spotted in advance, while those that do survive often do so against all expectations. When, at the end of the ceremony, I wish couples 'many happy years together', it is always a genuine hope but never a prediction.

Praying in vain

When Natalie phoned me tearfully to say that her husband had unexpectedly suffered a stroke and was in a coma, she asked me to say a prayer for him to recover. I felt very awkward. She clearly needed support and was desperate for a sense of hope, but I did not want to mislead her into thinking that my prayer was the magic wand that could achieve what the doctors were failing to do. In addition, I did not want her to feel God had let her down if her husband died, with her then blaming God for not answering the prayer. Of course, it was not the moment for a long theological debate, so I promised to say a prayer, albeit before making it clear that it would be both for him and for her, wishing them strength to face whatever happened in the coming days. As it happened, he did regain consciousness and made a full recovery, but I felt just as awkward when she rang to tell me: 'Rabbi, your prayer worked!'

To my mind, prayer cannot be used to *alter* reality, but instead should be a way of helping us *deal* with reality. Thus, if you are driving towards where you live and see a plume of smoke rising that indicates a house is on fire, there is no point saying: 'Please, God, don't let that be my house!' It already is or is not your house, while it is also fanciful to expect a celestial bucket of water to appear in the sky and suddenly put it out if it is yours. (Anyway, would you not want God to put it out even if it was somebody else's home?) Far better to pray for qualities: 'Please, God, help me cope with whatever I find… give me the courage to rebuild my life if I have lost any of my family.' Similarly, when taking one's driving test, there is no point saying: 'Please, God, do not let there be any other cars on the road' – however much we may want that to be the case – and much better to ask for calmness and confidence. The best prayers are ones that inspire us to be kinder, braver, more patient, more tolerant, more responsive. As the poet George Meredith put it so well: the person who rises from their prayers a better person, their prayer has already been answered.

My white lie

I could tell that I had annoyed Sandy with my sermon as she was never one to hide her feelings. I had posed the question of what happens when you attend a dinner party at which the food is badly cooked and the company dire. As you say goodnight to the host and hostess, do you say: 'What a terrible evening – never again' or do you murmur: 'Thank you very much, that was lovely'? I had raised it because the biblical passage that week was from Genesis, when Sarah laughs at the thought of having a child and says it is ridiculous that she should bear a child when her husband, Abraham, is so old. But, a few verses later, when God reports the conversation to Abraham, God says she thought it was ridiculous because *she* was so old and omits any mention of Abraham's age. Some would claim this is an editorial mistake, others say that it shows God deliberately modified her statement so as to protect domestic peace. I adopted the latter interpretation and therefore used it to discuss when it is or is not appropriate to tell a white lie. Sandy, though, took great offence at the idea of God condoning lies, whatever the motive.

I agree that white lies can be a dangerous road to take, as it is very easy to cross the thin line between a genuine desire to avoid hurting someone's feelings and using them to protect oneself or to flatter them falsely. Perhaps the guideline should be: what is my object? If it is anything other than to save someone embarrassment, it is not acceptable. The best solution is to be honest and positive, even if it involves some lateral thinking. So when leaving that ghastly dinner party, we can thank the hosts for all the effort they put into the evening (which is true, despite the fact it proved so unsuccessful). Sandy would still not approve as she believes in complete honesty. That is also the reason why she rarely gets invited to dinner parties.

Blasphemy

Do people have the right to blaspheme, whether they be of my faith or another? Of course they do! Freedom of speech means a healthy and transparent society, while every tyrannical ruler or despotic regime seeks to restrict it. Surprisingly, it has a religious history, originating with the Bible and the Hebrew prophets, whose mission was to protest against contemporary evils. Isaiah attacks not only the monarchy for exceeding its authority (1:23) but also the corruption of the religious hierarchy (1:11–15). Amos railed against the malpractices of the business community who grew rich at the expense of weaker members of society (8:4–6).

Religious satire or criticism may cause offence, but it is one person's right to express their view and another person's right to express that they are offended. Alongside the principle of free speech, there are also questions of practicality. Can we decide whom it is legitimate to criticise and whom not to criticise? There are faiths today which many would consider totally bizarre, such as Scientology, with its belief in space aliens who come to earth, or the Mormons with their gold tablets supposedly dug up in New York in the 1820s, which they hold sacred. Should they be exempt from laughter? They would say so. But if we exempt one, we have to exempt all, for blasphemy is in the ear of the hearer, and one person's sanctity is another person's idiocy. The cost of honouring all such views would be restricting free speech, and that is a cost too high. Sadly, there are plenty of religious targets that are worth hitting – from paedophile priests to bloodthirsty imams to rogue rabbis. They should not be exempt.

Religion cannot claim any special privilege or any unique exemption; it has to live with the possibility of being blasphemed, not just because of the principle of free speech, but in terms of its own self-respect. What does it say about a faith if it feels it cannot stand up to satire or criticism – is its God of the universe so fragile that he needs protection? Can an entire faith system be brought crashing down by newspaper columns or cartoons? How insecure must those believers be if they think that centuries of tradition can be blown away in a gale of laughter? A world without religious criticism – including what some consider blasphemy – would be a world that never progressed, and stagnated like still water that has grown putrid. That is not a religious vision, and the right to speak out should be defended by all God-fearers.

Who shall I marry?

Glenda wanted to see me as she had an urgent query. She was in her mid-thirties and had been a member of the community for a little while. We duly met and it turned out she was dating two men, both of whom had made it clear they saw a long-term future for the relationship, while she too was ready to settle down. Her problem was which one to marry, the difficulty being that, in her words, one was nice but non-Jewish, the other was not nice but Jewish. I was taken aback. It seemed so obvious that marriage had to be with someone you trusted and respected, and that there was no point forging a union with someone who would either be unpleasant to you or was a villain in the wider world. Being Jewish did not make them *kosher*. Yet, it was a genuine dilemma for her, perhaps reflecting her parents' wishes that she marry someone Jewish or her own sense of obligation to do so. I did point out that the nice non-Jew had the option of converting, be it now or at a later stage. I also mentioned that she had a third choice, to marry neither and wait for some-one who was both nice and Jewish. Unfortunately, she felt that her biological clock did not allow her that luxury and hence the need for a decision between the current suitors. I never found out the result as she left the area for work reasons before she had made a decision, but I did wonder how many other women were led to marrying someone with whom they were not entirely comfortable because of the desire for children? Conversely, how many children know they are the cause of their parents' divorce because they were the motive for their mother marrying their father even though she knew it might not work out in the long term? They were wanted, but he was not.

The secret missionary?

Greg was a Christadelphian who, because of the move-ment's strong attachment to the Bible in preference to later Christian teachings, had wanted to attend a synagogue service. I said he was welcome to attend, both as a ordinary visitor and knowing how much the Christadelphians had done to help resettle Jewish children who had come to Britain via the *Kindertransporte*. He seemed to feel very much at home and became a regular visitor over the next year. One day, though, he brought along some tracts about the beliefs of the Christadelphians, which he gave a few members he had come to know reasonably well. One of them pointed this out to me, and I had to have a word with him. Greg claimed that, having seen our faith, he was just sharing his faith with a few friends. I took a charitable view and said that there was a thin line between informing and encouraging, and as there was a lot of sensitivity within the Jewish community about Christian missionary activity – largely historic but still some pockets remaining – it would be better not to distribute material in future. He accepted that and continued to attend intermittently for another four years. When he then started distributing material again, and upset members in the process, I felt I had no choice but to ask him to refrain from attending. To be honest, I do not know whether he was a missionary, sent as a 'sleeper' to do nothing for a while and gain people's trust before engaging in more overt activity, or whether there was no plot and he was simply someone whose enthusiasm for his own faith led to him wanting to explain it. Unfortunately, his arrival coincided with Jews for Jesus – a very zealous missionary group – launching some high-profile campaigns and we were especially sensitive about conversionist activities at the time.

The baptised *batmitzvah* girl

This may have gone against the rules, but I reckon it was the right thing to have done. Barbara's parents were bringing her up dual faith, going with her mother to the synagogue's Religion School on Sunday mornings during term-time and accompanying her Christian father to church in the holidays. It was a neat arrangement that seemed to suit all three of them. When discussing her *batmitzvah* with her parents, I suggested a date that they vetoed on the grounds that she was having confirmation the week prior and they did not want to have two major family events so close to each other. Part of me felt very uneasy, for confirmation meant Barbara had already been baptised into the church as a child, and that she was now affirming her commitment to it. How could she be both Christian and Jewish? On the other hand, if she was having a Jewish ceremony, why should she not have a Christian one too? I know that many rabbis would have halted the discussion there and asked her, or her parents, to choose which route they wanted to take. They would have told them that she could not ride two horses at the same time. But I did not feel I had the right to force her to choose when she was clearly comfortable with both and saw no need to prefer one heritage over the other. It would also have made the family dynamics very difficult, with her feeling conflicted over the possible hurt it would cause to either parent, and with the parent whose faith was not chosen feeling their values and input had been cast aside.

Barbara's situation is not just an intriguing personal story but reflects a new religious reality. The 'either/or' attitude

of religious definitions that has existed until now is being
replaced by a 'both/and' one. Families that are used to serial
marriages and multiple step-relationships see no problem
with different faiths co-existing in the same household. The
old adage about 'the family that prays together, stays together' has long ceased to hold true. Judaism, meanwhile, is still
strongly attached to rigid definitions of who is and is not a
Jew. It prefers clarity to a laissez-faire attitude. But I suspect
it will have to adapt to the Barbaras of this world and allow
people to be 'Jew-ish' and let them find their own level of
observance and involvement. For my part, I was keen to keep
her options open – why let her attachment to the church prevent her from having the *batmitzvah* she clearly wanted and
which she was prepared to put in a lot of work to achieve? It
could be argued that baptism had made her Christian, but
equally it could be argued that having a Jewish mother gave
her Jewish status. But if the family was content, then why
should I introduce arguments anyway? Moreover, refusing
to go ahead would, in her eyes, have amounted to the synagogue rejecting her (and pushing her exclusively into the
arms of her other faith). When she reaches adulthood, she
will almost certainly find it difficult to sustain two faiths
simultaneously and veer towards one of them. Why force the
issue now, and especially as that would mean a 50 per cent
chance of undermining her Jewish allegiance? So both the
confirmation and *batmitzvah* went ahead, and while some
people might find that confusing, for Barbara it was perfectly
natural to her dual identity.

An under-age marriage?

I was approached by social services as to whether I would be prepared to conduct the marriage of Benny and Gertie, who were both Jewish and living locally. I said 'yes in principle' but asked why the couple themselves had not asked me. It transpired that they both had severe learning difficulties and were living in a care home. Benny was forty-two and Gertie was twenty-six, but their mental age was more like sixteen and ten. That immediately raised alarm bells in my mind. Was it legal to marry someone who was under-age in terms of their mental capacity? There were also ethical question marks: did they understand what love meant or what commitment involved? I was told they did fulfil the legal requirements, but I would have to determine other aspects when I met them in person to plan the ceremony. It turned out that there was a genuine affection between them and that they were a great support for each other. Before I agreed, though, I wanted to address a very practical issue with their carers, because Gertie was capable of becoming pregnant but not of bringing up a child. What precautions had been put in place? This, too, begged moral questions: sterilising her without her consent might be breaching her human rights, but relying on her taking oral contraception might be very risky. It was decided that, as they would be living in their own small flat, but still within the care home, administering the pill would be one of the tasks of the staff. The wedding went ahead just like any other wedding, with a blushing bride, nervous groom, tearful family and friends throwing confetti. Initially it was very successful, but, just like many other weddings, it ended with them splitting up after a few years. As Benny got older, Gertie could not cope with him behaving differently and being more demanding. They never actually got divorced, but she decided she wanted to live alone and moved back into one of the single rooms. I did not regret marrying them, as they had the right to have the same aspirations and feelings of any other couple; and if they eventually fell prey to similar problems, that was their right too.

To tell or not to tell?

I had visited Robin in Reading prison, where he was serving time for theft at work. I lost touch with him when he was transferred elsewhere, but was then surprised to have a phone call from him three years later. 'I've done my time, rabbi, got a year off for good behaviour and I'm out. I've settled nearby. Can I come to the service this Friday?' I said he was welcome, and he duly arrived and told me of his plans for starting afresh. I was delighted, and doubly pleased that he wanted to be part of the community, as being part of a good social milieu – rather than sinking back to dubious pre-prison associates – is often vital in changing course for a former inmate. But I also realised I had a dilemma on my hands. Intentions are one thing, reality is another. Should I warn those with whom he became friendly in the community, or with whom he sought to obtain a job, of his past? Is it unfair on them not to do so, or it is unfair on him to jeopardise his chances of gaining employment and a new life?

In the end, I decided not to say anything. Judaism believes in second chances. Every *Rosh Hashannah* and *Yom Kippur* we talk about making the new year a better year, forgiving those who have sinned against us and rectifying our own misdemeanours. It cannot just be pious theory but has to be translated into action. In Robin's case, there was a risk he might reoffend, but hopefully any employer would be alert to malpractices by any member of staff and have checks in place.

I took a slightly different attitude, though, in the case of Haim. He had also been released on parole and wanted to start attending communal events. He had been found guilty of sex offences in connection with children. Once again, I wanted to help rehabilitate someone and give them the chance to live a normal life, but not at the cost of exposing children to potential danger. Businesses may have security systems in place, but we did not. I therefore permitted him only to attend evening services, with the exception of *Purim* and *Simchat Torah*, and any one-offs at which children might be present. It was a compromise with which I was not entirely happy, but which I felt was the best way of including him but protecting children. In the event, he broke some of the terms of his parole and went back to prison. When he was eventually released, he moved to a different area. Perhaps some other rabbi is wrestling with the 'What to do with Haim?' question right now.

Should I report him?

Renee rang me in distress. She had been to a *kosher* butcher in London and seen him do something that was highly unhygienic. 'I won't go there again, but what should I do? I want to report him, but don't want to get a fellow Jew into trouble.' It was an attitude that reflected her age and the 'us and them' mentality with which she had been brought up by her Polish parents, and which viewed the non-Jewish world as inherently hostile. I reminded her that although it was not nice to have to report someone for breaking the law, it was only because they had done something wrong in the first place. In this case, the fault was his, not hers. I also pointed out that it was not just a matter of him doing wrong, but him potentially harming his many Jewish customers. Did she not feel they were owed the right to hygienic standards? Of course, that argument resonated more with Renee, as it was a Jew letting down other Jews and it appealed to her sense of tribal solidarity. But at least she cared enough to agonise over whether or not to report him, when so many others just shrug their shoulders, either not bothering to do anything or assuming nothing would come of it. Parents who are infuriated when their children say 'who cares?' or 'so what?' sometimes need to look in the mirror.

I promised my dying husband not to remarry, but…

Alison said she had a moral dilemma and asked if we could chat about it. It turned out that when her husband had died two years ago after a short illness, he had made her promise not to marry anyone else. She had agreed at the time, both to save him any distress and because she thought it unthinkable that, after a happy marriage of almost forty years, she would ever consider it. I was appalled at the promise he had demanded of her – many spouses would say the exact opposite and tell their partner that they wanted them to find happiness if they could. Still, I had known him for several years and he had always struck me as a very possessive person, so it seemed in character. It was obvious what she was going to say next. To her surprise, a friendship had developed into a relationship. Being in her sixties, she knew might enjoy another two or three decades and would much prefer to share them with someone rather than spend them alone. Was she bound by her promise?

My attitude was simple: No. The promise was (I decided not to mince my words) a very selfish one and should never have been requested. Moreover, she had agreed under duress, not wanting to deny her husband's dying wish. It is true she could have refused to agree to it, or said it was unfair to ask her, but that would have left him dying embittered and her feeling guilty. In addition, the crucial point was that she had been a loving wife through the marriage, and need have no qualms about having 'done her duty'. If he was still alive, she would have continued as his wife, but the marriage was now over and he could not control her beyond the grave. Alison was a little taken aback at my vehemence, having thought that I would want to discuss the arguments either way. 'Do you really mean that?' she asked, indicating instantly that, despite her hesitation, she wanted to go ahead. I conducted the wedding six months later.

Which husband should I be buried next to?

Connie said she was sorting out her will and needed some advice – could we meet? The issue was that she had enjoyed a happy marriage of thirty-six years to her first husband, and from which two daughters had resulted. After his death, she had remarried and it too had been a good match. But when her time came, was there any guidance as to which husband she should be buried alongside? I told her that it was entirely her decision and that there is no 'right choice' between two loves at different stages of one's life. When Connie said she had no strong feelings either way, I pointed out issues for her to take into consideration. One was whether her current husband would be hurt if she opted for her first husband. Logically, he would know that that was her longest relationship, but would he react badly? A second was how her children – now adults – would feel. Would they be horrified at their parents being in separate cemeteries, or would they understand that the second marriage was now the centre of her life? A third issue – though this should carry less weight than the other two – was whether her first husband's family would be upset if the plot alongside him that had been intended for her lay empty. I did add, though, that even if they did see it as a rejection or an insult, that would be unfair; what counted was whether she had been a good wife during his lifetime, not what happened afterwards. It would be a good idea, therefore, to do some discreet consulting before finalising her will. The one definite piece of advice I gave Connie was that, once she had made her decision, she should let everyone know, so that they all understood her reasoning and there were no shocked reactions when the time came.

7

Being Jewish in a non-Jewish world

The boy who did not kill Jesus

By the mid-1980s, most schools were teaching multi-faith studies in the Religious Education lessons. This was in recognition that Britain was becoming increasingly diverse in its religious life. Whereas, previously, the only non-Christians were the Jews, now they had been joined by a significant proportion of Muslims, Hindus and Sikhs, with Bahais, Buddhists and Rastafarians also having a presence. It was not just a numbers game, however, and also reflected a new mood of religious tolerance, seeing value in each faith and moving away from the idea that there was only one true path to God. Instead, it was recognised that there were many paths to heaven and which one you took was usually conditioned by your upbringing. This religious revolution was particularly apparent in the rapprochement between Christianity and Judaism. Despite having common roots in the Hebrew Bible, for centuries there had been hostile relations, with Jews being persecuted in Christian Europe, culminating in the Holocaust where six million – every third Jew in the world – were murdered. The Nazis may not have been worshipping Christians, but their policies were built on the well-prepared ground of what was known as 'Christian anti-Semitism': the notion that Jews killed the Son of God and were condemned to eternal suffering for their evil deed. A major reversal of this doctrine came from the deliberations of Vatican II – the Council called by Pope John XXIII in 1965 – which produced the famous document entitled 'Nostra Aetate'. It declared that Jews of the first century may have been guilty of the death of Jesus, but that guilt was limited to them and not applicable to subsequent generations. Instead, Jews were beloved of God and to be treated as 'our brothers'. It transformed Jewish–Christian relations and led to inter-faith dialogue groups springing up across the world, and especially in Britain, with local synagogues and churches – previously out of bounds to each other's members – often holding meetings together.

All this meant that what happened to Jeffrey was astonishing. He was eleven years old and, at that particular moment, was at school and sitting in the RE class. The teacher was talking about the death of Jesus. He explained the Gospel story of how the Roman Governor, Pontius Pilate, had offered to free one of those destined to die, Barabbas or Jesus, and the Jews had opted for Barabbas to be saved. The teacher asked Jeffrey to stand up and told him to explain to the rest of the class: 'Why did your people want to kill Jesus?' Jeffrey, you will not be surprised to know, found it hard to know what to say, unsure both of the exact details and what it had to do with him. I wrote to the Head suggesting he ask the teacher some questions. Such as – does he expect all eleven-year-olds to explain historical events that took place 2,000 years earlier? And did his question not imply that Jeffrey was directly linked to what happened in ancient Jerusalem and also that he bore some inherited connection with it? And would he ask a French child why his people invaded England in 1066? And was he expecting to learn something new from Jeffrey or was his intention to embarrass him in front of everyone else? And, bearing in mind that one of the few crimes worse than murdering a person is murdering God, did he think it was helpful to Jeffrey's relations with his classmates to publicly suggest that Jeffrey and his family had a distant involvement with it? I never received a reply, but hope that at least the Head had a chat with that teacher. Ideally, he would have updated him both on Christian teaching and classroom techniques. But, frankly, at worst, I would have been happy even if he had not reprimanded him and just said: 'Look, you have to watch how you tackle this issue – otherwise, those Jews will cause trouble for us.' Too right!

The puzzled prison governor

I was going into Reading prison for one of my monthly visits as chaplain just as the governor was coming out, so we stopped for a quick chat. 'One of your lot came in today who was very religious,' he said. 'How do you mean?' I asked. 'Oh, quite obvious,' he replied, 'big black hat, long black coat, beard, side curls – you know, the full works; and he's asked for *kosher* food.' 'Oh, what did he come in for?' 'Fraud,' he replied, 'massive amount, around £10 million I think.' 'In that case', I responded, 'he's not religious. He may be ritualistic, but not religious.' The governor looked at me, puzzled, started to say something, then stopped himself and said: 'Right, must be going, see you another time.' To this day I am not sure if he understood my point.

Animal sacrifices

For several years, the synagogue has opened its doors to local schools who come to visit us as part of their Religious Education studies. In the beginning, I was astonished at one particular question that the children asked, whatever type of school from which they came. It was: do Jews have birthdays? 'Yes,' I would reply, 'why not? They are good fun.' It puzzled me as to why this was always asked. Eventually, I realised. In every school, there was usually at least one child who was a Jehovah's Witness. They did not celebrate birthdays and were different from everyone else, so it seemed logical in the children's minds that, as Jews are also different from everyone else, they would not have birthdays either. A much rarer – and priceless – question arose from one eight-year-old: why are Jews commanded to leave their garage doors open at night? We are not! But why did he ask that question? Then it suddenly dawned on me: this little boy lived opposite a Jewish family who left their garage doors open at night, so he assumed that all Jews did likewise. It was a classic case of stereotyping, judging all Jews by the ones he knew and assuming that we are all the same.

The level of ignorance that many children displayed about Judaism was often matched by their poor knowledge of Christianity and the official faith of the country. It meant that I had to quickly revise the initial talks I prepared when I first went into schools and not use analogies that I thought would be helpful but in fact were just confusing. Thus, trying to explain the Passover, I mentioned that it was probably the same as the Last Supper – only to be asked by a puzzled child whether that meant the final meal before a nuclear war. I also gave up referring to the bread and wine Jews have on the Sabbath eve as being akin to the Eucharist when it was obvious the children missed the analogy and thought I was referring to a pop group, Eurythmics.

Still, it was a teacher's comment that disturbed me the most. After my talk and the round of children's questions, she asked: 'Thanks for all this, but the one thing you have not shown us is where you do the animal sacrifices – where does that happen?' Amazed at her ignorance, part of me wanted to be flippant and say that we do it in the kitchen so that blood can drain away safely, but I resisted doing so. Instead, I informed her that Judaism had abolished animal sacrifices almost 2,000 years ago and that they played no part in our services. She had read the Bible, which does contain much about animal sacrifices, and simply assumed that we had not changed since then. Although it was an appalling gaffe by someone who was supposed to be an RE teacher, she was not alone in not realising that Judaism has changed enormously over the centuries thanks to the interpretations and reinterpretations of the *Talmud* (rabbinic commentary on the Bible), expanding some biblical laws and effectively

negating others. I told her as gently as I could: that is why
we today are not known as Biblical Jews but Rabbinic Jews.

Sometimes it is difficult for the school to visit the synagogue, so I go to them. If it is a primary school, I often suggest that, before I come, the teacher asks the children to draw
what they think I will look like. Invariably I am depicted as
an old man, with long white hair and sometimes with a staff
in my hand and wearing sandals. It is quite an education for
them when I do arrive and look remarkably ordinary. I also
know that they find me quite disappointing – not at all the
exotic creature they had been expecting. Still, it is probably
the most important lesson of the entire visit. I do not care
very much if they go home without understanding what Jews
believe or not remembering any of the festivals about which
I spoke. What I really want them to say is: 'Mummy, I met a
Jew today and he was just like me.'

Hunt the Jew

Visiting a local primary school, I was told about a game
that some children played in the break, although the
teachers were trying to discourage it. Three or four children
would place a penny on the ground and then, when a child
came by, spotted it and picked it up, they would all leap forward and shout 'Jew!' Although it was disturbing, it was also
fascinating. Here was a group of five- to seven-year-olds who
had no concept of what being Jewish meant, may well have
not knowingly met a Jew, lacked any idea of their involvement in moneylending during the Middle Ages, and had no

reason to be anti-Jewish, yet were unconsciously perpetuating ancient stereotypes and imbibing anti-Jewish prejudices. It was like children dancing to 'Ring a Ring o' Roses' without any awareness of its connection to the Black Death – except in this case it was much less innocent in its effect, as it may have poisoned some of them in their attitude to Jews today.

Undoing 9/11

One of the many consequences of the terrible attacks of 9/11 was a feeling that individual lives were being caught up in global forces far beyond their control. What was frightening was not only what was happening but the feeling of being unable to have any control over it. Our lives were being dictated by what was taking place in New York or Afghanistan. As one very small way of reasserting our role, I approached the local imam with a plan. The result was that I went to the mosque and said a prayer for peace in Hebrew. He then came over to the synagogue and said a prayer for peace in Arabic. It was a small gesture but meaningful for us and others. There were many parts of the world where Hebrew in a mosque or Arabic in synagogue would be considered outrageous, but we were stating that in Maidenhead it was both possible and affirmative. Being a midweek morning, there were only a handful of people present, but we both preached about it at our respective services that weekend, while the local paper also covered it. It became well known locally and said very simply: whatever is happening in the rest of the world, here in our patch we know how to live side by side.

Learning I was different

I first came across anti-Semitism at my prep school, Orley Farm, in Harrow, Middlesex. It was very strictly run, so no verbal or physical violence for any reason was permitted. Then, one day, something extraordinary happened, though I have no idea what actually triggered it. The result was that Jews gathered in one corner of the playground during the lunch hour and Christians attacked them, or, rather, attacked us. I cannot recall how we Jews gravitated to that spot, nor whether it was by choice or compulsion. What made just as much impression on my nine-year-old mind was that, whereas up till then the school ethos was that you only spoke to others in your year, the fact that the ten to fifteen of us were all Jews magically overrode this sacrosanct barrier. We were vastly outnumbered by the Christians (there were no secularists in those days – just an 'us and them' society) and the fighting was largely fisticuffs and pulling each other to the ground. Then the bell went and we all trooped into class. This battlefield gathering occurred for three days in a row, at which point the Head stepped in and banned it. I dimly recall him speaking at the following morning's assembly about tolerance and living together. And that was the end of it. The ancient religious antagonisms disappeared as abruptly as they had started. I no longer spoke to Jews in the year above or below, and my Christian friends suddenly became my best friends again. School life returned to normal as if nothing had happened. But, even at that age, I knew something had changed within me. I realised that however much I had in common with my Christian friends, I would always be different. Conversely, I discovered that however little I thought I had in common with other Jews, actually there was always a connection. It did not stop me from leading a life that was very integrated with those around me, but from then on I knew that 'he's Jewish' was a hidden appendage I permanently carried around in their eyes.

Fighting back

I did once experience some individual anti-Semitism at that prep school, when a group of well-known bullies from school followed me on the way to the station shouting Jewish taunts and then jumped on me. I was hopelessly outnumbered but did make sure a couple of them had a punch in the face before I went down.

At my subsequent school, University College School, in Hampstead, London, there was a particularly unpleasant individual in my class called Bill. He was virulently anti-Semitic and also a bully. I remember, one day, the class was waiting for the maths teacher to arrive, Bill came in, saw another Jewish pupil sitting by the window, marched over to him, opened the window and shouted to everyone else: 'God, this place stinks of *kosher* meat!' I expected the boy – who subsequently became very prominent in the Jewish community – to hit him, but he was not of that ilk. I had been told enough times by my father that most bullies were cowards and that the best way to stop them was to fight back. 'Even if they win', he said, 'they won't want to attack you again and risk being hurt, so will pick on someone else next time.' Two weeks later, Bill and I happened by chance to be alone in the same room – he came over to me and sneered: 'Why don't you go back to Israel where you belong?' I suppose I could have taken it as a compliment that he recognised my ancestral homeland, but instead I hit him in the face. He hit me back and we both ended up on the floor. Even though I was sixteen at the time and it was many decades ago, I still have an unnecessarily large sense of pride that, although I limped away, he did not get up for a few moments. Perhaps I felt it was my personal equivalent of Cable Street. And Dad was right: after that, Bill always gave me a wide berth.

All Things Bright and Beautiful

The prep school above to which I went as a child had a Christian assembly every morning, using the hymn book *Songs of Praise*. As a result, I know 'Onward Christian Soldiers' off by heart, along with 'Hills of the North Rejoice' and 'To Be a Pilgrim'. I enjoyed singing them, but even at the tender age of seven always felt guilty about using the words Jesus or Christ or Saviour or Son of God. As a result, I developed the habit of staccato singing, as in 'Onward – soldiers, marching as to war/With the cross of – marching on before'. I found that the only song in the entire hymnal that I was able to sign the whole way through without interruption was 'All Things Bright and Beautiful'. It became my instant favourite, although most other boys hated it as they regarded it a namby-pamby tune with silly words. It was a school tradition that in their final term, leavers could choose one of the hymns to be sung. I always knew that when my turn came, that was the song I would select, even though I also knew that I would be the most hated boy in the school that morning.

The puzzled dentist

Another childhood memory that has somehow survived, despite most from that period disappearing completely, concerned visiting a dentist when I was fourteen years old. Somehow it arose that I was Jewish. 'Oh,' he said, 'so were you born in Israel?' I was astonished. Even at that age, I knew that dentists were supposed to be highly educated and university graduates. How could he think that Jews were not born and bred in England? I put him straight about my London origins very politely – not least because he was about to put a drill in my mouth – but remember thinking: 'Goodness, if someone as intelligent as him thinks that, what idea does everyone else have?' The rest of the appointment passed without further conversation, save for a few gurgles my end.

Try the Jews

On the day that I moved into Maidenhead, the house was deserted, as the removal men had been delayed and I was sitting in a totally empty building. The only item that existed was the telephone. Suddenly it rang, although in the furniture-less room, it sounded more like Big Ben chiming than an ordinary phone going off. It was my very first call as the Maidenhead rabbi. It was from someone non-Jewish who wanted his son circumcised for medical reasons. He had rung the local hospital and was told: 'We don't do that sort of thing anymore. Try the Jews.' We helped.

Another unexpected call came a few months later. 'I'm sorry to bother you, but I am stuck on a crossword. The clue is "a Jewish month" and it ends in "an", but I'm not Jewish so I thought I'd try you.' I was able to tell her that it was 'Nisan' and was rewarded with a cry of triumph: 'Great, that fits exactly!' There was even a group phone call one evening. One of the questions in the National Pub League Quiz Competition in 1985 was 'What is the *Beth Din*?' The table answering realised it was something Jewish but not exactly what, and so phoned me.

But it is not just non-Jews who can ring with strange requests. Some members of the synagogue tend to regard the rabbi as a live equivalent of the Yellow Pages. The most regular call is whether I can recommend a good plumber in the area, while on one occasion a member wanted my advice as how best to go about potty-training cats. This was despite knowing that I do not own cats. However, if you believe that a rabbi is the fount of all wisdom...

The anti-Semitic undertaker

As Maidenhead Synagogue covers a wide geographical area, I often officiate at funerals in far-flung areas and work with funeral directors I have not come across before. It means that some are not used to the fact that synagogues operate a very different funeral charging structure from churches. Churches have a standard charge for everyone of around £100, whereas synagogues do not charge for members, but do charge for non-members, perhaps around £500, sometimes considerably more. The discrepancy reflects the fact that members pay an annual subscription to join a synagogue, whereas non-members do not support the institution throughout their life that they then want to serve them upon the occasion of their death. It is a fair system, and everyone in the Jewish community is aware of it. However, the higher rate for non-members compared to the standard Christian rate can seem a stark contrast to the outsider. It obviously narked one particular funeral director in Basingstoke when I did a service there. As we stood next to each other in front of the congregation as the coffin was being solemnly brought in to doleful music, he leant over to me and whispered: 'Typical Jews, moneymaking cheats.' With the mourners looking on and the prayers seconds away from starting, it was not the time for a stinging rebuke, nor a detailed explanation of financial management systems. Without saying a word, I carried on looking ahead respectfully, seethed inside and made a mental note never to use that firm again.

How religions learnt to love each other

One of the great religious success stories of our time has been the leap forward in inter-faith dialogue, especially in Jewish–Christian relations, but extending much wider too. Whereas previous centuries were marked by persecutions, forced conversions, expulsions or massacres, the second half of the twentieth century saw a massive improvement. It could be argued that, for two faiths who are both based on the command to 'love your neighbour as yourself', this is long overdue, but it is still very welcome. Three short religious stories that have been in common currency in Jewish circles in the decades since then reveal the rapid journey from deep suspicion to mutual trust between the two faiths.

The first is from the 1950s: an elderly religious Jew is dying. It is the middle of the night, he lives in a cottage far away from the nearest town and a fierce storm is raging. He turns to his wife and says: 'My end is coming; please fetch the vicar.' She is aghast: 'You have been a pious Jew all your life. Why are you suddenly switching faiths at the last minute?' 'Don't worry,' he replies, 'I'm not – it's just that I wouldn't dream of calling the rabbi out on a night like this – get the vicar instead.' The story indicates that Jewish–Christian relations are non-existent; an 'us and them' attitude prevails; the punch-line is the thought of the rabbi sleeping peacefully at home while the vicar gets woken up and drenched.

The second comes from the 1970s: a Jew crossing the road is knocked over by a car; he is badly injured; a crowd gathers round and a nearby priest rushes to help. Bending over the man, he gives the Last Rites, saying: 'Do you believe in the Father, Son and Holy Spirit?', to which the Jew exclaims: 'I'm dying and he asks me riddles!' Whatever the quality of the story, it shows that Jews are aware of Christian practices and theology. They may reckon it is incomprehensible, but there has been a significant advance in knowledge. They now know what is going on in each other's traditions.

The third is much more recent: a Catholic priest and a rabbi are enjoying a meal together and swapping stories about religious lapses. The priest says: 'Tell me, have you ever tasted pork?' The rabbi pauses for a while and then confesses that he did do so once. 'Nice, isn't it?!' beams the priest. The rabbi thinks for a while, then says: 'OK, so let me ask you: have you ever had sex with a woman?' The priest blushes, but eventually admits to it. 'Ah,' replies the rabbi, 'nicer than pork, isn't it?!' What is significant is not so much the humorous ending but the context: the priest and rabbi are old friends, are socialising together over a meal and trust each other with personal experiences.

Jokes only work if they reflect realities that listeners recognise – hence the proliferation of mother-in-law gags – and often have a serious point behind them. These particular stories depict the inter-faith revolution that has occurred and from which our generation is fortunate to benefit. The only sadness is that there are still plenty of parts of the world where telling those stories, or ones involving other faiths, would result not in shared laughter but cries of heresy and death threats.

My Israel rant

In an age when there is widespread ignorance about the established faith of the country, it is no surprise that there is also much ignorance about a minority faith such as Judaism. But, while that is understandable, what is particularly annoying is the misperception of the role of rabbis. In many people's eyes, I am automatically seen as the foreign ambassador

of Israel and regularly asked: 'Why are you bombing Gaza?'
or 'What's the point of you staying in the West Bank?' Me!
Me personally! I am Jewish and it is assumed I have a hotline
to the Prime Minister of Israel's office.

I am well aware that the Israel–Palestine situation is a
mess and there is no obvious prospect for any immediate
improvement. My one piece of optimism is Northern Ireland. We tend to forget that for several decades Britain was
regarded by others as unstable and in the midst of a civil war
because of what was happening in our own backyard. Yet
what seemed impossible to reconcile did eventually end in
peace – it is a fragile peace, it took a long time, it involved
many deaths and much suffering – but my hope is that if it
can happen here, it can happen over there too.

The one misperception that annoys me utterly is the oft-
heard refrain that the key to all the troubles in the Middle
East is solving the Israel–Palestine problem. At this point,
I tend to go into a rant at whoever says it in my presence,
raising my voice with every succeeding sentence: Did Israel–
Palestine have anything to do with Iraq invading Kuwait,
or with Iraq fighting a war with Iran for eight years? Does
it have anything to do with the civil war in Syria? Or the
nuclear ambitions of Iran? Or Sunnis attacking Shias? Or
the Muslim Brotherhood trying to seize power in Egypt?
Or the strife in Tunisia? Or Yemen? Or Libya? Or Muslim
suicide bombers attacking mosques of 'the wrong sort of
Muslims'? Of course Israel–Palestine needs to be sorted out,
but I tell my, by now cowering, listener not to think for a
minute that it would solve any of those other conflicts.

The Christmas card

Every year, for the last fifteen years or so, a Sikh friend in Maidenhead and I send each other a Christmas card. Neither of us is Christian, but both are happy to use the common culture of the country as a vehicle for communicating. Of course, I also have no problem sending Christmas cards to Christian friends and have never understood those who shy away from doing so. Do they really think that sending a picture of a robin sitting on a snow-covered branch is going to compromise their Jewish identity and faith? For the same reason, I have no problem with schools putting on Christmas plays and despair of those who opt for 'Winter Festivals'. But I have noticed an interesting change in approach by many schools. Most schools have at least one or two Jewish pupils, and a disproportionately high percentage of them used to be asked to play Joseph or Mary in the annual Nativity play, so as to emphasise that they were not being left out. Now they still ask Jewish pupils to take those roles, but for a different reason: a deliberate policy of authenticity. Now that it is generally realised that Joseph and Mary were both Jewish, who better to play them?

Still, I was amused a few years ago when I was in the High Street and crossed the road to help when I saw that a lady had tripped over and her shopping bags were emptying their contents.

As I put the items back and handed them to her, she said: 'That's very Christian of you.' I just smiled, but said to myself: 'No, actually, it was very Jewish of me.'

Going public

If I am speaking to a non-Jewish group, I am sometimes asked why I do not wear a head covering. So I explain that, whereas some Jews do cover their heads all day, others only do so during prayer, which then leads into discussion on the differences between the Orthodox and Reform approaches. However, there was one occasion when I changed my pattern of behaviour for a short while. My grandfather had died, there was a week of mourning and, as a sign of respect, I decided to wear a *kippah* all day throughout that time. The internal effect was astonishing. Wearing it in the street, on the London Underground, inside shops, at a bus queue: it felt as if I had a ten-foot sign next to me saying: 'Hey, everybody, this person is Jewish.' It was just my self-perception, of course, and it did not lead to any reactions by others. But it did mean I was no longer just me, an anonymous person in the crowd: now I was a public representative of Judaism. How I behaved would now reflect on the entire faith and on all other Jews. If, for instance, I had failed to stand up in the train to give my seat to an older person, what would that have said about Jewish values? If I had found that a shopkeeper had given me fifty pence change when it should have been ten pence, and I did not spot it immediately and return it, what would that have signified about Jewish ethics? Of course, in theory, I should behave in an exemplary way at all times, whether or not I have a Jewish badge pinned to my head, but I certainly felt much more conscious of needing to do so with it on. Perhaps if I did wear it permanently that effect would lessen over time, but it was certainly an arresting experience and might be worth trying for a week yourself.

The gift of money I turned away

Luke was a leading member of a local Christian community whom I had met when invited to give a talk
there. He rang me a few weeks later to ask if he could come
to see me as he had a proposal to make. He explained that
the membership felt strongly that Christians in the past
had caused enormous suffering for the Jewish people. They
would like to atone for that black mark on the church's record
book by making a monthly donation to the synagogue. We
would be free to use the money how we wished. It was not
what I was expecting, but I had no hesitation in turning him
down, albeit very gently. I told him that the sentiments of
his members were much appreciated and did not need any
financial expression to back them up. After some discussion,
he accepted my stance and I asked him to pass on my thanks
to his members. However, while this was perfectly sincere,
there was another reason behind my decision. Accepting
regular income from the Christian community would make
us beholden to them, or certainly make us feel that way, and
that would not be a healthy state of affairs. I also wondered
whether, because it was a very evangelical group, it might
even be part of a long-term strategy for missionary activity,
or at least an attempt to draw us into their orbit. Curiously enough, another church group made the same offer two
years later. I turned it down too, with the result that we are
financially less healthy, but spiritually more independent.

8

Religious question marks

Revelation at a football match

If you are a teacher who is not managing to inspire the attention of children in your class, how do you know if it is because you are not being stimulating enough or because they lack the academic capacity to take in your lessons? This bothered Neville Ireland, a history teacher at my secondary school. He knew the children were not learning properly – but not where the problem lay, or the solution. One day he accepted an invitation to go with a friend to a football match and, while in the stands, he overheard some familiar voices in the row in front of him. It was two of his most hard-to-reach children. As he heard them chattering, he grew more and more astonished. They were not only comparing notes about which players had scored how many goals in how many games, but were reeling off statistics about former players and their records. 'Good gracious,' he thought, 'if they can recite goal averages for footballers, why can't they remember dates for kings and queens? It's not that they're thick, I'm obviously not making my lessons exciting enough.' It transformed his approach and, by the time I came into his class some time later, he was one of the most engaging teachers in the school.

Perhaps it was coincidence, but many years afterwards I too had a 'light-bulb moment' at a football match. I went to our local team, Reading, with one of my teenage sons. He was going through a totally non-communicative stage, with his daily conversation either being monosyllabic or restricted to grunts. Yet the moment the game started, he stood up and sang his heart out with all the others. Moreover, many of the others were not people you would associate with singing if you saw them in the High Street – in fact, if you did see them, you might cross the road, as they were more likely to go into a pub and ask for a glass of milk than lift up their voices in joyful odes. Yet, put them inside a football stadium and they miraculously discovered their vocal cords. I was particularly interested as, at the time, I was wrestling with how to improve the singing at our Sabbath services. People were attending, but not joining in. How could I transfer the passion so evident on Saturday afternoons to the musical black hole on Saturday mornings?

The puzzle was all the more intriguing because of the many parallels between the two events. They both involve ritual wear (football scarves and prayer shawls), both have their own hymns (albeit football fans mixing abusive ones with those full of praise), both rely on faith (whether facing relegation or a personal trauma), both have their own calendar (the regular matches and Sabbaths, the periodic cup games and festivals), affiliation to both is often handed down

tribally from parents to children. Both also involve important bonding factors such as camaraderie and a sense of
common identity, while the emotions inspired by both cover
exultation, despair, anger and hope.

The following Sabbath morning, I urged congregants to
think of themselves as football fans would when walking
through the turnstiles and do two things. First, greet others,
even those they hardly know, but who are sitting around
them. A smile, a handshake, a brief chat could make all the
difference to their day, between feeling ignored and feeling
at home. Second, to join in the songs even if their voice is
not that great, but add to the noise, be part of the communal
sound and get carried away by what emerges. 'Everyone
knows that Liverpool fans have an amazing anthem and
never walk alone,' I said, 'and if you both reach out and join
in, you will feel the same uplift.' To be honest, it did not work
that well, and I am still looking for that elusive goal – to make
the pews as boisterous as the terraces. Like all good fans and
rabbis, I have faith it will come one day.

And that is why we do what we do

I have often wondered how certain traditions developed,
whether in Judaism or other faiths, that do not seem to
have an obvious reason or cause. They may be justified by
subsequent religious interpretations, but it is obvious that
they are post-facto explanations and not the original ones.
To give a minor example, I visited a certain synagogue
where, during the usual parade of the scrolls around the

congregation on a Saturday morning, the person stopped and bowed, and then continued. Most synagogues do not do that, so why did they? No one seemed to know, except that they knew it was 'the tradition'. When I expressed my puzzlement to one member, he laughed and said: 'That's simple: in the original synagogue, before we extended it, there was a low arch at that part of the building and so whoever was carrying the scroll had to stoop to get under it.' It seemed that people were so used to doing this that they continued in the renovated building, even though there was no arch and no need to do so. Tradition!

I saw a living example of that happen at Maidenhead. When I came to the town, the annual *Shavuot* service was badly attended, even though it has the highly significant theme of the giving of the *Torah* at Mount Sinai, along with the recitation of the Ten Commandments. So, I instituted an informal cheesecake and strawberries study group after the service to make it more of an attractive event. This became a regular tradition over the next thirty years. One day I was discussing the theme of *Shavuot* with my Adult Education class and someone asked why we had those two foods every year. I asked the rest of the group if they knew why. They said the cheesecake was because it was the food traditionally associated with *Shavuot* and the strawberries because they represented the harvest background of the festival. The cheesecake answer was correct, but the strawberries one was not. I introduced strawberries simply because they were available at the time of *Shavuot*, usually around May, and because I thought they made a tasty combination with cheesecake. It was purely a personal whim based on my own taste buds, yet they had given it a religious gloss. What is more, their interpretation was highly plausible, but totally wrong. I subsequently found that most other members now associated strawberries with *Shavuot* and that, after thirty years, a whole generation had grown up believing they were the traditional food. Some of them were most surprised when they visited other synagogues and found they did not do likewise. How lapse of them!

The religious walk-out

I have been blessed with a very tolerant congregation. Even though I obtained a lot of media coverage for Maidenhead Synagogue (about which some were uncomfortable – 'Why draw attention to ourselves?'), took stances on controversial issues (such as welcoming those in mixed-faith marriages, opposing faith schools and supporting attempts to legalise assisted dying), they never complained. I have a theory (mentioned earlier) that, providing a congregation feels that their rabbi loves them, knows their names and is there for them in both happy and sad times, then they do not mind too much what else he/she does or says. However, there was one occasion when my words did rile someone beyond endurance. It was in 1985, when the Aids epidemic was becoming public knowledge, and I decided to use one of the High Holy Day sermons – when most of the community is gathered together – to talk about it. My object was to draw attention to the fact that it did not just affect homosexuals, but applied to heterosexuals just as much, and that, as many people had sex before marriage – and sometimes sex outside marriage – it was vital that they used condoms. At that point a prominent member stood up and walked out. I carried on but made a mental note to see her the following day. She was a dentist, highly educated and a woman of the world. I expected her to say she thought it was entirely inappropriate to speak about such sordid matters on one of the most spiritual days of the year. I was ready to counter that, in all other years I did indeed speak about more appropriate topics, but this year I saw it as my responsibility to look after members of the community and protect them from harm. She did not say that at all. Instead, she told me that it was a ridiculous sermon as Jews did not contract Aids. I was flabbergasted. We talked about the subject for a few more minutes. I said I was sorry I had upset her but that I stood by the sermon and then left. There was simply no room for discussion.

There was another person who resigned from the synagogue over my sermons, but in his case it was because of what I did *not* say. Apparently, I did not mention God enough. To be fair, he was a very God-centred person and felt he did not receive the spiritual nourishment he needed. I have never been that sort of rabbi. My ministry is about creating a vibrant community and pulling people together. My favourite saying is that 'To be a good Jew, you do not have to believe in God, just do what God says'. It is a little bit heretical, but not too much. Judaism has always been about doing. Unlike the Church of England, whose core document is the Thirty-Nine Articles of Faith, we have the 613 Commandments. When the then Bishop of Oxford Richard Harries reviewed my book *Faith and Practice: A Guide to Reform Judaism Today*, he wrote: 'This is a typical Jewish book: 280 pages on what to do and twenty on what to believe; if it had been a Christian book, it would have been the other way round!'

Swimming to synagogue

For several years, we have had the problem – in common with many other communities – of having too many people attend the High Holy Day services to accommodate them in our synagogue, which was designed for everyday purposes and not overflowing ones. Recently we have held them in the Magnet Leisure Centre, which not only has a large hall suitable for our needs, but also hosts many facilities, from badminton courts to a children's play area to fitness training. It also has a large swimming pool, which is why one year, as I greeted those entering, I noticed a member arrive with a prayer book under one arm and large towel under the other (no doubt with swimming trunks rolled up inside). He saw me notice his dual-purpose baggage and said with a smile: 'I thought I'd get some physical refreshment once I'd got my spiritual renewal.' It was an unbeatable argument.

In a previous decade, we had used a large scout hall at Altwood School, which had stacked in its roof twenty or thirty long pieces of tree trunks, no doubt to be used for some camping project, that were held above us by just three metal frames. If the bolts had not been secured properly and gave way, those logs crashing down on our heads would have caused a great deal of damage. It meant the services felt suitably precarious sitting beneath them, a very effective religious equivalent of the Damocles Sword, while those confessing their sins and praying for forgiveness seemed to have an added urgency to them.

In the decade prior to that, we had occupied the large hall of the Riviera Hotel. It was the right size but had the major disadvantage that it backed onto the kitchen, and every time someone opened the wrong door, out wafted smells of onion soup, roast duck or some other delicacy. It was distracting at *Rosh Hashannah*, but definitely unwanted during *Yom Kippur*, when we were supposed to be fasting all day and trying to forget our rumbling stomachs. At least we got extra points for managing to abstain that year despite the olfactory temptations. Still, the hall did have the advantage that the whole of one side consisted of windows looking straight out on the River Thames. Not only was it very pleasant on the eye, but it lent itself as an instant illustration for parts of my sermons, allowing me to sweep my hand in its direction as I spoke of 'not letting life flow by without us' or asked if 'we are the sort of people swimming against the tide or with it'. But I did try to limit the number of watery allusions, lest they became tiresome (and I sank in them).

The Christian rabbi?

I have always been grateful that Judaism has adopted a (to my mind) common-sense approach to religious dialogue, taking the attitude for some 2,000 years that there are many paths to heaven and that it does not particularly matter which one you take, so long as you reach that final destination and do not harm anyone else in the process. Judaism may have much to commend it, but it would be ridiculously arrogant to claim it has exclusive grasp of religious truth. This seems blindingly obvious the more one learns about other faiths and the extraordinary diversity of rules and beliefs they encompass. Can they all be wrong and only one be right? Is it not much more likely they are all imperfect attempts to pierce the veil and gain deeper understanding of who we are and why we exist? I cannot understand anyone who says that their faith alone knows the will of God, and I can only conclude they are either immensely simple or complete knaves. I am also keenly aware of the role of chance. I am Jewish because I was born into a Jewish family and given a strong Jewish identity. I strongly suspect that had I been born into a Christian or Muslim family that was just as committed, I would not now be Rabbi Romain but Reverend Romain or Imam Romain. And probably just as happy.

Sermon cricket

For several years, I was one of the panel of judges for *The Times* Sermon of the Year Award organised by Ruth Gledhill. The task involved whittling down applicants to a shortlist by a mixture of reading their sermons and listening to them preaching in their respective church or synagogue. We then had a finale of six contestants that was open to the public. I was astonished at one of the findings that quickly emerged in the first year and was largely repeated in succeeding years: Jewish sermons varied enormously, whereas Christian sermons were virtually the same. The rabbis tended to speak about a wide range of practical issues that arose either from the weekly *Torah* portion or from what was going on in the news. Thus they would vary from the food laws to abortion to business ethics to coping with cancer. The vicars, though, spoke about faith and having faith and reinforcing one's faith and the rewards of faith. Every sermon was based on the single theme of faith. It reflects the over-simplistic but partially true summary that 'Judaism is a religion of deed, Christianity of creed'. It is not that Christians are not engaged with the world, but Judaism, with its 613 Commandments, tends to concentrate much more on everyday concerns, with an opinion on how every single action, however small, should be conducted, from the way one washes hands to how many a times a week a couple should have conjugal relations. It seems, therefore, that the sermon, although similar in format in each faith, serves a different function. In Judaism, it is primarily to educate, while in Christianity it is there to exhort.

The thinking behind the award was to counter the prevailing image of sermons being endured rather than enjoyed, and to highlight the instances of excellent preaching. Unfortunately, the weekly experience of many parishioners meant that it was an uphill task. One result of bad experiences in the past has been the development of a survival mechanism known as 'sermon cricket'. This is a game played in the pews by which you score a run every time the preacher uses the personal pronoun, 'I', gain a six whenever he waves both arms in the air, and take a wicket when he says 'God'. Alternatively, one can play 'sermon alphabet': listen out for the minister to use a word beginning with 'A', then 'B' and so on throughout the alphabet. Time yourself and see if you can do better the following week.

Bearing in mind that much of the liturgy is the same each week, it is the sermon that is the one aspect of the service that can vary dramatically. When someone at home asks a returning worshipper: 'How was the service today?', what they often mean is: 'What was the sermon like?' An added complication is that it needs to be heard in different ways by different audiences: comforting the vulnerable but dis-comforting the comfortable. The best sermon is often one that challenges the congregation and provokes them into responding. As Rabbi Israel Salanter put it (in an era when there were only male rabbis): 'A rabbi whose congregation does not want to run him out of town is no rabbi; and a rabbi whose congregation does run him out of town is no man.'

My own inspiration comes from a much more secular source. When I was around ten years old, my parents took me on holiday to Brighton, during which we went to an open-air show on the beach. It started to rain and some people began to leave. 'Never mind the rain,' called out the presenter, anxious to reassure those of us left, 'the show will go on. Even if there is only one man and his dog in the audience, I keep going. And if the man goes to the loo and leaves the dog, I'll still carry on.' I have never forgotten his determination to persevere, and have always taken the attitude when facing a small congregation: never mind those who are not here, make sure the ones that *are* here have a great time.

I do recognise, though, that for some congregants there is a masochistic element at play. This applies particularly on

Yom Kippur, when they are supposed to be confessing all the sins of the past year, and they expect to be lambasted by me for their failings. Being told what hopeless wretches they are is seen by some as part of the cleansing process. When I took the attitude that, having the largest attendance of the year, it would far better to enthuse about a particular project or explore an intriguing topic, I had complaints from a few afterwards: 'Rabbi, you didn't tell us off!' They genuinely felt cheated of their annual slap-down and that they had missed out on a cathartic experience. It seems there is still a market – in some circles at least – for preachers who gnash their teeth, berate their flock for their utter worthlessness and thunder down hellfire and brimstone. The fact that most of those congregants will then disappear for the next 365 days suggests that, actually, this approach is not as effective as it seems.

A dangerous visit

One of the hallmarks of Maidenhead has been our outreach programme, part of which involved me finding Jews in the area who were not members of the synagogue, going to visit them and persuading them to join. It has meant entering the homes of people I do not know, something I never worried about till I went to see Nick. He lived in a fairly run-down part of Slough that was known for its social problems. The broken bottles and graffiti in the stairway to his flat was evidence of a neighbourhood that took little pride in itself. The doorbell was not working and there was no knocker, so I just banged on the door. Nick answered and welcomed me into a flat that was both dishevelled and smelly. I suspected he was unemployed, which meant little prospect of obtaining a synagogue subscription, but that did not worry me too much as we often reduce it for those out of work and maybe one day he would get a job. Nor was I overly bothered by the fairly menacing look he had about him. It was not necessarily his fault that he had a broken nose. What alarmed me more was the rows of knives which were the only decoration on his wall. I also realised that I was sitting on the far side of the room, whereas his chair was the one in front of the door. I made a mental note that if I survived that evening I would always choose the seat nearest the exit and not have my escape route blocked.

After fifteen minutes, I decided that it would be prudent to shorten the 45-minute visit I usually make and, sounding very positive and rising from my chair unexpectedly, said he would be very welcome to come to the synagogue one day if he had the time. I was by the door before he realised I was leaving, and, relieved to find it was not locked and I could open it, wished him a cheerful farewell. Of course, had I stayed longer, it might have proved a thoroughly pleasant evening, but my instinct was not to put it to the test. Since then, the advent of mobiles has made it easier to be tracked or call for help, but a lone visitor in unfamiliar territory is still a vulnerable person. This risk is perhaps even higher now that so many rabbis and vicars are female. It highlights how the job of clergy – often stereotyped as very otherworldly – can involve ministering to areas or situations where violence is frequently present and they can be victims too.

The missionary's son

Mitch seemed to fit a fairly standard pattern. He was in his late twenties, had a Jewish girlfriend whom he intended to marry, and he wanted to convert to Judaism so as to have a Jewish wedding and a religiously unified household for when children arrived. The aspect that made him different was that both his parents were Christian missionaries and, since he had gone to university, had spent their lives working in Africa. The sense of religious rejection, professional failure and personal hurt that would come their way when they discovered Mitch's plans would be enormous. We discussed it together and in particular how to inform them of his religious transition but also emphasise that it did not mean he loved them any less than before. In the event, they found it impossible to come to terms with his conversion and broke off relations.

Mitch was more typical in that a large majority of converts to Judaism do so because they meet someone Jewish. Whereas some people disparage those converting for 'the marriage motive', it seems to me irrelevant as to whether a person is introduced to Judaism through a partner or reading a book or having a religious experience or after a long personal search. What counts is whether they then feel at home in it. Certainly the Jewish community has benefited from those who bring a strong sense of commitment and vibrancy that some born Jews lack. In fact, a disproportionately high number of teachers at synagogue Religion Schools are converts, who feel enthusiastic enough to get out of bed and teach on a Sunday morning, while born Jews are still lolling around in their pyjamas.

Those converting to Judaism often fit a different profile to those joining other faiths. Although people can convert at any period during their life, the greatest number converting to Christianity are between the ages of fifteen and twenty years (a time of seeking identity); those becoming Muslim are very often between nineteen and twenty-six (a time of looking at a new direction for oneself); and adopting Judaism is most common for those in the twenty-five to thirty-five range (a time of settling down with family).

It also appears that each faith has different 'selling points': Islam is seen as providing a sense of purpose and direction; Buddhism as a path to self-knowledge and inner calm; Christianity as offering personal salvation and eternal life; while Judaism is good at community and camaraderie. Of course, each aspect can be found in all the faiths, but these are perceived as their distinctive characteristics.

Gender attraction is also markedly different: for every male convert to Judaism, there are five females (partly because of the off-putting requirement of circumcision for males, and partly because the children traditionally follow the mother's line, so her status is deemed more important). In Christianity, the ratio is two females for every male (perhaps because the popular image of being meek and mild is less appealing to men). Islam has an equal ratio of male–female converts and manages to give out an image that is both macho for men and protective for women.

Ju-bus

If Jews convert to another faith, they are much more likely to become Buddhists than to join any other religion. This is partly because its concentration on the inner soul appeals to those turned off by what they consider to be Judaism's over-emphasis on rituals and rules; it also lacks the historical baggage of persecutions of Jews within Christianity and Islam; that in turns mitigates any sense of guilt at leaving the Jewish fold. In fact, many Jews who adopt Buddhism feel that it does not present them with an 'either/or' choice or that they are abandoning their Jewish roots. They feel the two traditions can co-exist, with them being religiously Buddhist and culturally Jewish. The phenomenon of Jewish Buddhists is sufficiently recognised that they have acquired an affectionate name of their own: Ju-bus.

Still, Jews do adopt other faiths too. I remember being approached by a Jewish friend from youth club days with whom I was still in touch and who was thinking of becoming a Christian. She wanted to talk it over with 'someone Jewish who won't shout at me'. I guess she did not have a good relationship with her own rabbi. We talked over the issues, both her own spiritual needs and the impact conversion might have on her family. I also asked whether she had explored all the different options within Judaism, as synagogues can vary from the stultifying to the inspiring. But she was adamant about leaving. In the end I felt I had to be honest and say that the rabbis had always had a tolerant attitude to other monotheist faiths providing they had a moral basis. The reason we were not a missionary faith was that we did not hold there was one exclusive route to God. Although I was sad that she no longer felt Judaism could offer her anything meaningful, if she had now found a religious home in the church, then that was better than her remaining Jewish unhappily. I suspect some rabbis might disagree.

Religious mottos

'Rabbi, my old school had a motto, so did my university – why don't we have one for the synagogue?' Duncan asked me. It was a fair point, but I did not pursue it as it would obviously have to be a democratic decision and the thought of trying to get 800 families to agree seemed likely to cause more argument than harmony. Still, it did make me think what the possible contenders might be for a shortlist, especially as plenty of rabbinic soundbites might be appropriate. An obvious one is that of the first-century Hillel, who declared: 'If I am not for myself, who is for me? But if I am only for myself, what am I? And if not now, when?' In other words, we have to stick up for our rights, but without being self-obsessed, and while debating the balance is fine, there comes a point when we have to stop theorising and start doing.

Personally, I have always admired a contemporary of his, Shammai, who summed up his life's teachings as: 'Say little, do much, and welcome everyone cheerfully.' As a religious paraphrase, it is superb: it rolls off the tongue easily, but also covers a wide range of situations. Then there are the well-known words of Rabbi Tarphon, which have already been adopted by many Jewish groups as a slogan for their cause: 'It is not your duty to complete the work, but neither are you free to desist from it.' It has inspired those, for instance, battling against the odds to save millions threatened by famine, to inoculate children against polio, or to rescue animals caught up in an oil slick.

Of course, going back to the Bible, the five words of Leviticus – 'Love your neighbour as yourself' – are unbeatable as a general guide to life. Equally concise, and even more piercing, is the Genesis question: 'Am I my brother's keeper?' Modern rabbis have continued the tradition, such as Leo Baeck's 'Mere goodwill cannot replace definite ethical action.' My own ministry has been inspired by Harold Reinhart's 'It is not what people want that counts, it is what they ought to want.' I am also guided by Mendel of Kotzk, who declared: 'Take care of your own soul and another person's body, but not of your own body and another person's soul.' A plea for thoughtful moderation that is a powerful counter-blast to fundamentalists of all faith is offered by Louis Jacobs: 'Better to be probably right than definitely wrong', while Lionel Blue's assertion that 'Religious cooking is generous cooking' reminds of the importance of hospitality and always having an extra place at the table. Perhaps, to save arguing over which saying to choose, we should have a monthly motto that greets everyone and challenges us to turn fine thoughts into positive action.

The hearse

I was driving along the road behind two cars that seemed to be going very slowly for no particular reason. As I was running late, I overtook them both – only to discover that the first car was a hearse. I felt awful whizzing past the coffin. Logically, there is nothing wrong with that – it is not banned and the deceased certainly did not know – but somehow I felt I should not be in such a hurry for my next appointment when a person had recently left life altogether.

Is that just being over-sentimental or does it reflect something deeper? In previous ages, if a hearse passed by, those walking along the street would stand still, and men would take off their hats out of respect. In fact, there is still a Jewish custom that if that happens, you should stop whatever you are doing and follow the coffin for a few paces before resuming your activity. The thinking is that, even though you may have no idea as to who the dead person was, they were still a human being, had mattered to others, and so, in a small way, should matter to you too. Perhaps it is also acknowledging the natural cycle of life and death that will affect us too, as well as a reminder to make the best of the day ahead.

The only other time I overtook a hearse was when I had been delayed by an unexpected caller, just as I was leaving to take the funeral to which the hearse was going, and I needed to be there first to greet it.

The incomplete mosque

I was attending an inter-faith conference in Germany, which was supposed to coincide with the opening of a new mosque, and part of the programme was to be the first group to visit it. A problem arose when it was realised that there had been major delays and it was still several months behind completion. So, instead, we went to the site in the evening to be shown the plans and see how the mosque would eventually look. At that stage, just the main girders were in place, but we could imagine the grandiose shape it would one day have. Standing in its empty shell, with the wind howling around us, and the stars apparent through the gaps in the roof, our Muslim guide was very apologetic. But he had no need to be. If the building had been finished and decorated and bejewelled, we would have been full of admiration for the architect and the craftsmen, but not necessarily experienced feelings of God. By contrast, standing in the star-lit skeleton of the building, knowing it was reaching out to heaven, feeling the majesty of creation around us, carried a very powerful sensation of religious awe.

It is a message that is one of the forgotten parts of *Sukkot*. Usually we think of either the historical theme of the Israelites trundling around the wilderness, or the harvest theme of gathering in the ripe fruits. But it has a third theme: of the frailty and impermanence of life. By leaving our secure homes and living in a highly makeshift shelter (at least for a little while), it reminds us not to be fooled by thick walls and doors. They do not afford protection against the vicissitudes of life, while all our plans and ambitions can come crashing down as easily as the *sukkah* is blown over by a strong gust of wind. There is also a religious trap in having synagogues, churches and mosques that are so splendid that you forget all about the glory of God and reflect more on the wealth of the congregation. *Sukkot*, like that unfinished mosque, reminds us not to hide behind artificial edifices but concentrate on the religious values they seek to proclaim.

The odd couple

The wedding interview was going well until we came to the final question. We had talked about the couple and how they had met, along with the details about the ceremony, as well as their hopes for the future. I just needed to make a note of administrative details. 'What is your postal address?' I asked. He gave me his and then she gave me hers. I looked up in surprise. 'Aren't you living together?' I replied. It was a genuine question, as nineteen of the previous couples I had married were either at the same address, or, even if they had their own flats, had moved in together and rented the other out. I was not trying to make a moral point about sex before marriage, just be accurate as to their whereabouts. But they were shocked: 'Of course we are not living together – we are saving ourselves for the wedding. We believe very strongly in the sanctity of marriage.' It was said with the clear implication that I had severely gone down in their estimation for even suggesting such a possibility. Of course, I had no objection to their approach, but was surprised at how different it was to the vast majority of other couples who either lived together or had sexual relations beforehand. As a rabbi, what is important for me is not whether a couple have sex before or after they have signed the dotted line of the registration form, but the quality of the relationship.

I never worry about trying to define 'true love', as that is not what marriage is about. A couple can love each other dearly but be totally unsuitable for each other. For me, marriage is a partnership – almost a business arrangement – about how to go through life together with someone else successfully for the next forty or more years. The four key ingredients to my mind are:

1. How well do they *know* each other, and really understand what the other person is about?
2. Do they *respect* each other, and take each other's needs and personality seriously?
3. Do they *like* each other, and find that they enjoy each other's company?
4. Do they *care* about each other, and genuinely want the best for each other?

Frankly, it is impossible to promise eternal love or predict how one is going to feel about another person several decades ahead. But if a couple can answer 'yes' to those four questions above, then there is a solid basis for linking one's future together, whenever the sex starts… or finishes.

Heaven and hell

There is a story that I have heard quoted both as a Jewish tale and as a Hindu one. It may well be common to other faiths and I have no idea as to who was the first to tell it. But it fits a Jewish approach to heaven and hell exactly, so I will use the rabbinic version.

It concerns a rabbi who wants to know what hell is like. He is whisked there and shown a room full of people sitting round a pot of delicious stew – yet all starving. The reason is that they had spoons which were so long that they could not get them into their own mouths, and so they were wailing and moaning and crying out in hunger. 'That's awful,' exclaimed the rabbi with a shudder, and begged to be taken away from such a sight. When he went to view heaven, he saw exactly the same scene, with people sitting around a pot of stew all holding inordinately long spoons, but everyone healthy and content. The difference was that each person used their spoon to feed their neighbour, so they all ate and were satisfied.

It is doubly Jewish: first because it is really a message about how we should behave here on earth; secondly, it leaves completely unresolved the question of whether or not heaven and hell exist and, if so, what they are like. So, even if it is not our tale after all, it could be.

Taking opportunities

This is another story that I have heard in different guises, with the Jewish one being: a man is caught in a flood, and it is so high that he has to climb up on his roof. But he is not worried because, being religious, he prays to God for a miracle. Someone happens to come by in a rowing boat and offers him a place. 'No thanks,' he replies, 'God will save me.' The water rises higher, up to his waist. The man is unperturbed. When a helicopter flies overhead and lowers a rope to him, he waves it away, saying: 'No need, God will save me.' An hour later, he find himself knocking at heaven's gates, dripping wet and furious with God. On being let in, he rushes to the Divine Throne and complains: 'How could you do that to me? I showed faith in You, but You let me down.' 'Nonsense,' replies God. 'I sent you a boat *and* a helicopter – what more did you want?'

The power of the story lies not in the humour but the underlying message: that life is full of signals we do not always recognise and that God operates not just in stunning miracles, but in other ways too. It could be in the hand of friendship extended by a stranger. It might be a kind or perceptive remark that surprises us, and although our first instinct is to shy away, perhaps we should open up and respond. There is also the small still voice of our own conscience that urges us to take a path that is not attractive in the immediate future but might prove best in the long run. Perhaps it is an unexpected chance to start something new when we have got so used to our current routine that, even though we complain about it, we are unwilling to let go of its familiarity and miss seizing the opportunity we said we always wanted. As the man on the roof found out to his cost, it is often hard to spot a godsend.

The two stones

One of my favourite Jewish stories has a rabbi at its centre (who else?) but really concerns *Yom Kippur*. He was approached by two men the day before the festival who were not particularly religious but had both come to a point in their lives where they wanted to draw a line over their past and start afresh. They asked the rabbi how they could best repent for the faults they had committed and wipe the slate clean. The rabbi told them to go to a nearby field and collect stones whose size was approximate to the gravity of the sins they had done and bring them back to him. It seemed a strange thing to ask them to do, but off they went. One person was fairly villainous and had committed two robberies. He lugged back two enormous boulders. The other person had not done anything criminal, just the usual everyday lapses: he'd shouted at the children, been rude to his in-laws, been inconsiderate behind the driving wheel and cut a few corners at work; so he collected a large handful of small stones.

The two men presented the stones to the rabbi, who said: 'Okay, now take them back and throw them away.' They raised their eyebrows but did what he said and then returned to his study. 'Now what?' they asked. 'Well,' he replied, 'I'd like you to go to the field again and fetch those exact stones back.' They both objected and exclaimed: 'But you told us to get rid of them! What's the point of all this?' But he was adamant, so off they went. Of course, the man with the major faults immediately spotted his two boulders, but the other person had great difficulty in locating his small stones again. In fact, he could not identify them anymore.

The story is wonderfully appropriate for those of us who are not responsible for major misdemeanours, but have lots of petty small faults. The trouble is that they are much easier to sweep under the carpet and forget about. It means we never make up for them, by undoing the damage or apologising for the hurt, while it is also more likely that we will repeat them. Maybe that is why, although it is a tough call, the rabbis say that every night should be a mini-*Yom Kippur*, when we review the events of the day and determine to rectify them. We will never be perfect, but hopefully we will recognise the stones we scatter and gradually have less and less to collect.

God and the dinosaurs

It is not often realised that Darwin, despite his discoveries about the development of life on earth, was a religious Christian and was buried in Westminster Abbey. He may have been responsible for destroying the notion of the world being created in six days and humanity starting with Adam and Eve, but that did not affect his belief in God. For him, God was still the source of life and the process – be it through Adam or the amoeba – was mere detail. I wish this was better known, for it would save the countless conversations I have with those who feel that as Darwin has disproved Genesis, they can no longer believe in the Bible. My response is that they are using the wrong source material. If they want to know about dinosaurs, then they should not read the Bible but consult an encyclopaedia. If they want to know about how to behave and how to conduct relationships, then they should go to the Bible.

Adam and Eve may not be real characters, but they stand for all those who face temptation of any kind, who have to make choices, who must take responsibility for their actions and who face consequences when they go wrong.

Cain and Abel may never have existed, but what greater challenge is there to each of us than the piercing cry in that story: 'Am I my brother's keeper?', except this time it is we who must answer.

Noah may have been fictional but he sums up our situation, teetering between the constant threat of mass destruction and rainbows of hope for a better future.

The Joseph saga shows the ultimate dysfunctional family and warns of favouritism, sibling rivalry and how parents can mess up their children's lives.

The people who approach me have often been asking the wrong question, saying: 'Is the Bible true?' when they should be asking: 'Does the Bible contain truth and does it have anything to say to us and the way we lead our lives?' The holiness of the Bible does not lie in whose signature is on it – God, Moses, a series of editors – but whether it leads us to holiness and to lives that are better because of it. Darwin knew that.

Taking three steps backwards

There is a story told – true or not – about the American diplomat Henry Kissinger, who, during his famous Middle East peace mission, told a colleague that he had solved the problem of making a lion lie down in peace with a lamb, which the Book of Isaiah heralds as one of the signs of the messianic age and an era of universal peace. Kissinger duly showed him a cage with a lion and a lamb in it happily side by side. The diplomat was amazed, and for the next few days visited the cage. Sure enough, the lamb was still there, safe and well.

'It's a miracle,' he exclaimed, 'something for which we have waited for centuries! But tell me, Henry, how did you do it?'

'Easy,' replied Kissinger. 'Every morning I put in a new lamb.'

I am never sure whether that story is deeply depressing or marvellously realistic, but it certainly reflects the fact that we cannot lean back and wait for the world to improve of its own accord. It needs us to have the determination, and the vision, to improve it. This is highlighted by the remarkable prayer, the *Oseh Shalom*, which we not only recite but also take three steps backwards as we say it. It translates as: 'May God who makes peace in heaven help us to bring peace here on earth too.' But you cannot achieve peace by saying: 'I am right, you are wrong. Here I stand, I shall not budge.' You can only make peace by stepping back, seeing the other's person's position, giving way a little, and making room for compromise. Which is why we physically step back to reinforce its meaning.

Football and faith

I have always taken the attitude that the Bible not only addresses the key issues of its day, but has relevance to subsequent ones through the values it espouses. That does not mean it is the last word on any subject – I would certainly depart from its attitude to slavery or homosexuality – but it is worth consulting as one's starting point. In the pithy saying that is often used, the Bible has a vote but not a veto. However, there are some who reckon that, even if it is not obvious at first sight, the Bible secretly alludes to all future issues, from germ warfare to space travel, and you just have to have the skill to uncover it. With this in mind, I am asked periodically by the media to come up with biblical predictions as to how England's football team will fare in a forthcoming World Cup. (This is not a sign of religiosity but usually means sports journalists have started their coverage of the World Cup too early, have exhausted all the standard football comments and need to find punditry from other sources to fill the final days' gaps.)

In an attempt to be helpful – and with a tongue-in-cheek approach – I have advised England to take heed of II Kings 13:17, where it says; 'Then Elisha said "Shoot" and he shot', which is clearly nothing to do with firing arrows at the enemy, but everything to do with England hitting the back of the net...

If a free kick is given against England near their goal, they should pay attention to Nahum 2:5: 'They shall make haste to the wall thereof and the defence shall be prepared.' And also trust that Proverbs 1:17 applies to their opponents: 'Surely in vain the net is spread in sight.'

My advice for the English coach, should an injury occur, is to follow Deuteronomy 25:9 and 'to loose his shoe from off his foot', while I urge the referee to deal firmly with any delaying tactics by the visiting side: 'He shall pay for loss of time' (Exodus 21:19).

I also offer hope that the English captain never has cause to quote Psalm 139:16 to the referee ('In thy book all my members were written'), nor that any English player ever has to use Psalm 38:16: 'When my foot slips, they magnify themselves against me.'

Does it work? I was once told by an atheist that he could prove God did not exist. He had attended a football match at which Arsenal were playing Manchester United, and at which the Chief Rabbi and Archbishop of Canterbury – both Arsenal fans – were present and no doubt praying for victory. Arsenal lost. 'That proves that prayers don't work,' he told me triumphantly. It might also prove that God is a Manchester United fan.

My other will

At one of the High Holy Days, I gave a sermon that was ostensibly for others, but I realised afterwards that if it applied to them, it applied to me too. That may seem obvious, but it is very easy to talk about what others should do, but neglect it oneself (though I should add that this happens not just when speaking from a pulpit, but also when chatting over the dinner table or in a pub). The sermon was about ethical wills – the concept that as well as leaving your family instructions about your financial wishes, you also leave some moral guidance or reflect on the values by which you have tried to live. The idea is to bequeath something more than a bank account and the silver candlesticks, but also something of yourself. It goes right back to biblical times, although it was done verbally then: when the dying Jacob gathers his children around him and tells them the way in which they should live after he is gone (Genesis 49). It may sound simple enough, but writing an ethical will is not an easy thing to do, for it entails confronting yourself in a brutally honest way: summarising the essential truths you have learnt over the years, facing up to your personal failures, and deciding what are the qualities in life that really matter that you wish to pass on.

I know of one couple in the community who went one step further: they not only wrote an ethical will, but then decided to read it to their adult family. The astonishing thing was that the children were surprised to learn what mattered most to their parents, and the parents were surprised that their children were surprised, but the realisations led to a series of wonderful discussions and brought the family much closer together.

In fact, there are many aspects to parents' lives of which their children have little knowledge, and the ethical will can also be used to write some autobiographical details, particularly one's childhood or early adulthood, which are often completely unknown to one's children or grandchildren. I have lost count of the times I have visited a family in the community following a death at which they said about part of the person's life: 'That's something we never knew … we always meant to ask about but never did.'

But beware, it is difficult to sum up your ethics in a page. First, because it reminds you of all the times you have not lived up to them and you can become disheartened by all the 'if onlys' as you reflect on the course of your life. Second, because what you write has to ring true. When others read it, they must nod their heads, not look puzzled as if they did not recognise you. So they will not take words of sweetness from the person who always used to shout and scream at home. Nor will they believe lines about integrity if you were known for constantly taking kick-backs or greasing the wheels at work.

It took me several years before I sat down to write my own ethical will, and I found it both enriching to feel I had captured the best part of myself and depressing to think how much more consistent I should have been in adhering to those standards. Still, when they eventually read it, it is for my family to judge how well or badly I did, or if I was fantasising completely about who I thought I was. Why not gift your family something similar? Your ethical legacy could turn out to be more precious than any financial settlement you make.

The stigma

Sammy booked an appointment to discuss something that was worrying him. He explained that when he started a relationship with his wife, Josie, she was actually married to someone else. The affair led to her then husband divorcing her on the grounds of adultery. When she went to the Orthodox *Beth Din*, they granted the *get*, the religious divorce, but pointed out that Jewish law stated one could not marry one's paramour, the person who had been the cause of the break-up of one's marriage, and named Sammy. They warned that if this happened, any children arising would be regarded as *mamzerim*, illegitimate, bear that stigma throughout their life and also have the practical disadvantage of not being permitted to marry another Jew in synagogue. Despite this warning, Sammy and Josie went ahead, married and had a son. The son was now ten years old and what had not worried Sammy at his birth was now beginning to trouble him. What was his son's status and how could Sammy save him from being ostracised by the Jewish community?

The good news was that the son was in the clear. The bad news was that I had to explain a complex sequence of events. First, the *Beth Din* were right that in Orthodoxy one cannot marry one's paramour. Second, if the new marriage does go ahead, it is still valid, though ideally it should be dissolved. Third, as Josie had received a *get* before remarrying, the child was not a *mamzer*. A *mamzer* is only a child born out of incest or if the mother is married to someone else, whereas she was divorced from her ex-husband both civilly and Jewishly. The *Beth Din* had misinformed Josie about the child's status, perhaps deliberately so as to dissuade her from marrying her paramour. Fourth, this meant Sammy and Josie need not have any worries about their son's status or his ability to marry anyone Jewish in synagogue. Fifth, Reform synagogues did not maintain the law against marrying a paramour if the adultery was technical, for example if it was a symptom of the marriage having already broken down, rather than being the cause of the breakdown. Sixth, Reform did not recognise the notion of children having the status of a *mamzer*, as that puts the punishment of the parents' incest or adultery upon the child rather than on them themselves. This is monstrously unfair, and an unfair law should not be a Jewish law. Sammy went home very relieved, and also more knowledgeable about Jewish law.

The circumcision question

Michelle and Nigel came to see me, officially to tell me that she was pregnant with their first child, but actually to discuss what would happen if it was a boy. Whereas once I might have said: 'I can give you the name of a reliable *mohel* to do the circumcision,' now I am more inclined to say: 'Were you thinking of having a circumcision?' In their case, that was the right response, because, despite both being Jewish, they were not sure if they wanted to go ahead with it. They are not alone and reflect one of the noticeable changes in Jewish attitudes to religious rituals. Previously it was taken for granted; now many Jewish parents worry about it, discuss what will happen and what will be the effects. It is hard to know whether this is due to opposition to the concept of circumcision itself, or because couples are more prepared to question and probe. Another factor is that circumcision – common in certain circles, including the royal family, in previous decades – is now out of fashion and attracts negative comments. There may also be the influence of friends or family in mixed-faith marriages, who often do not opt for circumcision because the non-Jewish partner is not comfortable with it. It is noticeable that, whereas in the past when someone asked a pregnant Jewish woman if she knew what sex the child would be, the stock reply was: 'So long as it's healthy', nowadays 'We're praying for a girl' is also heard. It is striking, though, that there are other Jews who ignore countless commandments – who cheerfully eat pork and disregard the Sabbath – yet who do observe this particular command. It illustrates that circumcision is primarily an act of identity and transition: saying: 'However good or bad a Jew I am, it is still important to me to pass my Jewish heritage on in this way.' It is as much a marker for the parents as for the child.

The issue for Michelle and Nigel was the actual level of pain that their putative child might suffer. There is no doubt that the baby does feel some pain, though it is mitigated partly by the anaesthetic cream that is usually put on his penis beforehand, while there is also the Jewish tradition of letting him suck a finger that has been dipped in wine – equivalent to an adult downing half a bottle of whisky. The objection that used to be raised by some parents – 'It will make him look different at school when they all have a shower' – is rarely heard now that there are often Muslim children in classes too. Fears about psychological damage are sometimes mentioned, but these hold little weight as no one has ever claimed to have been able to remember what happened to them at eight days old. Having attended countless circumcisions, I reckon that the parents suffer much more than the child, both worrying in advance and on the day, with the mother often in tears and the father wanting to murder the *mohel*. My role is two-fold. Partly to prevent the latter, but, more importantly, to position myself behind the father in case he faints and needs supporting. The last time it happened was with a dad who had previously been an Israeli paratrooper. He had faced plenty of trauma in battle, but whereas armed opponents could not knock him out, the sight of his own son's blood did.

Having talked through the issues, Michelle and Nigel decided to go ahead with a circumcision if it was a boy. They were keen to maintain the tradition once they had reassured themselves that they were not recklessly endangering their child. On a more light-hearted note, I told them that one of the characteristics of Jews through the centuries was that they had been less prone to alcoholism than the surrounding populations. Various sociological reasons have been suggested, but there is also the argument that it is due to circumcision and the awful associations they have with their first taste of wine! It was not this that convinced Michelle and Nigel, but it did lighten their mood.

The coat bought on the Sabbath

Tracey was a vivacious 23-year-old and never without a boyfriend. They tended to last for two months and then be ditched as she had no intention of settling down for a while and was interested in having fun, not getting involved. Dating Motti was a new experience as he was Orthodox and, for instance, would only travel to see her on a Saturday evening once the Sabbath had gone out. On their third date, he had arranged to pick her up at her home on a Saturday night. As she came out, he commented on what a lovely coat she was wearing. 'I'm glad you like it, it's new,' she said. 'I bought it shopping this afternoon.' It was the wrong thing to say (or to have done), for he immediately said he could not go out with her wearing a coat that had been purchased desecrating the Sabbath. He asked her to go back and fetch another one to wear instead. Somewhat shocked, she did so. When I asked her why someone as strong-willed as her had meekly acquiesced, she replied: 'Frankly, I felt like slapping him, but he had bought theatre tickets to a show I wanted to see.' I was not surprised to hear shortly afterwards that he did not even make the two-month limit. Of course, had the relationship developed into a more serious one, it would have begged the wider question of how compatible they would have been, given their different levels of religious observance. While this might apply to all faiths, it is particularly acute in Judaism, where so much of the religion is home-based. Even if a couple manage to work out a compromise for their own activities, it becomes even more of an issue with the arrival of children and what direction they are given. Unless either Tracey or Motti were to have changed their lifestyle completely, a scenario of constant clashes would have been likely. The coat was a useful early warning sign.

Religious prejudice

Beryl gave me enormous frustration. She was Jewish, had lived in the area for many years and had a strong Jewish identity, but steadfastly refused to join the synagogue. Why? Because we were Reform and, in her eyes, only Orthodox Judaism was the real thing (even though she had chosen to live out here, far away from an Orthodox community). Yet, she did not even join a London Orthodox synagogue and have a long-distance membership. Why? Because her husband was not Jewish and as she had thereby broken one of the most deeply held Orthodox taboos, she felt she would not be welcome. So she was too heretical for the Orthodox, but too traditional for the Reform! What I could not understand was why she had deliberately chosen to occupy a religious wilderness when she could at least have contact with us, the local Jewish community. She replied it was to do with her principles. Personally, I reckon it was more to do with her prejudices.

Religious madness

Very few people had heard of the Yazidis until they began to be persecuted by Islamic State in Iraq in 2014. It is an ancient faith, dating back some 3,000 years. What struck me most about the attention they suddenly received – apart from the needless human suffering they were having to endure – was the strange nature of some of their traditions. Yazidis are forbidden to eat lettuce, banned from wearing blue, while they revere peacocks. When I first read this, I laughed out aloud. Then it occurred to me that the same astonishment might greet those coming across Judaism for the first time and who hear that we are forbidden to eat pork, banned from mixing wool and linen in our clothing, while we circumcise male children when they are eight days old.

To mangle a line from a third faith (which demands celibacy for its priests and forbids unhappily married couples from divorcing): 'Let he who is free of strange customs throw the first stone.'

Why did God allow this to happen?

Rabbis – no doubt vicars too – need to be on their guard whenever they hear this plaintive cry, not because it is a difficult question, but because of the emotional disconnect between the person asking it and the minister hearing it. When someone utters that question, they are usually reeling from the loss of someone they loved and who died in a tragic way or at a young age. Their pain is real and raw.

For the minister, though, it is hard not to be wearied by one of the oldest theological questions in the book, or frustrated that those who never praise God for the good things that happen to them readily blame God for the bad ones that occur. Instead, we have to take a deep breath, respond to the hurt in front of us, and try to help the person navigate a way through it. Sometimes, that is sufficient and what they want, with their question being more a blast against the woes of the world than a real enquiry. Other times, people do seek an answer that will help them make sense of how the world works and what they can expect of it. Rabbinic responses range enormously, particularly as it begs the question of to what extent God is an intervening God. God may have been very proactive in the Bible, but it is assumed by many that just as the gift of prophecy ceased at its close, so did God's active participation in daily affairs.

For some rabbis, especially the Orthodox, whatever happens is the will of God. We may not like it or understand it, but it is part of the divine plan and, within the larger picture, makes sense. Reform rabbis tend to opt for the view that we are the ones responsible for what occurs in the world, whether by what we do or what we neglect to do, and it is irresponsible to shift the guilt onto God. Whether it be Auschwitz, a drunken driver or a terror attack, the question is not: 'What was God doing?' but: 'What were people doing?' There are also rabbis, myself included, who would challenge the assumption that life is fair and orderly. That is as naive as believing in fairies, but whereas we have jettisoned the latter, we still cling to that idea about life. In many ways, it is the role of religion to try to bring fairness and order into a world often ruled by chance; to turn the jungle in which we find ourselves into something more resembling a garden. The commands not to kill, steal or commit adultery are only there because the natural instinct of many is to kill, steal or commit adultery. For me, religion can never answer the question 'Why did God allow this to happen?' because it is based on a false premise. Instead, religion answers the question 'How do I respond to what has happened?' and helps us to make our own lives meaningful and the world a better place.

9

Family and other traumas

The mother who bullied her son
once too often

There was no doubt that Miriam was a very caring mother and would do anything for young Tom. However, she was also a very dominating character who not only insisted she knew what was best for him in any given situation, but made sure Tom knew she knew and obeyed her. Luckily, he was an accommodating child and also sensed she only meant well, and so the constant friction that might have occurred as he grew up was largely avoided. But, as he approached thirteen, he began to be more independent and flex his muscles. He was beginning to change, but Miriam was far too set in her ways to either notice or see any need to alter her behaviour. In the week before Tom's *barmitzvah*, she took him shopping for new clothes. Naturally, she felt she knew what suited him best and although he argued that he really didn't like the suit she chose and much preferred another one, she went ahead and bought it.

The day dawned. He said he wanted to wear his old suit instead of the hated new one, but she told him he was being ridiculous and forced him to change into her choice. Having got her way, as usual, she started looking forward to the rest of the day. That was her second mistake.

When they arrived at the synagogue, I just saw a family that seemed full of the nervous yet excited anticipation that characterises most families on their *bar/batmitzvah* day and was blissfully unaware of the slumbering volcano that was about to erupt. The service was scheduled to start at 10.30 a.m. At 10.25 a.m., I got the family, at that point milling around noisily greeting relatives and friends, to take their seats in preparation for the start of the service. Except Tom decided not to sit down, but to walk out. One minute he was in front of me, the next minute he was disappearing through the exit door. Everyone else was still chatting away and had not noticed his act of auto-ejection, so I quickly raced after him. 'What's going on?' I asked as calmly as possible but sensing that I was not going to like the answer. 'I'm not having my *barmitzvah*,' he replied simply.

It was now 10.26 a.m. 'Let's sit down and have a chat,' I suggested, and, less calmly, asked why he had made that decision. After some inarticulate replies, the story about the suit gradually came out, as well as the larger issue of Miriam's total control of his life. It had been fine before, but now it felt suffocating. He did not know how to stand up to her, but walking out of the *barmitzvah* and embarrassing her in front of all her guests was a way of punishing her. It was certainly very effective.

I made him promise to stay put, while I went back to the

synagogue and explained that there would be a little delay before the service started, assured Miriam that there was absolutely no need for her to go after Tom and I would sort things out, then repeated it so that it actually sank in and she stayed put in her seat. I dashed back to where I had left Tom, felt elated that he was still there and then deflated when I realised that the much harder task of getting him to come back inside still remained. Conscious of the clock ticking and those in synagogue becoming increasingly perplexed, but also realising that Tom would need time to assess what he had done and would do next, I gave him time to blurt out his pent-up feelings. I chose not to disagree with a word he had uttered, and suggested that he really needed to have a direct talk with Miriam (with someone there as a referee if he thought that helpful) to express his opinions to her too. I then added that I reckoned he had achieved his object of making his protest, while it would be unfair to all those who had travelled long distances if he did not reappear. To my indescribable relief, he agreed. We went back to the synagogue together, I told Miriam I would explain everything later and, fourteen minutes late, we started the service and Tom duly had his *barmitzvah*.

In the end, I never had the conversation with Miriam. She was not in a fit state to do so, yo-yoing between delight at having so many people witness her darling son's moment of glory and fury at nearly having her careful plans sabotaged. She was not in listening mode. Instead, I spoke to her husband, Frank, the lack of whose mention in this story so far reflects the inconsequential role he played in family decision-making. I told him the truth, and emphasised the irony of the situation. *Barmitzvah* is supposed to be when a person 'comes of age' and begins to take on more adult responsibilities. It also means parents stepping back, letting go and allowing the teenager to think and act for themselves. By insisting on what suit Tom should wear, Miriam had been keeping him as a child and undermining the whole concept of *barmitzvah*. It may have seemed to her a relatively innocuous matter, but in his eyes it was highly significant. I warned Frank that unless they adapted to the man-child they now had in the house, they might risk a complete breakdown in their relationship with him.

Did Miriam and Frank pay attention? Yes. A few weeks before their second son, Ben, had his *barmitzvah*, I had a chat with them about the family dynamics and, among other things, asked what Ben would be wearing. 'I'm leaving it up to him,' replied Miriam, with the sweet triumph of the newly righteous.

Embarrassing moments

It is always a moving moment when, at a *bar/batmitzvah*, the boy or girl stands up and recites the Ten Commandments. We know they might end up not keeping all of them, and that many listening in the congregation break them from time to time, but it is an affirmation of a code of values and sets a level of behaviour to which we aspire. It is difficult, though, in cases when the pupil reaches the seventh command – 'You shall not commit adultery' – and I know that explains why the mother and her family are sitting on one

side of the synagogue and the father and his family are sitting
on the other side.

The girl who spoke just in time

She was a lovely little girl, very sweet and quite clever,
but desperately shy. So much so that she virtually never
spoke in class at the Religion School on Sunday mornings
if she could possibly avoid it. That meant not talking to the
other children, and certainly not volunteering answers to
any questions that I asked the class generally. If I addressed
something at her directly, she would respond, but with the
minimum amount of words and almost inaudibly. This carried on from the time she entered the Religion School when
five years old. She was now thirteen. How on earth was she
going to stand up at her *batmitzvah* and recite aloud – in
Hebrew – in front of a packed synagogue consisting of both
familiar faces and complete strangers? The day drew near,
she had rehearsed with the *batmitzvah* tutor and worked at
home on it, but never let her family listen in. Standing next
to her at the reading desk, I reckoned that so long as I could
hear her, that would suffice, and I could then say something
diplomatic like: 'For those at the back who couldn't quite
hear, she did it perfectly.' Instead, I was totally redundant.
She opened her mouth and a loud, clear, strong voice rever-
berated around the building, and as melodic as a nightingale.
She was not just reading the text, but coming out of her shell
and revealing who she was. It was the best *batmitzvah* ever,
not so much in terms of her performance level, but in the

root purpose of the ceremony: marking the transition from childhood towards adulthood, standing up to be heard, asserting her own identity and having the courage to become the person publicly she already was deep within. Everyone who knew her was stunned, not least her parents, who had typecast her as a wallflower who would always live in the shadows and constantly need their protection. Suddenly they had to reassess the child they thought they knew so well, and it was a moment of transition for them as much as for her.

But the *batmitzvah* was significant in another respect. It is a good example of how the original symbolism of a ritual can be superseded and bettered. Back in the second century, when thirteen was designated as the age of maturity, it really was adulthood and you were probably out earning a living and with marriage not too far away. Two thousand years later, it serves a very different purpose: at the very age when the spotty teenager goes monosyllabic, resentful and wants to hide away in a corner wearing a hoodie, what happens? They are thrust centre stage, have a spotlight shone on them, asked to perform publicly in a language that is not natural to them. It is totally counter-intuitive, but it works, and it says to them: you are important, you count, we value you. And that just so happens to be the message they most need to hear at that difficult stage in their life. Although there are some exceptions, most children grow five centimetres that day, physically or metaphorically, and walk tall. What is more, although it is not cool to admit it, especially to parents, they are really pleased with themselves. It is a landmark for the parents too, albeit in a different sort of way: if your son or daughter is now thirteen, then it means you are no longer eighteen anymore, and things are moving on in your life too. So, although many parents look on with pride during the day, that evening many look in the mirror with a certain apprehension. It does not need to say anything, for they can read the message all too well. They are no longer Peter Pan, and their child is taking over.

The parents who ran away

Rosemary had a wonderful childhood. She and her twin sister, Agnes, had a loving home and thoroughly enjoyed school. Her parents made it clear they were devoted to both of them and attended all of their school plays, hockey games and music recitals. Their friends were always made to feel welcome and birthday parties invariably turned out to be fantastic surprises, each one better than the previous. This blissful existence even continued into their teenage years, when relationships might have become more fraught. The struggles and angst that friends had during this period were almost unknown by Rosemary. It was with profound shock, therefore, that the two of them came home after school during their last term in the sixth form to find a note left on the table for them. Their parents wrote that they had done all they could for the two of them and had been the best possible parents they could be. As the girls were now eighteen, they now felt that they had fulfilled their duty and could relinquish their responsibilities. They had taken the car, were going off to lead their own lives and would have no further contact with them. They wished the girls well and left details about the house and financial support.

Agnes collapsed into hysterical sobbing, whereas Rosemary – always the more measured of the twins – at first thought that they might have been kidnapped and had been forced to write such a note under duress. The common factor was that neither girl could comprehend what had led to such a volte-face. Was it a sudden decision by their parents, or had they long planned it?

Why had they not explained everything face to face with them?

Did it imply they had loved them only out of duty and that the stable family life was only an emotional charade? In the event, they never received any answers, for the parents never did make contact again. Fortunately, both girls had already secured university places and so had a structured future ahead of them for the next three years, which allowed them time to slowly adjust. Agnes still wanted answers and for a long time kept trying to find out what had happened. In contrast, Rosemary found herself too impatient to get on with the new life that was unfolding around her to want to delve into the past. As for the parents, it is hard to believe that they could not foresee the hurt they would cause the girls by suddenly cutting themselves off.

It would have been more understandable if they had previously been totally self-centred and neglected the twins, but the contrast between the love they provided and the suddenness with which they snatched it away was astonishing. Agnes met someone at university whom she married shortly after graduating. I am pleased they are still together, as I had worried that it might have been an attempt to find a parent substitute rather than a love match. Rosemary is a free spirit who travels the world as part of her glamorous job. I sometimes wonder if it is a way of subconsciously looking for her parents, not so much a deliberate hunt for them but more a matter of being open to possibilities. But no one has seen them or gained any insights as to their thinking. Perhaps they never had an adolescence themselves and this was their way of rejecting conformity? It remains a complete mystery.

The stony silence

When Lucy died, I visited the family and sensed there were tensions between her two daughters and son. I spoke to her husband about it afterwards and he confirmed that there had been a major fall-out between Lucy and her son some years back, and they had not been on speaking terms from then until her death. When it came to the stone-setting a year later, I asked, as usual, to see the wording in advance before it was given to the mason. I noticed immediately that it declared that Lucy was much mourned by her family, and named her husband and the daughters, but not him. I queried the omission and was told that the other two did not want his name alongside theirs. I warned that this could be a big mistake for several reasons. First, because she did have three children and stones were a matter of historical record, not value judgements. Second, the absence of his name would publicise the family rift and make it highly visible to those who did not already know about it. Third, the son might well be upset by it and so it would perpetuate the quarrel rather than heal it. Fourth, if they did manage to have a reconciliation at some stage, they would look back and wish they had included his name. Unfortunately, their emotions were such that they chose to keep the omission. Some years later, when officiating at a funeral nearby at the same cemetery, I noticed that the engraving had been altered and the son's name added. I guess they had made up after all.

A fight to the death

When Malcolm died at home, I had an unusual role to play: preventing his wife and granddaughter from killing each other. Both blamed each other for his death: the wife blamed the granddaughter (who had lived with them for many years owing to a rift with her mother) for causing his heart attack by her continual rudeness and disobedience; the granddaughter blamed the wife for wearing him down by her constant nagging and bullying. They were punching each other and tearing at each other's hair over his dead body. I managed to separate them and send one off to call the doctor. Of course, they had both loved him dearly in their own way, but had been totally dysfunctional in the manner they showed it and interacted with each other. Families can be wonderful vehicles for love when they work well, but can also be highly repressive in other circumstances. The problematic line in the Ten Commandments about the sins of the fathers being visited upon the children and grandchildren makes sense when seen in the context of abusive behaviour that occurs in families – be it physical, sexual, emotional or verbal. The children who grow up in such a climate may hate it, but then often go on to replicate it when they have families themselves, seeing it as normative and causing a variety of social ills to cascade down the generations unchecked.

Surprisingly, he died peacefully

When Donald died in his eighties from cancer, the family phoned me. He had not been a member of the synagogue, so I knew nothing about his life or circumstances. His son told me that his mother, Donald's wife, had died a few months earlier, but that 'her death was a great relief'. I took that to mean that she had been suffering from a painful terminal illness and the family had been pleased that she was no longer in pain. Quite the contrary. She had had a heart attack out of the blue at a time when she seemed perfectly healthy. Instead, the 'great relief' was that the son had always worried that his mother would knife his father to death. It had not been a happy marriage for many years, she had felt unable to leave and he had long expected that one day she would be in the kitchen, pick up a carving knife and plunge it into Donald. The fact that the family no longer had to be on perpetual standby for a phone call asking them to visit her in the police cell and him in the mortuary meant that they had felt much more relaxed for the last few months!

Definitely not Walt Disney

Most of the inmates I met in prison were in for petty theft or drugs. It was impossible to say that they looked like criminals – who does not in a passport photo? – with some looking very ordinary and others having a disreputable demeanour to them. But one person stood out. Harold was in his mid-fifties, had thick silvery hair, a kindly face and twinkling eyes. He looked like Walt Disney's idealised favourite uncle, someone you could trust or cuddle up to. He was the only one inside for murder. It was not part of a criminal activity, such as a bank robbery, but at home: he had killed his wife. It was yet another example of the fact that so much assault is domestic, with most violence occurring behind the living room curtains rather than in the High Street.

I remember the shock in the Jewish community at large when Jewish Women's Aid was launched, both to draw attention to the problem of abused wives and to offer refuge for those being hurt. The shock was real: surely Jewish men do not hit their wives? Unfortunately, such wishful thinking was totally naive: Jews do take drugs and abuse children and commit any other criminal act that non-Jews do. Jewish crimes may often be more 'white collar' rather than 'blue collar', but that is because we tend to be middle class rather than because we are Jews. On the positive side, the fact that we often have the benefit of family life, the structure of a community around us and an ethical basis to our identity, means that the rate of some crimes is less than that of the wider community. But we are not immune to fault-lines – as the fate of Harold's wife shows.

The husband beater

Violence by men against their wives is totally wrong, but, unlike in the past, at least it is now recognised as unacceptable and women are much less constrained about seeking help. Unfortunately, there are often three time-lags: the first is between being hit periodically and accepting that these are not one-offs but part of a pattern; the second is between thinking it is one's own fault for being negligent in some way and realising that the blame is with one's partner for being manipulative and violent; the third is between acknowledging one is living in an unacceptable situation and summoning the courage to end it by leaving. These time-lags may be very lengthy, in some cases taking several years, with the victim becoming adept at deceiving both themselves and outsiders. In Maisie's case, she had a low sense of self-esteem and so thought that Paul's violent behaviour was often justified by her own forgetfulness or stupidity, accepting it as 'punishment' for her 'misbehaviour'. It was only when she fell pregnant and Paul hit her in the stomach, potentially injuring the foetus, that she woke up to the fact that if an unborn child did not deserve to be punched, then nor did she. She left the following day while he was at work, obtaining a court order that ensured he never saw his daughter once she was born. There was a steep learning curve for even those who wanted to help abused women. At first, posters about Jewish Women's Aid were placed on synagogue notice boards. It took a while to realise that no woman wanted to be seen reading the poster and writing down the helpline number. The result was that they were transferred to women's toilet cubicles, so that they could be noted in private.

While such instances are contemptible, just as harmful are wives who beat their husbands. In some ways, they are more problematic in that there is much less public awareness and those husbands do not know where to turn to for help. In addition, there is the stigma of admitting that, in those relationships, the 'weaker sex' is apparently much stronger than the 'stronger sex'. When Gavin told me that he was experiencing problems at home, I assumed he was going to tell me it was to do with the usual problems of arguments or non-communication. It took him a while to blurt out: 'She keeps on hitting me.' After both going to counselling sessions, initially separately and then together, the irony emerged that she was angry that he was not the strong character she wanted him to be and therefore bullied him. His inability to stand up to her enraged her even more and so the violence became a regular occurrence. Whereas other abused husbands have left their wives, Gavin chose to take a course in self-assertion, and the marriage, although not wonderfully happy, has survived to a manageable degree.

Home influences

In the house where I spent much of my childhood, two framed pictures were hanging on the wall of the upstairs corridor leading to the bedrooms. One was a charcoal drawing of a dishevelled street urchin pushing a little boy in a wheelchair. It was accompanied by the caption: 'I cried because I had no shoes, till I met someone with no feet.' I do not know which of my parents put it up, but seeing it daily throughout my formative years meant it became ingrained into my thinking. In fact, whenever I have been upset about something, or in pain myself from some ailment, it has not been long before that saying flashes through my mind. I realise that whatever my woes, they are inconsequential compared to the sufferings of so many others, and I get on with the job at hand.

The second picture was that of Rudyard Kipling's magnificent poem 'If'. Again, I walked past it every day year after year, imbibing its advice to trust yourself when others doubt you, not to give way to hating, and to greet triumph and disaster just the same. But what resonated most was the counsel to 'fill the unforgiving minute / With sixty seconds' worth of distance run' and I have always used whatever time I have available to the maximum possible effect.

Hating your brother

Occasionally our members hit the national headlines because of their prominence in various fields, such as media entrepreneur Michael Green, MP Evan Harris and entertainer Frankie Vaughan. However, Ray achieved less worthy attention. He had a long-standing feud with his brother Bobby, although it was a one-way feud and the latter bore him no ill will. It had involved Ray making abusive phone calls and sending excrement in the post. Despite being both in their late seventies, it erupted into violence when Ray took a car-jack handle and repeatedly hit Bobby with it, causing injuries to his face and arms. He then smashed the windscreen and window of his car. The case received national attention, both because of the age of the protagonists and because of the dramatic breakdown in sibling relationships. The High Court judge sentenced Ray to a term of thirty months in prison, but in view of his advanced years, it was suspended, but with a strong warning that any further misdemeanours would result in him going to jail. The judge's remarks summed up the pitiful nature of the case when he said: 'Heaven knows, we have a short time enough on this earth – you and your brother rather less than most … I shall be rather more impressed if your (stated) remorse is demonstrated by a real effort to make peace with your brother for the few remaining years allotted to you.' Unfortunately his words were in vain, for the brothers left court without saying a word to each other.

There have been other family battles within the community – often after the death of the person who had acted as matriarch or patriarch, with the adult children then falling out either because there was no strong central force to hold them together, or because they argued over the terms of the will. Families are such strange creatures – capable of being a wonderful source of nurture and support, but equally able to be a destructive pit of anger and humiliation.

The uninvited step-children

When Bernie married Cynthia, his parents were pleased that the 38-year-old was at last settling down, but were not impressed by his choice of wife. They objected to the fact that she was divorced and had two daughters by her previous marriage, now aged fourteen and sixteen. Whenever they invited her and Bernie round for tea, it was without the two girls. Cynthia found this very hurtful and refused to leave them if it was not a Sunday that they were spending with their father, while it left Bernie caught in the middle. After several months of trying to justify his parents to Cynthia, as well as trying to explain her absence to them, he came to see me. 'I can't carry on like this,' he said, 'I'm piggy in the middle and it's wearing me down.' He had asked for an hour's appointment, assuming it would be a long and involved conversation, so was surprised when it ended after ten minutes. 'It is very simple,' I told him, 'you have to tell your parents that unless they accept your new family, you will ditch them.'

He looked amazed, and said he thought that the command about honouring one's parents was sacrosanct. I had to correct him and say that although this is true generally, it does not apply in all cases. The rabbis held that if parents do not act as parents should act, then they no longer count as parents and forfeit the honour that is due to them. In his case, for instance, his parents had the right to give their opinion about Cynthia's suitability while they were dating. Hopefully they put it sensitively, and judged her in his best interests, but even if not, they had that right. But once he had married her, then they should have accepted the reality of the situation and made the best effort to accommodate her and support him. Banning her children and placing him in an impossible position was neither right nor loving. He needed to speak to them plainly, give them the option of accepting his wife and step-children or losing contact with him. I did point out that there might well be other elements at work that were completely irrelevant to Cynthia's previous marriage, such as their reluctance to accept any bride for their son, or their desire to control his life as much as possible. Bernie nodded at both these suggestions and admitted that deep down he realised he was going to have to confront them. As so often happens, people know the solution to their problems, but need a chance to articulate it with someone else, as well as find the courage to implement it. Hearing the words out loud, instead of them running round your head, can create the climate that enables that next step. When we next spoke, some two months later, he told me that the four of them had recently had a nice afternoon at his parents'. But even if his parents had rejected his ultimatum, he would still have been in a better position than before.

The non-wife

I was very pleased for Geoff. After a difficult marriage and an unpleasant divorce, he had met Doreen and they seemed ideally suited. After a few months, she moved into his flat and rented out her own. They talked about marriage, but decided that there was no urgency and they would wait till there was a lull in their respective businesses, when they could have the ceremony and then enjoy a long honeymoon abroad. Sadly, these plans were derailed when Geoff died in a car accident. Worse was to come. As they were not married, she had no legal status. Geoff had not rewritten his will since the revision after the divorce, so the executor was not her, but the bank manager. The hospital refused to deal with her over the funeral, while she had no say in the disposal of his ashes, even though she knew what he would have wanted. She had not yet met all the family, nor all of his friends, so was not treated as the widow or as the main mourner by them. A week after he died, she was asked to hand over the keys to his flat, but she could not go back to her own one as the tenants were there, so she temporarily stayed with a friend before looking for rental accommodation of her own. It meant that anger dominated her emotions – partly at 'the system', partly at Geoff for not revising his will, and partly at herself for not foreseeing this possibility. Her grief at his death, and the loss of her anticipated future, were suppressed by the waves of resentment that crashed over her. It was a lesson about making wills and planning ahead that I have frequently quoted to other couples. Geoff was a very popular person and so his funeral was packed. What was almost as sad as his untimely death was that the loneliest person there was Doreen.

The death-bed revelation

Adrienne had been going downhill for a while, and I had promised to visit her next Sunday. But she rang up on the Thursday and asked me to hurry round. She told me she felt she was dying and needed my advice urgently. The reason was that her son Andrew was not actually the son of her late husband. Instead, he was the result of a brief affair she'd had. Nobody knew and now she was wondering whether she ought to tell him the truth. What did I think?

I am not an automatic believer that 'honesty is the best policy'. Some secrets need to be kept a secret, for the sake of those whom the truth may hurt. If that means the person with the secret has to carry the burden of knowledge to the grave, then that is a price worth paying. So my instinct was to be cautious, lest telling Andrew helped her but left him angry or confused. Two aspects, however, made me veer the other way. First, Andrew had never got on well with his supposed father and had always wondered why they had so little in common. This happens in many father–son relationships simply because of personality differences, but in Andrew's case his true paternity would explain it. Secondly, his supposed father had a history of depression and I knew Andrew worried that he had inherited this trait and would one day be prone to it. He would be greatly relieved to know that this was not necessarily his fate.

So I said that it might indeed be a good idea for Adrienne to tell him the truth, not so much to relieve her, nor out of piety, but to help him come to terms with his identity. My only caveat was that if she was to do so, it should be as soon as possible, to give him time to digest it while she was still alive. I did also warn her that it might backfire and that he might be resentful at the deception for so many years or feel guilty over unkind words he had said about his supposed father. He might also be exposed to pain if he tried to contact his real father and was rejected. There was no guarantee what the consequences of knowledge might be. I know of two people, for instance, who only found out they were Jewish when a parent who was dying told them just before passing away. In one case, it made no difference to them at all; in the other case, the person decided to learn about Judaism and joined the synagogue.

I still came on Sunday, as planned, by which time she had deteriorated further, but she whispered to me: 'He knows,' and her smile indicated it was the right decision. I smiled back, but felt like whooping out aloud, as it could so easily have had a disastrous outcome, with angry exchanges and her dying in distress.

When to abandon family

Jews are as prone to addictions as anyone else. It is enormously painful seeing someone self-destruct, but just as horrible seeing partners being dragged down with them. In one terrible month, I had to deal with someone whose husband had a gambling problem, someone whose wife was an alcoholic, and someone whose son was a drug addict. All three had been coping with their loved ones' addiction for years and had now either reached the end of their ability to cope or were hitting serious financial problems as a result. What is more, they had all pursued the obvious steps, albeit in different ways, such as learning about the problem, seeking support groups, obtaining professional help, and all to no avail. I decided it was time for them to hear a message that some might consider brutal, but which I thought was more of a lifeline:

'You have attempted to help them and exhausted yourself in the process; you had a duty to try to rescue them, but you do not have a duty to drown with them. While you are obliged to give help, they have to be willing to receive it; and so far they have ignored it and failed to take back control of their lives. You should set an ultimatum: that if they have not started to make measurable progress by a certain date, you will ask them to leave the home/cut off contact with them. If the addicts do not change – and we know it is tough, but also that it is possible – then staying with them just colludes with their refusal to change course. It helps neither them nor you. Yes, they may continue in their twilight existence, but there is no reason why you should be worn down by it anymore. You are not doing this to punish them, but out of self-preservation.'

In two cases, they did let go, albeit with great sadness and much guilt – the woman with the gambler husband and the parent of the drug addict. The husband with an alcoholic wife refused to do so. He proved unable to help her, but he did manage to reorganise his own life so that it was independent enough for him to carry on relatively unscathed. None of the outcomes could be judged a success, it was more a matter of how best to minimise tragedies.

Hello, I'm adopted

A new family had just moved into the area from Manchester. When I went to visit them, their six-year-old opened the door, stuck out his hand and said: 'Hello, I'm Jake and I'm adopted.' His mother beamed and said – as if to pre-empt my thoughts – 'We don't have any secrets in this house.' That is admirable but I thought it was still disturbing that

Jake defined himself in that way. Most children opening the
door to a stranger would have just said hello, some might
have added their name and others might have said 'and this is
my home'. I noticed that he introduced himself in exactly the
same way when he came to the Religion School the following
Sunday for the first time: 'Hello, I'm Jake and I'm adopted.' I
wondered if his parents had not crossed a line between being
honest and giving him a complex. I have seen other parents
pursue the opposite approach, not telling their child about
their true parentage and then building up problems later on
for when the truth has to be told, or, even worse, is discovered by accident. A more savvy way was taken by Max and
Marlene, who told their adopted daughter that they loved her
not because she happened to come out of Mummy's tummy
but because they thought how great she was when they first
met her. It made her feel valued and special.

It just goes to show: you can't ever tell

Ritchie and Penny took their Judaism seriously and certainly wanted to pass it on to their children. He came
from Hull, where there was a small but close Jewish community, whereas she came from north-west London, where
the whole world seemed Jewish, so they had a lot of different experiences to call upon. They had an active Jewish life
at home, brought their three daughters to Religion School
every Sunday and sent them on Jewish summer camps.
The result? After they had left home, one became ultra-
Orthodox, one joined a Reform synagogue, and one married

someone not-Jewish. Three totally different outcomes from the same home and upbringing. Moreover, they were not the only family in which such dramatic variations occurred. Although the offspring were also subject to influences outside the home, it suggests that nature is at least as important as nurture. It also led to an unexpected reaction from Ritchie and Penny. They had always opposed mixed-faith marriage and had seen marrying within the faith as important both for religious reasons and for the harmony of the relationship. Yet they now found that they got on very well with their non-Jewish son-in-law, but intensely disliked their Jewish ultra-Orthodox son-in-law. In fact, in an unguarded moment, Ritchie confessed: 'I never thought I'd say this, but the daughter who married ultra-Orthodox has caused more problems than the one who married out.'

And all because they didn't get married

Martin and Jilly were both retired and were both living alone after their respective spouses had died. A mutual friend introduced them to each other and they hit it off immediately. It was very touching to see their late romance develop, and eventually they moved in together. I was chatting to Martin by himself while at a synagogue event some two years later and their relationship came up in the conversation. He said how lucky he was to have found Jilly, so I took the opportunity to ask if they intended getting married. 'Oh, no,' he replied, 'things are fine as they are, and it's not as if we're going to have children, so there's no need.' When I said that marriage was not just for the children but for each other, and about making a public statement about their private feelings, he responded: 'Maybe, but we're already living together, so what's the point? Anyway, we don't want to complicate things with inheritances to our respective children.' It is an increasingly common scenario, with many in a second long-term relationship, after being divorced or widowed, deciding that there is no need to marry. It is partly a matter of circumstance – many divorcees reckoning that their original white wedding had not stopped the marriage going sour, so why bother this time? For their part, many widows and widowers think that the new relationship may be wonderful but they do not want to feel they are undermining the importance of their previous marriage by having a repeat ceremony.

There is also the issue that Martin highlighted, that a new marriage nullifies any previous wills and so assets that had been intended for their children would now automatically go to each other after death unless they wrote new wills that protected the inheritance their children – often grown up by this stage – would have expected to enjoy. At the same time, social mores have changed, so that retired couples who, in their youth, would not have dreamt of living together without being married, now happily move in together without any paperwork. Nor do they worry about commitment for the future, partly because sharing the same address is seen as sufficient proof of intentions, partly because their financial positions are often relatively stable, and partly because the future is not that long anymore.

However, Martin did make the wrong decision. Perhaps others in his situation will find the same. He and Jilly lived together very happily for another four years, but as their health began to deteriorate, fissures appeared. When he developed the beginnings of Alzheimer's and she became frail, her children felt it was unfair to expect her to look after him (as she would have done for as long as physically possible had they been husband and wife) or for them themselves to have any responsibility for Martin (as they might have done had he been their father-in-law). The result was that Jilly's children took her away to live with them, while Martin's children's took him to a care home. They never saw each other again. It was not that their respective children were particularly uncaring, but that they simply did not think in terms of Martin and Jilly being a married couple. The fact that they had never married had given out a message – unintentionally – that this partnership was based on mutual convenience, and so once it was no longer convenient, there was no need for them to stay together. Of course, another set of children might have felt more of an obligation to keep the couple together, or may have had a deeper relationship with their non-in-laws, which transcended any legal standing. However, there is no doubt that by Martin and Jilly not signing the marriage certificate, it lessened their relationship in the eyes of others. Instead of 'till death us do part', their status was 'till family loyalties us do divide'.

10

Special moments

'Pay me to shut up' – the offer they couldn't refuse

In 1984, the *Maidenhead Advertiser* participated with other local newspapers throughout Britain in a joint project to purchase a lifeboat. Having a father who served in the Merchant Navy during the war, I have always been sympathetic to seamen and wanted to help. But with so many other good causes constantly demanding people's money, my attempt at fund-raising still needed to capture people's imagination. I like to think my sermons are reasonably interesting, but then so does every minister, yet if you ask people what key words they associate with 'the sermon slot', they may well respond with 'boring' or 'snooze-time'. No wonder that those training preachers often remind them that 'giving sermons is like drilling for oil: if you find you don't strike your target soon, stop boring'.

Personally, I like the story about the young rabbi who was appointed to a congregation and gave his first sermon. At the end, everyone shouted 'Encore!' The rabbi beamed and duly obliged. When he finished, once again everyone shouted 'Encore!' He blushed deeply and said: 'No, I couldn't possibly do that.' At which point one of the elders of the congregation stood up and said: 'Young man, you will keep on giving that sermon again and again until you get it right!' So I hit on the idea of giving a sponsored non-sermon: if people really do not like sermons, then here is their chance to have their way and stop me from giving one. With the help of the *Advertiser*, it was announced that I would be going through the High Street the following week, stopping in every shop to give a forty-minute sermon on some worthy subject. However, if the shopkeeper did not want to hear it – or, more likely, did not want his customers put off and rushing away – then all he or she had to do was put £1 in the box. Simple!

It was sufficiently novel to elicit a good response. I did actually prepare the most appallingly boring sermon just in case anyone refused, although only for five minutes. One person did say he'd like to hear it before deciding whether to pay up or not, and thankfully gave in after three minutes. The one hostile reaction came from a person who declared: 'I'm not giving money to help people sail around in boats,' missing the point that lifeboatmen were there to save other people. I did gently point out that if he was swimming and carried out to sea, he might want them around, but my attempt to appeal to his peace of mind on future holidays failed miserably and I decided that this particular shop might be a sermon too far. Everyone else, though, responded positively and I learnt that the best donors were in pubs, as there were lots of people with loose change and a merry heart. By the end of the day, £250 was raised and went into the pot that eventually resulted in a new lifeboat. It was named *The Newsbuoy*, was launched later that year by the Duke of Atholl, then chairman of the RNLI, and based at Mallaig in Scotland to serve the north coast and surrounding islands.

The following Sabbath, as I stood up to give the sermon, I wondered whether I might be greeted with a hail of pound coins and have to quickly sit down again. None arrived, so I tried to give them a different perspective on sermons by telling the story of another rabbi new to his congregation, who gave his first sermon and was praised by all who heard it. The following week he gave exactly the same sermon again. People were a little puzzled but, okay, it was worth hearing again, so they said nothing. The third week came and he delivered the sermon a third time. This was too much. The following day, he was summoned to a delegation of board members who complained about the repetition. The rabbi listened quietly and then said: 'Just remind me, what was the sermon about?' They looked at each other blankly, muttered a few inconclusive words and eventually replied: 'Well, we can't actually remember, but it was definitely the same one.' 'You are right,' said the rabbi, 'and I will continue giving it until you remember it.' You have been warned.

Did you hear the one about the rabbi and the priest who went into a bar and…?

In May 1985, a nearby school in Stoke Poges took some pupils on an outing to Land's End. It was one of the many that the school ran every year, except this one was to become notorious as four eleven-year-old boys drowned in the sea, including one from Maidenhead. The families were devastated and the entire school was in mourning too. The parents decided to turn their grief to a constructive outcome and set up a campaign to fund a lifeboat to be based in the area. They could not bring their children back to life, but they were going to take steps to ensure it never happened again. I was very moved by the tragedy – both by the loss itself and by the way they were coping with it. We cannot argue with death, but we can determine how we respond to it – shrieking, giving up, fighting on. And, while the past is beyond our control, we can try to shape the future.

I wanted to help the campaign, but with dozens of groups already doing sponsored table-tennis or swimming lengths, I knew I had to come up with something very different lest people suffered from charity fatigue. It was obvious. I am not a natural comic, but everyone likes a laugh, so I decided I would get together with other local clergy and we would do an evening of sponsored religious jokes. It was novel and it would culminate in a fun event that people would enjoy. It might also shift the view of clerics from being stodgy and out of touch. Of course, if our stand-up skills proved lacking, there was a danger we might be laughed *at* rather than laughed *with*, but it was for a good cause. Surely we who thundered down from the pulpit every week could lighten up a bit? Six local vicars had the courage to join me and when the local paper gave us a lot of coverage, it got picked up by the national press and television. Excruciating headlines abounded such as 'Religious rib-ticklers' and 'the Sacred Seven'. The most cringeworthy was 'Rev-olutionary humour', no doubt leaving those who had declined to join in feeling either smug or relieved. Still, each article, radio and television appearance led to more donations, not to mention enormous publicity for the evening itself. It was held in the hall of a local church, and the turnout rivalled Christmas. For two hours, the five of us told gags that gently poked fun at ourselves and our respective faiths. Why should the Devil have all the best jokes?

Certainly that night we made sure we did. It was also a wonderful exercise in inter-faith relations (at that time, the Muslim, Sikh and Hindu communities were less involved, but if the event had been held now, it would have included them too).

What was the best joke? It depends who you ask, but, personally, I like the one about the rabbi, the priest and the vicar in the USA who were good friends and liked to play poker. However, they were in a town that banned gambling, so they had to do it covertly.

One evening, they were playing together when the sheriff burst in and arrested them. They were taken to the judge, who first summoned the priest and asked: 'Were you gambling?' He crossed his fingers behind his back and replied: 'No, sir, it was just a game of cards.' The judge then asked the vicar the same question. He whispered under his breath: 'Forgive me, Jesus' and also denied it. Finally, the judge turned to the rabbi and said: 'So, were you gambling?', to which the rabbi replied: 'With whom?'

There was also the rabbi who said he could give an instant sermon on any subject, whereupon he was challenged to speak about constipation. Completely unfazed, he gave a talk about Cain who was not able (Abel), Moses who took two tablets, and Solomon who sat for forty years.

The best bit, though, was that the evening raised £2,000 and, a few years later, a lifeboat was established at Sennen Cove, Cornwall, close to Land's End. It was officially launched by the Duke of Kent and named *The Four Boys*. Thirty years on, the four families still have a great sadness in their past that resurfaces from time to time, but at least it was a case of tragedy leading to tangible good, rather than, as tends to happen more often, tragedy leading just to pain and despair.

To eat or not to eat – that is the orange

In the 1970s, the then Soviet Union was notorious for the way it treated its Jewish population. In theory, everyone was equal in the Communist state, but in reality Jews were often oppressed. This was nothing new and dated back to the rule of the Czars. Ever since the 1917 revolution, religious life had been suppressed for all groups and the two million Jews had been forced to subsume their identity. However, the Six Day War in Israel in 1967 – when the young Jewish state gained an unexpected victory over the Arab armies trying to destroy it – had led to a resurgence of pride in their Jewish roots. This worried the Soviet authorities, who adopted a curiously contradictory policy. Jews were often denied promotion in their careers, be it in academia, business life or the judiciary, and made to feel unwanted, yet when they applied to leave and settle elsewhere, they were refused permission. The latter was due to the mindset that said: life in the Soviet

Union is perfect, so why should anyone want to leave? Such requests cast aspersion on the idyll that had been created. Unable to lead a normal life, but also unable to leave, they became known as the Refuseniks.

In a remarkable show of solidarity, Jews around the world tried to help by protesting publicly against the policy and by urging their own governments to put pressure on the USSR to change. There were also hundreds of Jews who travelled to the Soviet Union for the sole purpose of visiting the Jews trapped there. It was partly to show that they were not alone and to give them comfort, like visiting someone in hospital who was in for a potentially long stay, and to keep their spirits from flagging. The visits were also to boost their Jewish knowledge, which was severely limited owing to the Soviet ban on religious education, by giving classes about Jewish life and taking in Jewish books and artefacts. Gaining visas for individual travel in the Soviet Union was very difficult, so they joined official tours but slipped away once in the country.

The authorities were highly displeased by this development, resenting the negative image the country was receiving and upset by the protests that regularly accompanied flagship Soviet events abroad, such as tours by the Bolshoi Ballet or Moscow Symphony Orchestra. They were also worried by the flow of Westerners who, in their eyes, were bringing seditious material into the country, stirring up anti-social activity and undermining the state. A cat-and-mouse game ensued, in which foreign Jews tried to carry out visits and the Soviet secret service, the KGB, tried to stop them. The first time I went, I was let into the country without any trouble, but once it was apparent that I was not on the tour bus every day, I was occasionally followed. It was unnerving but not dangerous, while the Refuseniks whose homes we visited were not worried. This was because, if the KGB knew the West was in contact with them, this was a form of protection, for if they disappeared suddenly, their plight would be publicised and their release demanded. The families in greater danger were those being monitored by the KGB, but not known to the West and whom nobody would miss if arrested. What was also dangerous was teaching a group who had gathered in someone's home, for this could be construed as political activity and breaking the law. Once, when I was addressing a class, someone on look-out duty spotted a KGB car drawing up outside. I was told to tear up my notes and flush them down the toilet and was then promptly whisked away. The rest stayed and got ready to pretend it was an informal get-together of friends. I was definitely not '007', but it did feel as if I was in the midst of a spy film. The constant vigilance under which the Soviet Jews lived was epitomised by the joke: 'How many television stations does the Soviet Union have?' 'Two. Channel One is the government programme with state-controlled news. Channel Two is a KGB officer telling you to turn back to Channel One.'

When I went back to the Soviet Union the following year, they immediately took me aside at passport control, opened my suitcase and confiscated the books on Jewish history I had brought with me. Fortunately, they did not take the medicine that I had obtained for one of those I intended visiting and who found it difficult to obtain prescriptions for his heart condition. The rest of the trip was uneventful and I did what I had planned without interruption. However, on my way out

I was not allowed to board the plane, but taken to a cubicle, stripped naked, and interrogated with a soldier standing guard next to me and the butt of his rifle resting a few centimetres from my bare foot. It was intimidating – as it was intended to be. What they were after was names of new Refuseniks that I was taking back to the West, and which they wanted to intercept. I had put them in code in my diary, which is usually dense with dates and notes anyway and virtually impossible to read. Despite the officer going through it carefully, they were not spotted and I was eventually allowed to leave. I was very conscious, though, that had I not had a British passport, I would be as trapped as the Refuseniks, and I was at my most worried when they took it away 'for checking'.

I realised there was no point packing any books the following year just to have them taken away. So this time I did something that not only worked but turned out to be much more powerful than I had envisaged. I packed twenty Jaffa oranges. The thinking was that many of the Refuseniks wanted to emigrate to Israel, they could not get there, so I would take a little bit of Israel to them. The border guards did query why I needed so much fruit, but I explained I had a Vitamin C deficiency and they let me proceed with them. At every house I visited, I took an orange as a present and it was humbling how thrilled they were with what for most of us in the West would be such an ordinary gift. In fact, it also left them with a dilemma. At that time, the Soviet economy was in a poor state and fruit was rare and expensive. On the one hand, they wanted to permanently display on their mantelpiece this living symbol of the Jewish homeland. On the other hand, they were keen to eat the delicacy, and before it went off. Most compromised by keeping the orange for a couple of days and then eating it. Several years later, when they were allowed to emigrate freely, they were able to actually walk through the orange groves from which their presents had come. As for me, the following year my entry visa was withdrawn and I was banned from entering the Soviet Union. I was clearly a threat to the state, but the work of visiting and teaching was carried on by hundreds of other activists, and the fruits of their labour is now a historical fact.

Hearing lost voices

The synagogue obtained two scrolls to replace the two that we had had on loan for many years, but now had to return. One of the new acquisitions had a remarkable history and, a few years later, had a major impact on the community. It was from the famous collection of Czech scrolls – scrolls that had been collected by Jews during the war to save from the Nazis. When the latter rampaged through eastern Europe, they would not only massacre Jews but burn down the synagogues, turn them into horse stables or denigrate them in some other way. The silver ornaments from the scrolls would be melted down to help the German war effort and the scrolls themselves destroyed. The Czech Jews could not save themselves but did manage to save over a thousand of their scrolls, transporting them from rural communities to a warehouse in Prague, where they survived the war and, astonishingly, lay neglected until 1963. At that point, they were brought to England and rehoused at Westminster Synagogue, where the

Memorial Scrolls Committee undertook to repair the damaged ones and send them to synagogues around the world, both as memorials to those destroyed communities and to be used once more for Jewish life. Maidenhead was given the scroll that once belonged to Kojetin Synagogue, a small town 225 kilometres south-east of Prague. The Jewish community had started in the sixteenth century and had once been a flourishing community of over 500 individuals. As Jews had become more urbanised, it had gradually declined and by 1939 had consisted of some seventy members. Not one of them survived the war, all being taken to concentration camps and murdered in either Auschwitz or Theresienstadt. Thanks to the thoroughness of Nazi records, we know exactly their names, ages, time and place of death. There were two consequences of the Kojetin scroll's arrival in Maidenhead. The first was a dedication service in 1979, which, because of its emotive history, attracted a large congregation of both members and invited local dignitaries. As the scroll was opened up for a short reading, there was an acute awareness of when that had last happened: a Sabbath morning in 1942, the weekend preceding the mass deportation. Once chanted from on every Sabbath, it had lain silent for several decades. We wondered how many *barmitzvah* boys had read from that scroll over the years, and how many had later been taken off to be exterminated.

The second consequence was that a member of the community, Len Brown, who came from Czechoslovakia, took an interest in exploring the history of Kojetin. It was he who pointed out that 1992 would be the fiftieth anniversary of the community's demise and that we should mark it by organising a trip there. Not only did eighteen members express an interest in exploring our scrolls' roots, but so did the pastor of Kojetin, whose Hussite church had been established in the synagogue building after the war. What took us totally by surprise, though, was the response of the rest of the town. When we arrived at the synagogue-cum-church, we expected to be greeted by the pastor for a short memorial service. Instead, the mayor was there, as was the national press, and the building was packed full of local people. It was their first chance to remember officially too. Many, now in their sixties or seventies, cried when we read out the names of all those carried away by the Nazis. Afterwards, they told us: 'I sat next to him in class' or 'I bought bread from his shop every day.' The trauma of the war and then the struggle to survive afterwards under Communism had meant that there had never been any thought given specifically to the town's Jews. For them, everything now came flooding back. We were as much moved by their reaction as by the occasion itself. That, too, was mesmerising, for as we said the *Shema* and *Kaddish*, we were conscious that it was the first time in fifty years that Hebrew had rung out in the building. It was as if, after half a century of silence, echoes of those lost voices were briefly audible again and the walls smiled at hearing the ancient tongue once more.

The name-changers

Bernard Feldstein had been a long-standing member of the community and served for many years on the council, including as chairman. In conversation one day, he told me that his father's surname was Feld. This struck me as very strange because the usual pattern for a change in name is to make it less obviously foreign or Jewish, not more so. Thus a Hertzberg became a Harding, a Cohen turned into a Collins, and Levinsky ended up as Lewis. What had happened in his case? It turned out that his immigrant grandfather had been a Feldstein, but had anglicised it to Feld so as to give his father a better chance of assimilating into British society. Bernard, who had fought for Britain in the war, and who had a professional qualification as an architect, felt no need to prove his patriotic credentials, but did feel proud of his Jewish roots. He therefore reversed the trend and readopted the former family surname. Thereafter, I always thought of him as a good example of a person equally comfortable in both the worlds he inhabited – Jewish life and wider society – and willing for both to be known.

Another member kept their surname, but changed their forename. When Maurice became Mike, it had nothing to do with his Jewish identity but his self-perception. He had been a late developer, always felt nervous in the company of others and unsure of his own direction. His teenage years were traumatic emotionally and he found university life a three-year endurance test. It was only in his mid-twenties that he began to feel there could be a better version of himself, more confident and outgoing, and he concocted the idea of that side of him being called 'Mike'. Whenever he encountered situations, he began to think: 'What would Mike do?' and forced himself to follow that lead. It worked, and the gawky Maurice gradually transformed into the assertive Mike. In his mind, 'Maurice' became associated with all that was limiting and unattractive about himself. Eventually, sometime after crossing over between the two personas, there came a point when he wanted to discard Maurice completely, and when he changed job and moved house, he introduced himself as Mike to those he met for the first time. Having known him under both names, I commented on the process and said that, although he had developed this technique by himself, there were several biblical precedents for a name swap signifying a change of identity. The most obvious was the fairly shady and unlikeable character called Jacob becoming the family head and spiritual leader known as Israel. Mike disagreed: 'I'm not sure if that is completely parallel. Jacob's name was an outer recognition of his inner change, something that had already happened. In my case, changing my name was a vehicle for forcing myself to live up to my image of who I wanted to be.' It was a good point, and maybe more of us should follow Mike's lead.

A family screamed here

On the way to visit a family on Winter Hill in Cookham Dean, normally a simple drive and with only a handful of cars coming and going, I found myself stuck in a queue. Someone had come off his motorbike. While waiting, an ambulance rushed past taking the person to hospital, and once the traffic began to move under police supervision I saw the mangled bike, the damaged car that he had hit, a helmet still lying on the verge, crying relatives who must have lived nearby and been summoned, along with general debris littering the road. On my return an hour and a half later, I was greeted by an astonishing scene. No road block, no bike or car, no helmet or debris. There was just a clear road and nothing to indicate that a major physical accident – and emotional trauma – had taken place less than two hours earlier. If I had not known that it had happened, I would have never have guessed that blood and tragedy had been in evidence there such a short time beforehand. Indeed, the cars that I passed, who may well have not been there when I was, would have been blissfully unaware of the brakes that were slammed on too late, the horrendous thud of flesh against metal, the screams of those who saw it happen, the dreadful wait till an ambulance arrived, the genesis of the nightmare that would haunt the car driver for months to come. Of course, it happened whether they knew about it or not, but it seemed to add to the tragic nature of it all that such a terrible accident could go unrecognised only ninety minutes later.

Where did those blossoms come from?

After Gerald had recovered from his heart bypass, he came to synagogue to give thanks – as he put it: 'I'm not sure to whom, but I want to say it anyway.' He spoke about the first walks he had taken outside the house, just a few minutes each day initially and then slowly building up. 'It was amazing, I walked along the pavement and I saw things I'd never noticed before, even though I've lived there over twelve years. I noticed the fences, the trees that were beginning to blossom, the way the sun streamed through the branches. It was if I was opening my eyes for the first time. I know it's because of my operation, but I felt an astonishing sense of wonder, as if seeing everything for the first time, and appreciating what I normally take for granted and virtually ignore. Certainly I was looking at the world with new eyes.' I suspect Gerald is speaking for everyone who recovers from a major illness, operation or accident and feels they have rediscovered the world in which they find they are still alive. But only a few manage to maintain that sense of awe for long before familiarity breeds complacency.

The day the *barmitzvah* boy died

Arnold was due to have his *barmitzvah* in two weeks' time. He was nervous but excited. We had a dress rehearsal and all went well. His family had been keeping the date in their diary for months and were not only looking forward to the occasion itself but the clan gathering that such events usually involved. Suddenly, I received a phone call to say that he had suffered a fatal heart attack. Arnold was no ordinary *barmitzvah* boy: he was about to celebrate his eighty-third birthday. He had never had a *barmitzvah* at the standard age, owing to the outbreak of the Second World War, during which time he was evacuated to an area where there was no synagogue and no tuition facilities. His thirteenth birthday came and went, and was just one of many casualties of the war. He never lost his Jewish identity but did not pursue Jewish involvement when he grew up, married someone who was not Jewish and assimilated away.

Many years later, well into his retirement, I came across him living in Reading. He decided it was time to renew contact and, with his wife accompanying him, he became a regular attender. When he mentioned the story of his *barmitzvah*, I suggested having it the following year, which would both give him time to prepare and be on the seventieth anniversary of what should have been the original date. He thought it was a wonderful idea and immediately set to work.

Two weeks before the due date, the heart attack intervened. If he had been an actual thirteen-year-old, what happened next might well not have occurred. But, in his case, the family decided to go ahead in his absence. They all came together in synagogue as planned, different relatives took the parts he would have done, and another read out the sermon he had planned to deliver about his life story. Far from being sad, the whole service had an appreciative and joyous feel to it. By the end of it, everyone was sure that Arnold had indeed had his *barmitzvah*, not only seventy years late but posthumously.

The photograph album

One of my earliest childhood memories is sitting down with my mother and going through the family photo album with her. I remember her pointing out this cousin or that aunt. I was surprised, as she had often said that she regretted having no family. As the list of names continued, many of which were not ancient relatives who might have passed away, but looked the same age as she did, I blurted out: 'But I have never met any of them.' She shut the book suddenly and just said: 'No, and I'm afraid you never will.' She clearly could not speak about it, and changed the subject. It was some time later that I realised that they had all been murdered in the Holocaust, and that she and her parents had been among the few that had been able to leave Germany in time. She had actually had a large family, but that was before the war. After the war, it was just the three of them. Such was the legacy of a whole generation – trauma and loss – and, although it is hard to know which conscious and unconscious influences affect us most, it is perhaps why I always wanted to have a large family of my own and eventually had four sons.

Postscript: Something that embarrasses me personally is an uncomfortable truth: I owe my life to Hitler. It is horrible to have to express gratitude to such a vile person, but if he had not come to power and instigated his anti-Semitic policies, my German mother would never have left Leipzig, sought refuge in England, met my English father, married him and had me. I feel more at ease saying 'I owe my life to the war', but deep down, I know it is him. Yugh.

The two ladies

Gill and Maureen had been renting a house together for as long as anyone could remember. Both wafer thin, both spinsters, both passionate about pottery, they would spend Sundays scouring car boot sales or visiting galleries. They lived near to the synagogue and used to cycle there every Saturday morning, and I often wondered whether they would eventually invest in a tandem. One day, they spoke to me after a service: 'Next month we will have been together for twenty-five years. We still love each other dearly and would like a ceremony to mark the occasion. Nothing public – just you doing a blessing in front of the Ark for the two of us.' I was a little taken aback, partly because I had thought they were companions and hadn't realised they were lovers; and partly because this was in the 1980s when such ceremonies, common today, were hardly heard of. But, amid my double surprise, and, to be honest, slight discomfort, I knew deep down that the response had to be 'why not?' They were a loving, stable, committed family unit, who had a 25-year track record. I knew that if it had been a heterosexual couple who had approached me, I would not have hesitated to reply affirmatively. Perhaps that moment epitomised the journey that many people went through during that period, intellectually having no doubt that gay couples should be treated equally in every respect, but emotionally having reservations based on either habit or prejudice.

There was no doubt which of the two was the right response, and a few weeks later the ceremony took place. It was obvious how much it meant to them, both as a recognition and a reinforcement, and I was glad to have been challenged out of my 'comfort zone' and forced to take a step forward. As for the biblical texts condemning homosexuality, they may be problematic for the Orthodox, but Reform has no hesitation in saying that it reflects a bygone age, just as do the texts about stoning rebellious children or subjecting women accused of adultery to drinking a potion of water that has been cursed, so as to tell whether they are innocent or guilty.

There is much about the past that is to be admired and pre-served, and also much to be jettisoned as no longer applica-ble today. Gill and Maureen, quiet pioneers, just wanted to be happy together but surfaced after a quarter of a century to claim their right to Jewish acceptance.

The miracle

If you discount the miracle of seeing a child being born, which I have mentioned already, then I have only wit-nessed one miracle in my life, but as that is one more than I expected, I count myself lucky. It took place during a retreat for rabbis. Part of the programme was a meditation led by Lionel Blue. We were all sitting in a circle, and there was an unlit candle in the middle. Lionel spoke for a while about how hard it can sometimes be when we try to think about God and the meaning of our lives. Then he said he would light the candle – it would be a useful image to focus on as we entered a period of silence and contemplation. But, for some reason, the candle would not light – it was a large, fat candle, had already been used before and the wick had burnt down into a hollow within the candle. Someone else tried to light it, but also failed. 'Never mind,' said Lionel, 'we'll just have to imagine it burning', and so we got on with being silent. After a while, perhaps half an hour, he said that if people wanted to share anything with the group they could do so.

A few people did, and then one person, Desmond, said how upset he had been that the candle would not light. For him, it signified something that had gone wrong in his own life recently, and how he had lost confidence in himself as a result. During that half-hour silence, he had been unable to think of anything but the candle and he had been trying mentally to relight it, and at the same time to rekindle the inner spirit within himself. While he was saying this, I was looking at the candle and gave a start, for it seemed to me that there was a tiny light. I leant forward in my chair – perhaps I was mistaken – perhaps it was just the reflection from a wall light. But there was a nervous flickering, and other people had begun to notice it too. Within a few moments, it had become a bright flame, steady, confident and definitely ablaze. Desmond gasped, was astonished, and then smiled broadly.

Had Desmond lit the candle by sheer willpower? Had God lit the candle as a sign that his period of turmoil was over and a new light was dawning? Or had the candle been smouldering invisibly all the time and had then gradually become more obvious? Lionel and the person who had tried to help him were both adamant that they had not lit the candle. Actually, the answer did not matter very much, because the significance of all miracles is not how they happen, but what their effect is. In this case, it was the impact it had made on the despondent person who had felt hopeless and who now felt a new sense of enthusiasm. So often, it is a matter of inner blindness: being blind to the possibilities around us and then suddenly seeing the light. That is the real miracle, without any thunderbolts overhead or earthquakes below, but when something inside us moves, and our eyes are more open than they were before.

My nightmare

Ever since I heard this story, early on in my career, I have been terrified of it coming true for me and determined to avoid it. It is about a man who was retiring from his job after working for five decades in the same company. There was a special ceremony and he received the traditional gold watch for long service. Everyone connected with him turned up, and the managing director made a speech praising him and saying that he hoped he had enjoyed his fifty years with the firm. The man replied that, actually, it was not fifty years' work, but one year's work repeated fifty times. The anecdote, which may well be apocryphal, typifies the rut that we can all get into, and how much easier it is to 'play safe', stick with familiar patterns and fail to take up new opportunities. I know that many do have to remain at jobs that are not very fulfilling simply to make sure the bills are paid, but I am saddened by those who look back on a lifetime of work and feel they have neither enjoyed it, nor achieved much in their own eyes. It is one of the great contrasts between 1 January and 1 Tishri: whereas the secular new year is a time of merriment and enjoying the moment, with a semi-serious, semi-jocular attempt at resolutions for the next 365 days, the message of *Rosh Hashannah* is that a new year brings new possibilities, and it urges us to make it a better year than the one that has just passed. Of course, we do not necessarily do that, but at least we have fifty annual reminders before we get to the gold watch stage.

A Buddhist tale

When preaching or writing I tend to stick to stories from rabbinic lore, but there is one from the Buddhist tradition that I have often used. Its message is so appropriate, and in keeping with Jewish teaching, that no one has ever queried my quoting it. Anyway, if they did so, I would reply that truth can be found in many quarters, and what is important is not the source but its validity.

The story is about a monk who was returning with one of his disciples to their ashram, their monastery. They belonged to a group that had two major vows: one was silence and the other was to avoid physical contact with women. During their travels, they came to a fast-flowing river. There they saw a beautiful young woman, who was crying. She said the current was too fast for her to get across to where the rest of her family lived. 'That's no problem,' said the older monk, and he picked her up, put her on his shoulder and carried her across. The disciple was astonished – his master had broken both of their vows, but, under vow of silence himself, he said nothing. However, two days later, he could no longer restrain himself. 'Master, master,' he blurted out, 'how could you have done that? You spoke to her. You even picked her up in your arms.' 'My goodness,' replied the monk, 'are you still carrying her?'

It is a tale of those who are able to unburden themselves of the past, and those who cannot do so. It ties in directly with the High Holy Days, when we focus on our faults. But once we have made up for those committed against other people in a practical way – through an apology or restitution of some sort – then we can take their weight off us and stop carrying them.

The smile

I read this story when I was aged eleven or twelve, and it has remained fixed in my memory for the five decades since then because of the wonderfully transformative effect about which it speaks.

It was Thursday morning and Ollie was on his way to work. He had had a lousy week so far. Nothing had gone right for him, and now he faced two more days of slog and then nothing to look forward to at the weekend. Standing in the crowded bus, he felt very unloved. Suddenly, he noticed that an attractive young woman at the other end was smiling at him. 'Gosh, smiling at *me*,' he thought, and then checked himself. 'No, she's probably looking at someone else.' He glanced in her direction again, but this time there was no mistake: she was smiling at him. 'Hmm,' he said to himself, 'maybe today's not going to be so bad after all,' and he found himself inadvertently brushing his hair with his hand. Just then, the bus came to a halt and she turned to get off. He was disappointed, but still cheered by the fact she had thought him worth smiling at, and had a spring in his step when he got off a few moments later. What he did not realise, because of the crowd in the bus at the time, was that she was carrying a white stick, and he had not seen how she cautiously tapped her way along the pavement once she got off.

That is not a shaggy rabbi story, but about what could

happen to you or me later today, and about how a little thing like a smile from someone else can help change our mood entirely. It also highlights that, however down we may feel, a friendly face can make all the difference to our day. And, of course, if it works for us, then it works for others too. So if you see someone looking like Ollie, whether you know them or not, try a smile, because it might be just what they need. Maybe he in turn will pass your smile on to others, and that split second of human warmth will travel across the country and last a long time. Best of all, a smile can do as much good for the person giving it as it does for the person receiving it. Have a try and see if I am right.

A near-death friendship

Holly and Bruce had been firm friends at school together, kept in touch for a while afterwards, and went their separate ways. She was shocked when, twelve years later, she read about him in the national papers. He had been driving in Ireland on business when his car had veered off the road and had become submerged in a bog. Because it was such an unpopulated area, the accident was not discovered for another forty hours. During that time, Bruce had managed to curl up with his head in a pocket of air near the foot pedals. After a day had passed without anyone rescuing him, he had become convinced that he would die there. It was almost the end of the second day till he was found. Although suffering from pneumonia and hypothermia, he was not injured and made a full recovery. Meanwhile, Holly had seen the story in the papers – billed as a 'miraculous' survival given the odds of him never being discovered or found too late – and recognised his name. She no longer lived in Maidenhead, but he still did, and she was able to trace his whereabouts and made contact. They re-established their friendship – always a platonic one – and have been in touch ever since. Bruce periodically quips that the silver lining to his accident was them teaming up together again, but that he would have preferred a more conventional route.

The fleeting meeting

I have often been intrigued by the few seconds' worth of social interplay between me and passers-by: for instance, as I am waiting to cross the road, the traffic light turns red and a coach draws to a halt. I see some of the people on it, glimpse the expressions on their face, notice what they are wearing or holding, and can sometimes tell if they are off to the seaside or heading towards the office. Then I cross the road and never see them again, never find out if they reached their destination, never know if they had a wonderful or terrible day. I am equally conscious that it applies the same in reverse.

I get a similar sensation about anonymous inter-dependence when at airports (though this could apply to many other areas of life). When I take a flight from Heathrow to Paris, for instance, I tend to think just of myself – have I packed properly, have I got my passport, have I allowed enough time – whereas my short trip is only possible because of the thousands of people who are part of the process: from taxi-driver to airport staff to aeroplane designers and man-ufacturers, as well as those who make the paint that is used on the signs or grind the coffee that I have on board, or print the safety instructions that I read, or clear the plane of rubbish left by previous passengers. The list is endless, and involves the efforts of people I rarely ever meet, yet depend on totally.

Watching people fall

Like many rabbis and vicars, I double up as a social worker, trying to help people in the community cope with a variety of personal or domestic problems. They include de-pression, drug dependency, failed relationships, alcoholism, financial incompetency and many other problems that make their lives utterly miserable. I have spent countless hours with individuals giving them support, exploring options, making suggestions. Sometimes, it pays off and the person is able to help themselves and chart a new course. Other times, it is totally wasted because the person cannot change. This might be because they lack the strength to do so, or feel trapped in their current situation and reckon nothing can be done for the better. There are also those who, though they would deny it, do not *want* to change. The prefer the hell they know how to navigate to something different where they fear they would feel out of their depth or lack the control they think they have currently. Some of these people I have known for over twenty years, and whereas once I would have become very animated at their cries for help, now I still respond but with no expectation that anything will improve. I have watched them cry bitterly over their lifestyle and then go back to it with a comforting sense of familiarity. They are constantly falling and I have learnt the painful lesson of knowing that in some cases I can help, whereas in others I can do nothing save look on as they fall yet again.

But what shall I say to her?

I had asked Maggie to pop in to see an elderly lady who lived near to her, and who was very alone. She did so and agreed to go again in a fortnight, but in that time the lady had slipped in the bath, broken her ankle and was now in hospital. Maggie was still willing to visit her there, but told me that she had never done a hospital visit for someone she hardly knew and was worried about what to say. 'I'm not a great talker… and I certainly don't want to put my foot in it. What is the right thing to say?' It was a typically honest question by her, though I suspect she is not alone in finding that visits can sometimes be difficult, particularly if the person in hospital is not able to communicate well or does not have that much conversation of their own.

'The main thing is going,' I said. 'That in itself says that you care and have made the effort. It is also worth thinking in advance of topics to mention – such as what has been going on in your life, what you have watched on television and what is happening in the news generally – as it is very easy for their horizons to become very limited in hospital and you can offer a window onto the world outside. You can also ask about them, not just their current condition but their life before they knew you. Some people are very happy talking about themselves or reminiscing about "the good old days". But don't be shy of talking about yourself too; it makes it more of a two-way relationship and not just an official visit. It would be wrong to unilaterally introduce difficult subjects they may not wish to discuss (e.g. "Are you afraid of dying?"), but if they hint at a worry ("I'm very scared here") then you should certainly follow it up ("What of? Is it the staff? Or is it the thought of death that frightens you?"). You can also ask: "Is there anything you would like to discuss?" to see if there is an issue on their mind that concerns them. They may say: "No, nothing", but at least it gives them an opportunity to do so, be it dying or something less dramatic but still weighing on their mind, such as their cat, their freezer or missing a grandchild's birthday party. A warm handshake, smile or kiss at the end of the visit is also important and can more than compensate for any gaps in the conversation.'

The *Lammed Vavnik*

I will never know for certain, but I am sure that Russ was a *Lammed Vavnik*. *Lammed Vav* is the Hebrew for 'thirty-six' and refers to the rabbinic legend that there are thirty-six hidden saints who exist in every generation. They are ordinary people, but who do remarkable things, and do them quietly and unnoticed. No one knows who these thirty-six are, they do not know who each other are and, such is their modesty, they probably would not consider themselves to be one of them. There are always exactly thirty-six, and when one of them dies, another comes to take their place, and without them, the world could not exist.

What made me think of Russ as among their number? His wife left him for another man whom she married. Sadly, some years later, she caught the Aids virus from her second husband. He was unable to look after her, so Russ stepped in and took over. He nursed her devotedly, despite his own pain, still raw, at her departure. He was there for her throughout all the unpleasant stages and right up to the very end. He had no formal responsibility for her, and it would have been so easy for him not to have bothered, and understandable. But you cannot measure compassion by a rule-book, and he kept going long after others went home.

I have also wondered about Carla, who was born to be a mother, grandmother and great-grandmother – it was part of the DNA – yet never married. But a small detail like that was not enough to stop her. Instead, she adopted all who were lost or lonely or single or divorced or bereaved or new to the area. She fed them love by cooking for them, whether it was meals at her house or taking meals to their house. Along with her cooking, she dished up warmth and ladled out kindness. Carla did this year after year after year. In fact, it became decade after decade after decade. By the end of her life, more people had passed through her house and her care than someone with twenty grandchildren.

Beverley might be another contender. She used to collect second-hand clothes for a local charity shop. This is not so unusual, but what distinguished her was that she used to collect them from people who had suffered a bereavement. They suddenly found they had lots of unnecessary clothes on their hands, but these were items that belonged to a loved one, so they did not want to just bin them, while even the thought of sorting through them to give away caused them distress. Beverley would offer to help the person when they felt up to it, not just taking the clothes away, but going through them together first, sorting them, chatting about the memories they provoked, stopping for a little cry, having a cup of tea together and listening to the person's tale. When she finished, she took away the clothes, but left behind grieving people who felt they had been helped and understood.

Last word

R eaders may have noticed with some surprise that, for a book that is about the experiences of a minister of religion, the word 'God' has not been a dominating feature. It is certainly true that I have not been interested in expounding theology, and instead I have been immersed in people and the issues they face. 'Seek God in the people God has created,' the rabbis of old used to say. If that is true, then I have been engaging with God all the time.

Glossary

All terms are Hebrew words unless stated otherwise

BARMITZVAH – coming of age ceremony for thirteen-year-old boys

BATMITZVAH – coming of age ceremony for thirteen-year-old girls

BETH DIN – rabbinic court, often used for status issues

BROIGUS – quarrel (Yiddish)

GET – document of Jewish divorce

HANUKKAH – festival celebrating the victory of the Maccabees

KABBALAH – Jewish mysticism

KADDISH – memorial prayer

KIDDUSH – blessing over bread and wine

KIPPAH – head covering

KOL NIDRE – evening service for the Day of Atonement

KOSHER – food that is suitable (also used colloquially of behaviour)

LAMMED VAVNIK – one of thirty-six mythical righteous people

MAMZER (plural: *mamzerim*) – illegitimate child

MATZAH – unleavened bread eaten at Passover

MEZUZAH – container, with biblical verses on a scroll inside, attached to one's front door

MOHEL – person trained to perform a circumcision

PURIM – festival celebrating the liberation of Jews in Shushan

ROSH HASHANNAH – Jewish New Year

SEDER – ritual meal eaten to celebrate the festival of Passover

SHAVUOT – harvest festival that also celebrates the revelation at Mount Sinai

SHEMA – prayer famous for its declaration of faith in God

SHIVAH – service during seven days of mourning after a death

SIMCHAT TORAH – festival, the Rejoining of the Law

SUKKAH – temporary hut built at festival of Sukkot

SUKKOT – harvest festival

TALLIT – prayer shawl

TALMUD – fifth-century rabbinic commentary on the Bible

TORAH – the Five Books of Moses

YESHIVAH – rabbinic seminary

YOM KIPPUR – Day of Atonement

About the author

Rabbi, writer and broadcaster Jonathan Romain is minister of Maidenhead Synagogue in Berkshire. He writes
for *The Times*, *The Guardian* and the Huffington Post, as well
as the religious press, and is often heard on the BBC. *Confes-
sions of a Rabbi* is the sixteenth book he has either written
or edited. In 1999, he was part of a small group of British
Jews invited to an audience with Pope John Paul II. In 2004,
he received the MBE for his pioneering work nationally
in helping mixed-faith couples, and two years later he was
presented with the Inter-Faith Gold Medallion for fostering
religious dialogue.

He is chaplain to the Jewish Police Association, chair of
the Accord Coalition for inclusive education, and chair of
IFDiD (a clergy group which campaigns for the legalisation
of assisted dying). For several years he was a judge for both
The Times Preacher of the Year Award and the BBC's Frank
Gillard Awards. He is a past chairman of the Assembly of
Rabbis UK and is on the Council of St George's House,
Windsor Castle.